SQUARE PEG, ROUND BALL

SQUARE PEG, ROUND BALL

Football, TV and Me

NED BOULTING

BLOOMSBURY SPORT

LONDON · OXFORD · NEW YORK · NEW DELHI · SYDNEY

BLOOMSBURY SPORT
Bloomsbury Publishing Plc
50 Bedford Square, London, WC1B 3DP, UK
29 Earlsfort Terrace, Dublin 2, Ireland

BLOOMSBURY, BLOOMSBURY SPORT and the Diana logo are trademarks of
Bloomsbury Publishing Plc

First published in Great Britain 2022

A catalogue record for this book is available from the British Library

Library of Congress Cataloguing-in-Publication data has been applied for

ISBN: HB: 978-1-4729-7926-1; eBook: 978-1-4729-7929-2

2 4 6 8 10 9 7 5 3 1

Typeset by Deanta Global Publishing Services, Chennai, India
Printed and bound in Great Britain by CPI Group (UK) Ltd, Croydon CR0 4YY

To find out more about our authors and books visit www.bloomsbury.com
and sign up for our newsletters

CONTENTS

1

Anpfiff

FC ST PAULI 1–0 FORTUNA DÜSSELDORF.
17 November, 1989. Millerntor Stadium, Hamburg.

In which it begins.

I was 20 when it happened. It was a dark autumn night, on the banks of the river Elbe, the coal fires of Hamburg's stolid and crumbling tenements adding their chemical tang to the evening's damp mist. I'd been handed my match ticket as we left Feldstraße U-Bahn station and then headed up the stairs in a one-way throng. Everyone around me was singing, stamping and letting fall emptied cans of Holsten. They rattled percussively on the walkways. Through the turnstiles with a creak, mumbled thanks, a drop of fag ash and half a ripped ticket pushed back. Then up the dozen steps and into the Nordkurve just as Hans Albers' *Auf der Reeperbahn* started to splutter and crackle through the megaphone speakers fixed to the overhanging roof of the main stand and the stanchions. Smoke and steam rose from the crowd, thousands of shining eyes turning towards the dew-speckled field as kick-off grew near. Someone brought me a Bratwurst with a ripple of sweet mustard along its glistening top edge and a foaming beer in a plastic glass.

Just then, the teams ran out, a roar went up, a floodlight failed and everybody laughed. I laughed, too, so loud I almost spat out some sausage.

'So, *this* is football!' I thought. And everything changed.

*****

This is mostly a book about football, but it's also a book about me. That's unavoidable, because I wrote it from things that I felt, saw, heard and said over a peculiar 30-year period of my life in which football often dictated the terms. It skips lightly over most of my early years, since they were pretty uneventful, to be honest: Action Man, *The Pink Panther Show* and latterly E.L.O. were all fairly unchallenging milestones and anyway, the 1970s have been gloriously transcribed by greater Parker pens than mine. So, we can gloss over a decade or two.

What this story really tells is that far trickier bit of the human condition to negotiate; those torturous steps that start when the legal age of adulthood has been reached and yet never seem to end. Growing up is the unfinished journey that sits at the heart of this football adventure and for many years it co-existed, often exuberantly, sometimes uncomfortably, with the biggest game in the world. Football is the marked-out green landscape in which my almost-adult life began to play out. Stumbling into a career, parenthood, responsibility and self-determination is a process most normal people have mastered by the time they ripen into early middle-age, or at least they appear to. Not so with me. Even as I pass into my sixth decade on this planet, I'm still grappling around in the dark trying to establish who I think I am. The one thing I now realise with a degree of understanding and surety is that football, and my bumpy relationship to it, has taught me more about myself, my values, shortcomings, loves and fears than any expensive course of Gestalt therapy might.

This, then, is the tale of my slow, late discovery of the game, my escapist and total immersion into it, my awe at moving close within its stellar orbit and ultimately my dejected understanding, as I retreated from its core heat, that something was wrong. Either with me, or with the game, or maybe both.

This narrative, as scattergun as it is, plays out on the terraces of a cult Hamburg club, before, accompanied by TV cameras, it leaps with puppy-like abandon and clumsiness across endless acres of Premier League car parks, hundreds of miles of players' tunnels in the great cathedrals of the world's game, landing toe-to-toe and face-to-face with a succession of the game's greatest exponents. At some point half a lifetime ago, football and I entered a kind of unspoken symbiosis that came about in a haphazard fashion and fell loosely asunder, equally without a plan.

But the story never strays far from its befuddled core: me, football and my quest to figure out my place in its world. I suppose that's the point. It's a kind of footballing *Bildungsroman*. I like to use German words, you see; that's a part of me, too. *Anpfiff* is another good one. It means, 'The whistle blast that denotes the beginning of a game.'

2

Football is the Game

ARSENAL 2–3 CHELSEA.
31 August, 1949. Highbury, London.

In which resides the wonder.

This story begins with Dad, because in most football books it does. In fact, in most books it does, even the Bible.

Disappointingly perhaps, there's no conventional football trajectory. No heartening paternal kinship or love of the game nurtured through the turnstiles of some tightly bound common history. There was no home town club, whose fairytale terraces provided the furnace in which our family bonds were forged. The lineage of support in our family has guttered and stuttered. We were middle class, which needs stating. We didn't say 'toilet' or 'couch', but 'lavatory' and 'sofa'.

Dad was a teacher. I was a small boy. And there we begin.

I grew up in a village in Hampshire, and then in Bedford, a part of England so inoffensively devoid of difference that it slips between the fault lines and lies hidden in the country's imagination as effectively as a 10 pence coin that has dropped down the side of a car seat.

Bedford boasts no proper football club for miles around. Twenty miles away, David Pleat was doing marvellous things on a plastic pitch with Luton Town, it was true. In fact, I think I went to see Ricky Hill play there, but I can remember nothing about it and I can't be certain it's not a false memory. Many years later I got a flashback of some long-forgotten visit as I waited outside the main entrance at

Kenilworth Road for Mick Harford to emerge and discuss something or other. I even considered bringing up the subject of my possible attendance at Luton Town as one day, 35 years later, I rushed David Pleat through Madrid airport to catch a connecting flight to Valencia. 'Are we nearly at the gate?' he'd enquired with a look of near panic in his eyes. And on we'd hobbled.

Sometimes, when I was almost a teenager, we would drive down to London to visit our cousins, the children of my dad's only full brother, Nik. My cousins were Chelsea fans, like Dad. They lived in Wandsworth and were close in age to both my sister and me. Yet, culturally, we were miles apart. For a start, they were Londoners. And more to the point, Uncle Nik swore with insouciant abandon. Moreover, and to my astonishment, I understood that it was seemingly OK for my cousins to swear, too. Kate, who was roughly my age, would freely tell her older brother to 'fuck off' with no regard to the fact that their mother was within earshot. I was scandalised.

My Wandsworth relatives were 'football crazy', as the rather quaint expression goes. Uncle Nik was, and still is, a season ticket holder at Stamford Bridge. These rare family get-togethers would sometimes descend into a list of strongly held opinions about Chelsea's current shortcomings. Grievances were aired about the brothers' beloved dysfunctional club in the rougher end of Europe's most fashionable quarters. Expressions such as 'fucking Bumstead' would jostle for prominence with some mournful yearning for the return of Ron 'Chopper' Harris.

On these occasions I would catch a glimpse of a different side to Dad from the playful, indulgent man who sat at the centre of my world, reading the paper, and letting the smoke from his Embassy cigs wreathe around his fashionably luxuriant sideburns. This London, football Dad had an edge of otherness I couldn't quite define.

It was only much later in my life, reflecting back on those long-distant days of mysterious adult conversation drifting around the room at head height that I saw it all for what it was: the glint in his eye, and the snap and bite to his language, were nothing more than the increasingly distant echoes of a series of childhood experiences receding at life-speed across the event horizon. Football stuff sits deep and gains in potency with time.

*****

The first match I ever saw was at Stamford Bridge in the very early 1980s. I was about 11, probably.

We had driven down from Bedford in a red Datsun estate, passing through London's endless parade of wet pavements and off-licences, my sister and I with our noses pressed to the steamed-up window gazing out at the capital city, whose grandiosity and decay never failed to awe us into silence. The closer we got to Chelsea, the quieter Dad became, until eventually we parked up in one of those streets of white-fronted houses hemmed in by the rumbling of the District Line. Taking care that every door was locked, we set off in the same direction as the donkey-jacketed masses, following the alluring scent of softly piled onions being thrown into pasty baps by frightening women.

I don't remember much about the game, except for the sour tang of the February turf rising from the muddy pitch. I can blurrily recall the swell of the Shed End crowd penned in, so Dad told me, by an electric fence. And I clearly remember feeling that strangely hollow sensation of watching a football match without commentary.

From time to time the crowd broke into a song in which various people whose names I didn't know and couldn't make out were instructed to 'fuck off'. And every time the unmistakable consonants filled the darkening air, I tried to sneak a look at my dad from the corner of my eye.

One very clear memory: midway through the second half, my sister Emily was struck on the nose by the ball, after Micky Droy had hoofed it into the stand. She cried and some boys from a couple of rows back passed her some sweets. One of them advised her never to wash the mud from her face, as it was sacred Micky Droy mud.

Then we drove home, leaving London behind, with its otherworldly football grounds, its underground stations and long, dark, wooden escalators that led to the hidden world of my father's childhood. I didn't know this then, but as we drove past St John's Wood on the Bakerloo Line we were passing the tunnel that led to Dad's past. I was dimly conscious of his connection to London, but understood little about the capital city, football or Dad.

*****

Dad's genealogy is total chaos, more like an Italian parliamentary coalition than a working family tree. When he first met Mum, for example, she told him she had a sister called Joanna. Dad replied, 'I think I've got a sister called Joanna, too.' He's still not totally sure whether he has or not.

He is the oldest son of John Boulting, who, together with his twin brother Roy, formed a formidable partnership in the British film industry in the 1940s and 50s. Alternating between roles as producer and director, the Boulting Brothers made films such as *I'm All Right Jack* starring Peter Sellers, and they are often credited with having launched the career of Richard Attenborough when they cast him as Pinkie Brown in the well-known adaptation of Graham Greene's thriller, *Brighton Rock*. Between them they were married nine times and had 13 children.

Much is shrouded in mystery and family myth. Certainly, by the time I knew of their existence, whatever relationship Dad had with his famous film director father was all but over. John Boulting didn't attend Mum and Dad's wedding, choosing instead to place some rather dismissive words in the press about my dad's shortcomings. My maternal grandmother kept a scrapbook with newspaper cuttings.

I never met my grandfather John and he was not often talked about, not even when one of his films would pop up on BBC2 on a Sunday afternoon. From time to time, since Boulting is quite an unusual surname, a hotel receptionist or bank clerk would, on writing the name down, enquire of Dad, '…as in "The Boulting Brothers"?' Vaguely chuffed, but also embarrassed for Dad, we'd look blankly ahead, afraid to catch a glimpse of his reaction. He'd nod, but not say anything.

My dad's parents split up when he was young, and though he still saw plenty of his father throughout a disrupted childhood, it was his mother, an Irish woman originally from a family of wealthy tea importers just north of Dublin, who raised him. After their separation, she lived for a time in Grove Court in St John's Wood in one of those monolithic red brick blocks of flats near Lords Cricket Ground. Veronica (she hated her name and preferred for some reason to be called Davide) was a wry, stylish lady with short-cropped hair. She used to drink in a pub called the Princess Royal, where Dad would sit, clutching a soft drink and gazing at the cuttings on the wall from the *Evening Standard*. They were Chelsea match reports, framed.

The Princess Royal was a model of modest urban architecture, built in the 1930s. Its rounded corner carried the legend Charrington's Ales. Just one simple dark door led to the dimly lit interior that the sunlight could barely touch through the narrow, heavily draped windows. Yet on the inside, as my dad discovered, the pub was home to a legion of Chelsea fans, an isolated flock of Blues in dangerously North London territory. They took over the pub, supping, smoking and swearing they'd never seen a worse full-back in all their lives, while my granny-to-be sat or stood at the bar, lighting the next John Player Special from the last, a gin and French in the other hand. Dad took in the sights. It must have seemed wildly exciting.

Growing up, Dad still had frequent contact with his father, despite his parents' divorce. That contact could be distant, almost negligently so. He remembers, for example, hanging around the tube station accosting respectable elderly ladies for sixpence so that he could spend the rest of the day riding round the Circle Line, because there was nothing better to do. But from time to time, Dad was taken by his father on a special treat.

One such occasion was in August 1949 at Highbury. John Boulting had tickets to see his team: Arsenal. That day they were to play Chelsea and he took Dad along, who was just eight years of age. It was the first match he can recall seeing. The identical East and West stands, the Clock End and the North Bank! The famous Art Deco façade, built at vast expense and way over budget. This place was a temple to modern, swashbuckling football.

Seventy years on he can still recall much of the detail: 'A most unlikely hero figure. Knee-high to a not-more-than-average-sized grasshopper, balding, but he could play a bit!' he says of one player. 'Freddie Cox was Arsenal's tricky winger. Bow-legged of course from rickets. The result of a bad diet,' he remembers with a chuckle.

I do a quick internet search and Cox's face comes to life – side-parting, benignly smiling, running at a retreating defender with his handsome chin in the air. Freddie Cox DFC, having flown fighter planes for the RAF during the war, resumed his preferred trade of torturing full-backs when football resumed in 1945. He signed for Arsenal from Spurs in July 1949 and a month later was on the losing side at Highbury as Chelsea beat them 3–2.

This, despite the fact that Cox had been brilliant that day as Dad recalls, giving the run around to Stan 'Killer' Willemse, the ex-marine and uncompromising Chelsea defender. What a line up! Roy Bentley, the famous league-winning Chelsea captain, Bill Robertson, the keeper, who'd retire to run a newsagent near Heathrow. And for Arsenal, the famous brothers, Leslie and Dennis Compton. There were few bigger stars imaginable.

But as the late 1940s gave way to the '50s, John Boulting did something unforgivable for a football fan. He dropped his support for Arsenal and transferred to Chelsea. It happened, as far as can be reasonably pieced together, like this.

My grandfather had first worked with Richard Attenborough on his directorial debut, *Journey Together*, a war drama in which everyone talks like Jacob Rees-Mogg in flying jackets. The two became friends, with Attenborough openly admiring of John Boulting's real-life participation as an ambulance driver at the battles of Belchite and Brunete in the Spanish Civil War for the International Brigades. Their collaboration continued with *Brighton Rock*, by which time Attenborough was well on his way to stardom.

But it was this role that quite extraordinarily brought about my family's continuing, if fractured, relationship with Chelsea.

Considered too chubby to play the lean, menacing Brighton gangster Pinkie, Attenborough was sent on the recommendation of fellow actor John Mills to train with Chelsea for a fortnight before filming.

During those mornings jogging around the perimeter of the training ground, certainly doing star jumps and probably throwing medicine balls at other men, Attenborough embarked on a love affair with Chelsea that would last until his death. In the 1970s he became a director at the club, donating almost a million pounds to help save Chelsea from having to sell Stamford Bridge. In 2008 he was appointed Life President.

In the early days of Attenborough's love for Chelsea it was, among others, my dad who was the beneficiary. John and Roy Boulting, invited to Stamford Bridge by John Mills, now started regularly to take their place 'in the centre of the East Stand, just to the left of the half-way line' as Dad recalls. He remembers the clouds of bluish cigar smoke rising towards the eaves of the roof. And on the pitch, a procession of players, each one recalled in a hi-def of memory, which the footage of the era cannot hope to replicate. On occasion he would even stand on the terraces, once being passed down over the heads of the crowd to the front so he could see, in true post-war cliché fashion. From his spot in the front row, he took it all in.

'I had a blue and white bobble hat, a rosette, definitely,' he pauses in the retelling. 'But I don't think I had a rattle.' Dad did, however, have a scarf. His mother, the quiet, put-upon, patient woman that she was, indulged his fandom. She made him a scarf, hand-stitching the names of all his favourite Chelsea players onto it. Years later, when Dad was a young man, she'd drive him and his friends half-way across the country so that they could all attend some Chelsea game or other. My grandmother would trudge into the away end with them, sometimes taking a book with her, which she read until the match was over. Then she would drive them all home again.

Dad met Mum while they were both students in Dublin. He was returning to the land of his birth in a successful attempt to gain an almost entirely mediocre qualification in Classics from Trinity College, and she was attending a teachers' training course overseas in a bid for adventure after a stifling convent school education. I imagine their lives together in a kind of 1960s black and white, a stylish swirl of mini-skirts and drainpipe trousers, cigarette smoke (Dad only) and Guinness glasses being slowly drained of their blackness. But Dublin was just a staging post. They continued to meet back in London, during holidays, and after they had finished college. Mum by now was teaching in Hackney, but living in a posh Chelsea flat in Upper Cheyne Row with a tiresome-sounding friend called, appropriately, Venetia. At weekends Venetia would go off to Twickenham with her suitable friends to watch 'rugger', while Mum would meet up with Dad and head off to Stamford Bridge where he'd treat her to a 'DoozleDog', some sort of awful Chelsea frankfurter that Dad has never stopped talking about for my entire life to date. I have a dim recollection of him forcing one on me when I was a child like John Selwyn Gummer with a burger; it was a sloppy cascade of oily onions and pasty pink meat in a rapidly disintegrating roll. Of those trips to the Bridge, Mum remembers with a mixture of horror and nostalgia the rickety staircase she'd have to climb up high in the stand to access the only ladies' toilet in the ground.

Then they married and soon thereafter left London. England won the 1966 World Cup, though neither of them cared much since 'Peter Bonetti was the only Chelsea player and he didn't get a game.' A year later, my sister Emily was born. That didn't stop them going on a driving holiday in a knackered old Bedford van with broken windscreen wipers to San Sebastian, where, in a pre-planned twist of fate, Chelsea just happened to be on a pre-season tour. They went to the match, then followed the team bus back to the hotel in their van. Properly obsessive.

Then I came along on 11 July, 1969, 10 days before the Americans landed on the moon, and that was that. Dad pretty much stopped going to the football as his family grew up.

He did try, though, to hand on the tradition; attempted to instill some sort of Chelsea habit in us. Saturday afternoons were high jeopardy affairs when I was six or seven, nervously awaiting the teleprinter's message of triumph or disaster to rattle across our badly tuned, black and white TV, as we huddled around the Calor gas fire.

We knew the rules. If the number next to Chelsea's name was bigger than the number next to the opponents when the letter F and T clattered into finality, a great victory roar would go up. While Emily and I parroted back a swift and lusty rendition of *Blue is the Colour*, our minds were on the bigger prize: if Chelsea won we all got to swig from a massive bowl-sized victory glass that Dad would collect from the kitchen and fill with ginger beer.

Yet somehow, football slipped through my grasp and, as I grew older, I paid less attention to it rather than more. We still watched all sorts of sport on the telly together: cricket, Formula 1, golf and athletics, as well as wrestling, of course. Football was part of the mix, with its commentary-down-a-telephone line sense of drama, and FA Cup Final *Abide-With-Me* pageantry. But it wasn't *special*. At least, not yet. Besides, pretty soon I was into David Bowie, tippexing flowers onto my Marantz ghetto blaster, and hanging around the bandstand in Bedford Park wearing an army greatcoat, eyeliner and about 30 bangles. This was not a look that would have gone down well at Stamford Bridge in the John Hollins era.

Perhaps it disappointed Dad, I don't know.

*****

The last match I saw with him was at Selhurst Park. I think it must have been 1997. We sat in the stand among the sparse Wimbledon crowd singing 'shitty ground' over and over again as Chelsea's player-manager Ruud Gullit idly choreographed the total destruction of Joe Kinnear's side. By now, I was already smitten with the game and Dad was revisiting his old habits after decades away from football. Across all this expanse of time a fragile unspoken bond was forged in the sour air, among the wet coats and drifting smoke, the singing, occasional silences and isolated echoing shouts.

We walked away together feeling the acute strangeness of the situation. As we reached the car, certain building blocks of our family's history that had remained indefinitely suspended dropped silently into place. It had become my game now, as well as his.

3

The Man With the Cone Upon His Head

LIVERPOOL 0–1 WIMBLEDON.
14 May, 1988. Wembley Stadium, London.

In which lessons are learned.

By the time I left school, Dad had completely given up inculcating the football gene in me. I seemed more intent on writing poems about nuclear war and playing the saxophone barely adequately. A career path of uncertainty opened its scrawny arms and beckoned me thither.

That summer I worked in Bedford for a local engineering firm in a temporary clerical job for which I had to wear a tie. I was, improbably, charged with ordering hundreds of thousands of pounds of raw steel every week – a task that I often mismanaged. Then I spent another somewhat implausible four months working for a logistics firm in Germany, despatching parcels around Europe. I endured the winter of 1986–87 in a blisteringly cold and bleak suburb of Munich, typing and receiving telexes in the offices of a long-since defunct freight company, surrounded by heavy-smoking profane Bavarian women who oscillated wildly between considering me too pathetic for sympathy and simultaneously worthy of endless pity. I rented a tiny fusty room in a tower block apartment that belonged to a terminal alcoholic. He didn't move from the couch on which he lay draped, one hairless thigh revealed by his gaping dressing gown. All day my landlord would languish in front of a VHS recording of the violent goring of the matador Francisco Rivera Pérez, known simply as 'Paquirri'. One weekend, simply to get out of the flat, I walked 10 miles in the sleet to the concentration camp at Dachau and back. It was a strange part of my life.

But for all the time I spent in Munich, I didn't even realise that I was living so close to the Olympic stadium. The famous stadium was still home to a Bayern side, that featured a young Lothar Matthäus with whom I would one day natter amiably to for the entire duration of a Champions League group match at Stamford Bridge. Bayern also boasted an exotically recruited Mark Hughes with whom, many years later, I would walk along the banks of the Moskva river in the middle of the night. Of course, I could have had no inkling of what my future might hold, and besides, I wasn't remotely interested.

Indeed, the only visit I paid to the proximity of that famous concrete bowl, with its instantly recognisable sail-like roofing, was one freezing cold Wednesday night, when I staggered through knee-deep snow in the surrounding park, on my solitary way to see the Paul Simon Graceland Tour, not knowing that I was passing one of the great cathedrals of the world game.

*****

In September 1987, one warm late summer's day, I arrived at Cambridge University having somehow gained a place to study modern languages. I could not quite believe I was there.

Moving into my student accommodation at the top of a long wooden staircase on my first day, I became aware that the adjoining room was already occupied. I was about to meet my new neighbour. As I came and went through the door to my room, carrying boxes with dictionaries, cups, a squash racquet I would never use and a kettle, I could hear dance music thumping through the thin partition wall and slipping through the gap under the door. There was a smell of Lynx deodorant in the air.

Later that afternoon, after the awkward-yet-landmark parental goodbyes had been ineptly performed, and Mum and Dad had driven the not-very-considerable distance back to Bedford, I shyly introduced myself to my new flatmate with whom I was about to share a tiny corridor/kitchen, equipped with one electric ring and the noisiest fridge in England.

Simon was a fourth-year linguist and prodigiously talented, as it turned out. I think he graduated with a first-class degree, something I palpably didn't do. But Si was decidedly different from most other of the white middle-class stodge that made up the indeterminate mass of our college. For a start, he was from Liverpool. In fact, he was the first scouser I ever met, which now seems an outlandish claim to make, given how much of my subsequent life I have spent on Merseyside. He had a twinkle in his dark brown eyes, was as sharp as a razor, and had a friend called Billy who came from Glasgow and once punched me so hard he knocked me out. I think I probably deserved it. I'd never met anyone from Glasgow either and hadn't been warned that you weren't advised to attempt to imitate their accent.

Si was a Liverpool supporter. It was a good year for them, of course. Kenny Dalglish was well on his way to guiding them to the second of his three titles in charge. But this didn't stop Si from suffering. He kicked and screamed and fretted his way to his final year as a student of modern and medieval languages, while simultaneously agonising over every tortuous twist of fate thrown in the path of the 'Redmen' as they marched towards their inevitable victory.

For Si, these matches, however distantly consumed (radio snippets being the only resource), were everything. Their overbearing weekend importance gradually built throughout the week and would seep into the beginning of the following week, either imparting their toxins, or bathing the days in a soft-focus contentment, before, by Wednesday, the anxiety might start to build again. In his case, too, a long way from home, he must have keenly felt the pull of the Kop. From him I learned that Liverpool were good. I mean, they were really, really good. Many years later, I would narrate a footballing biopic about the career of Kenny Dalglish. The footage of his rampaging authority on the pitch, the sheer *command* of the man, with all that movement around him. If Dalglish was a seriously good player, going about serious business, then Si was a serious fan. He too wasn't messing around.

Sharing such close quarters with a genuinely fanatical football supporter quickly taught me to be wary of Saturday afternoons, when the dance music would give way to BBC Radio 2's football commentary from around the grounds. Howls of anguish, limbs hitting plasterboard, deep, visceral groans of despair. Si was an incarcerated beast, chained to his love for Liverpool Football Club, tossed raw meat from time to time, and on other occasions subsiding in whimpers and in tears. Genuine tears. Football actually, often, and almost uncontrollably, made this man cry. Trying not to listen from the room next door, I would put my coffee cup down very quietly and sneak out without letting the door bang. It was like an unspeakable illness, what Simon had. No one knew what to do.

Si also played for the college football team, along with a couple of my other friends. They took it all very seriously indeed. Only once or twice did I actually bother to watch them play, but never with any great interest. It just seemed like an overly long-winded way of running around, getting muddy and shouting. Sometimes I'd meet them for a pint in the pub after the match, but always felt excluded because I hadn't run around, got muddy nor been shouted at.

But, at my desk, with my window open, in the grip of a Sunday afternoon essay crisis, I could hear the match in progress, and I envied them their commitment to their blunt and boisterous cause every bit as much as I envied them the fact that they weren't having to write 1,500 words on Stendhal's *Le Rouge et le Noir*, or desperately trying to learn my lines for whatever student theatrical production I was involved in. I took to the stage at Cambridge with all the amateur commitment and full-hearted sense of adventure with which my sporting peers applied themselves to winning games of football.

My friend Sean, who I fondly imagine played centre-forward in the cultured style of Teddy Sheringham, but with only perhaps eight per cent of his talent, was a fiercely intelligent intellectual from Nottingham. Ever the contrarian, he had decided from a young age to support Derby County, since, in Brian Clough, he saw a reflection of himself. Late at night, in the college bar, he sounded like Clough, too.

And Giles, an ex-Etonian student of Russian and Swedish, with long flowing blond locks, had a strong affection for Wimbledon Football Club. This was reasonable enough, since he had grown up in Wimbledon about a mile and a half from Plough Lane, albeit about 100,000 miles outside its cultural catchment area.

Giles really loved football. He didn't love it in my flatmate's slightly unhinged way. He just enjoyed watching it, talking about it, playing it, talking about it, watching it and talking about it and reading about it. Unlike Si, he saw humour in the game, and rejoiced at the shortcomings of the players he supported every bit as much as he admired their strengths. He would have a lifelong affection for Lawrie Sanchez, who he would regularly decry as having been the worst player he'd ever seen play for Wimbledon, despite having been responsible for the club's greatest-ever achievement. Happily for him, Giles would go on to become a publisher of sports books, and would eventually commission a book jointly written by Dave Bassett and Wally Downes about the Crazy Gang. With that milestone many years in the future, he would want for no more in life and, last I heard, he now spends most days tending his allotment and probably still thinking endlessly about football.

If there were a match on the telly Giles would often be found in the much under-used common room, sat on his own. From time to time, idly, I'd join him. By my final year, ever more frequently. Together, we watched the away leg of Manchester United's first round encounter with Peski Munkas in the much-missed European Cup Winners' Cup. We did this because we wanted to know what 'Handball!' sounded like in Hungarian. Every time we heard the crowd shout it, we dissolved helplessly into uncontrollable laughter. We were students, you see, on full grants.

Even I, an apprentice fan in the company of young men with a far greater stake in the game, could feel football's hardcore tug. Though the detail and the history still eluded me, there was enough to admire in the huge and unexpected waves of delight and despair it could elicit in my friends. A move breaking out of defence, a shot out of nothing tipped over the bar, a sleight of foot to get out of a tight spot on the touchline, a thunderous tackle, a defender up within a second, ball at his feet and pointing as a sudden cheer dissolves into applause. Even on telly, this was great theatre, and it beat having to analyse Thomas Mann's political intentions in *Der Zauberberg*.

In May of our first year, just as our exams had come to an end, the much-maligned Lawrie Sanchez somehow headed the ball past Bruce Grobbelaar to give Wimbledon the lead against Liverpool in the 1988 FA Cup Final. Somewhere in the world, perhaps already at home in Liverpool having finished his exams, Si would have exploded with a fury exceeding any furies he had previously unleashed. As if mimicking the life cycle of a star, he may have burned with anger until collapsing in on himself, only once more to expand with hot rage, reaching 20 times his standard incandescence, before shrinking to a point of black singularity, lifeless and devoid of energy. What could be done? Nothing could be done for Simon.

Giles, in the meantime, was actually inside Wembley stadium. He'd taken the train down for the match and was going to return that evening as he had exams the following day. Many, many hours after the final whistle and Lady Diana had had the honour of being introduced to Dennis Wise, the door to the college bar swung open, and Giles sauntered in, walking in a crouched position and with a traffic cone placed with enormous inevitability on his silkily groomed locks. He was trying to sing the Wombles song: '...dergroun...vergroun...' bling freeeeeee! Womblsss of Wbldn commonareweeeeee.'

How strange, I thought, looking at Sean, the black polo-necked academic centre-forward of our college team. 'He's won the FA Cup,' Sean mused. 'That's why he now has a traffic cone upon his head.'

Then, in 1989, I went to Germany again, and it suddenly all started to make sense.

4

Brown and White Dynamite

GERMANY 1–2 BULGARIA.
10 July, 1994. Giants Stadium, New York.

In which decisions are due.

For the third year of my languages degree, I took a placement as an English teacher in a funny little town in Schleswig-Holstein called Quickborn. It was very near Hamburg.

On the day I arrived, the school was shut, because I was a week early. Sitting, confused and slightly panicky, on the wall outside the main entrance as the light faded around me, I was wondering what my next move should be.

By luck, I was rescued by a history teacher who happened to be passing. She said she could put me up for a while and took me to her family home, where I was straightaway introduced to her bearded, long-haired, important-looking husband. Over awkward tea and cakes, I asked him what he did for a living.

'Oh, you know,' he said, significantly. 'This and that.' He paused again. 'Singer. Songwriter. Poet. Politician.'

I glanced up at the framed photos on the wall. He picked up his coffee cup and wandered back to his atelier in the higher reaches of his bohemian house set in the most conforming suburb in this highly contradictory country, leaving me to try to figure out where the hell I'd ended up and who he was. Days later I discovered that he was Franz Josef Degenhardt, Germany's equivalent of Bob Dylan, and that it was he in the photos beaming out radiantly over a sea of black and white faces with a guitar across his midriff. This was going to be a bizarre year, I already sensed.

I was indisputably a substandard teacher. For a start, I was not much older than some of the kids in the school. And for another thing, I managed to mix incompetence with a certain arrogance in a quite heady cocktail. I lasted a matter of weeks in the job before the head teacher called me into his office to suggest that perhaps it would be better if I left his school and never came back. I agreed with him that was a wise course of action and wondered how I would fill what remained of my entire academic year, before I was supposed to return to university to complete my degree.

I needn't have worried. I gravitated immediately to Hamburg, the wonderful, coal-smoked, rugged harbour city. It seethed with night life and hidden, dark corners and crannies. I got a room in a shared flat with a heavy metal guitarist called Werner and set about falling in love with the place.

This was a city built in the bleak, romantic Hanseatic tradition. Its understated beauty dripped through the thinking of Thomas Mann, inspired Richard Brahms. Hamburg had survived Operation Gomorrah, when it all but burnt to the ground under the weight of Allied carpet bombing. Hamburg is where the Beatles came of age.

And Hamburg is the city that had been the making of Kevin Keegan. They still adored him there. Many years later, the legendary commentator Brian Moore's son, Simon, would tell me how Keegan had come to their family home for Sunday lunch, during which he had offered to put him and his girlfriend up over the summer. A few weeks later, Simon spent some time in a smart suburb called Blankenese, laying a patio for Keegan while he went off to training with SV Hamburg. Between them, they'd normally just about manage to carry and lay two slabs in a morning. But Keegan used to come back from training and cheerfully lift two entire slabs all on his own, then jog back to the garden with them. I love this image. I can see him in his blue and white Hamburg SV tracksuit running to and fro with his curly locks bouncing around his upturned collar.

Hamburg was the obvious place for an epiphany.

*****

In the end it was a cheerful actor from Stuttgart called Georg who was almost solely responsible for my falling headlong in love with football. One evening, drinking in our favourite Turkish bar, he presented me with a ticket to a football match for the following night, telling me that his pal couldn't make it. He asked if I could come with him: 'Hier. Komms'te mit?' Then he extolled the virtues of the particular club in question, 'Pauli.' He meant FC St Pauli, Hamburg's second club. I didn't know anything about them really, except that they played in a brown kit. Nonetheless I told Georg that I would very much like to come, although I really wasn't sure.

And so, in 1989, I made a discovery that changed the course of my life. I can recall that the experience cost 10 deutschmarks, the price of maybe two packets of fags. But straight away I realised that Pauli were special. Their much-loved Millerntor ground, which has since undergone immeasurable changes, was a terrifyingly atmospheric, ramshackle mess in the late 1980s, a description which applied to Hamburg generally back then, shortly before the fall of the Berlin Wall and the torturous process of reunification.

Hemmed in at one end by the eastern end of the infamous Reeperbahn '*Sex-Meile*' and a giant Nazi bunker called Flakturm IV at the other, it was bordered on either side by a vast, empty expanse of crumbling tarmac, which bore the optimistic name 'The Field of the Holy Spirit'. Twice a year, this nightmarish urban vacuum would fill up with a huge mobile funfair, called, for some reason, the '*Dom*', or 'Cathedral'. From the back of brightly painted trucks, massive log flumes, chairoplanes and rollercoasters would improbably unfurl, jostling for position with wall-of-death centrifuges, prize fighter boxing rings, halls of mirrors and, I swear I remember, freak shows: the bearded ladies of Hamburg were still gainfully employed when I first discovered the city. After matches, fans would spill into the fair, adding to the sense of barely contained chaos.

The visiting team on my first trip to Millerntor was Fortuna Düsselfdorf, a crashingly average side who succumbed to a near total annihilation at the hands of a St Pauli attack that had seldom known success on such a scale. At least that's how I choose to remember it. In reality, the prematurely balding son of Hamburg, André Golke, scrambled home the game's only goal in the 35th minute, after which Pauli started to hang on. It was the hanging-on that had me. The goal was the goal, but the agony of nearly conceding was the thing I remember more clearly. The shredded nerves of watching wave after wave of Düsseldorf attacks! The evening passed in a riot of entertainment, which left me without a voice, but happier than I had been since arriving in the city.

Within days of that first match, I had begun at breakneck speed to transition into a fully functioning, genuinely obsessed, badge-kissing, local paper-scouring fool whose emotional life was carved into regrets about two points thrown away or the hopeful medium-term expectation of points accruable over the next three games.

Without Georg's free ticket, I would have continued perhaps indefinitely rubbing along with humanity on its own terms, rather than having my horizons simultaneously shrunk and expanded by the fixtures of the Bundesliga. Without him, I would never have learned that a Brazilian striker could be as inept as Leonardo Manzi, that a song about deploying a helicopter to rescue an opposition player could be so riotously funny or that the smoke of grilling pork sausages drifting through a fine drizzle could catch with such arresting beauty in the cold blue light of a night match. All this would have eluded me.

I assumed that going to watch Pauli was always going to be that good. It wasn't. En route to finishing in a largely ignorable 13th spot in the league, Pauli's victories were few and far between. I saw FC Nürnberg, an under-performing big city side who flattered to deceive come away from Pauli with three points. In the cup, I admired the visit of SV Meppen, for whom the Pauli fans had a moderately amusing song, which translated along the lines of, 'Take the wellington boots off the Meppeners!'

Despite the fall of the Berlin Wall in November 1989, Germany was an unhappy, divided country. Not just physically, by the slowly unravelling barbed wire and sectioned concrete of the Iron Curtain, but culturally across perpendicular lines. And one of those fault lines came to the surface at Millerntor, where the alternative German scene had decided to congregate. Anti-establishment, anti-fascist, anti-authoritarian, the club pulled in the waifs and strays of the surrounding run-down streets, packed to the gunnels with squatters, musicians, artists, political firebrands, layabouts, chancers, pleasure seekers and, weirdly, me. Even their keeper was a non-conformist. Volker Ippig was Pauli's talisman; a long-haired former dockworker who lived in a squat near the ground, worked with disabled children, visited Nicaragua and took to the pitch with a clenched fist salute. How the crowd adored him! How I would go on to admire him! Pauli represented open revolt to the mores and conventions that bound, and still bind, Germany more tightly than we might imagine.

I was just 20, you see, and I loved it as only a 20-year-old can. I even loved the ritual of the pre-season friendlies, played between Keegan's old club SV Hamburg, the never-relegated founder members of the top-flight, and the band of brothers in their brown kits who turned out for the other lot.

Pauli didn't like SV Hamburg, for all the obvious reasons. The SV supporters would often come from the outlying suburbs and tended to have real jobs, making things or at least mending them, perhaps on board one of the Chinese container ships moored in Hamburg's vast harbour. SV fans, weaned on successful football teams, often came with a different attitude towards politics. In short, Pauli's fans all thought SV were Nazis and SV thought Pauli were all violent anarchists who needed socially cleansing. The truth was, of course, probably nowhere near either of those extremes. But these are the games people play, in life and in football.

All the best action during a succession of these ill-advised friendly fixtures was on the terraces, as line after line of green-clothed, white-helmeted riot Polizei, with snarling Alsatians on leads, would charge at both sets of rival supporters in the Südkurve. 'We are brown! We are white! We are Pauli dynamite!' we'd chant vigorously in English, before breaking into Monty Python's *Always Look on the Bright Side of Life*. Once the game had been irrelevantly concluded or even abandoned, everyone would leave the stadium to chase each other around the fairground shouting about Nazis, occasionally stopping breathlessly to roll a cigarette.

For the first time in my life I watched the game closely, moving unconsciously where I stood as the patterns of play swept across the pitch like ripples on a wind-touched puddle. The stretching and shrinking of a back four's fragile line of defence, the loneliness of the goalkeeper, the snap and tussle of the centre where mini-battles for possession flashed like grenades igniting in no-man's land. The sheer astonishment of a goal! The utter improbability of scoring and the unreal sense of it having just happened, right in front of your eyes. Sometimes you could hear the player scream in delight just a fraction of a second before the crowd cottoned on, caught up and ignited their roar.

Football is mostly an impossible proposition. It's like catching water in a sieve. Most moves break down, most shots fail. That's why, when, for whatever reason, something goes *right*, the sense of release is amplified. Stick 60,000 people in a stadium and that release becomes euphoria, spreading pheromones through the air at light speed and creating at one stroke a herd. A tribe.

Football, unlike hockey, for example, or cricket, or anything else, is a fundamental nonsense. To control a hard ball, faced with 11 players who want to take it from you, the only sensible thing to do would be to pick it up and run. Yet the laws of the game expressly forbid this and so you are left with the next best thing – a foot. Seriously, a foot. Feet are great for walking, standing and running. But not much more than that. There is a clip on the internet in which Thierry Henry talks about the best Lionel Messi goal he ever saw. Messi does something so deft and unlikely with his left foot, controlling the ball twice, seemingly without asking his standing right foot to contribute in any way, that Henry is left looking to the camera and asking in exasperation, 'How did he do that? How is that possible?' Then his right foot finishes it off. 'I mean, how?'

Lionel Messi was still in nappies back then. And besides, St Pauli were no Barcelona. Yet my affection grew on each subsequent visit.

This is how a football club insinuates itself. This is how the game gets in, slowly but surely, as you get to know the actors.

I fell in love with all of it. All 90-minutes-plus-time-added-on-for-injury of it. I felt now that, in my own way, I had gate-crashed the world that, back in Cambridge, Sean, Si and Giles already intuitively understood. I had become a fan. A little late, but I'd done it on my terms.

*****

I returned to England to finish my studies. Since I'd been away, the '80s had ended.

I spent the summer of Italia '90 waiting for university to start and working as an operating theatre assistant in King's College Hospital in Camberwell, mopping up blood, removing amputated body parts for incineration in yellow bio-hazard bags and picking up extra bags of blood from the stores when the operation wasn't going quite to plan. Then I took the bus home to Putney for the football on the telly.

Like millions of others, I was entranced by the spectacle: Pavarotti, Steve Bull, Jack Charlton, Graham Taylor in the studio, Roger Milla, Des Lynam, Frank Rijkaard, Rudi Völler and all. I was living in a bedroom of a shared house with a group of unemployed actors – friends of friends. Although I was actually still a student working as a hospital porter, I aspired one day to become an unemployed actor just like my housemates – and would go on to fulfil that noble ambition. But, for now, they were wildly exciting company and it was a wildly exciting summer. Tony Head, at the very height of his Gold Blend fame, used to come round to watch the football with us and I followed England's progress with total awe. I saw Platt's Belgium volley hit the back of the net in a riotous pub in Southfields with my long-haired college friend, Giles, as the pint glasses flew in the air. Then I blacked out. Lager, you see. Football and lager.

I watched England edge out Cameroon in our back garden, eating burned sausages and talking to the bloke from the coffee advert. Then, weirdly, and for reasons I can no longer recall, I had to watch the semi-final defeat to Germany (of all countries) in a semi-deserted pub near the station in Twickenham. Leaving in a state of total desolation, I felt genuinely like the world would never feel whole again. I was not the only one, I suspect, who felt that way.

But football doesn't work like that. You just recalibrate. Before too long I had returned to the final year of my studies at Cambridge and continued my quest for a tribe. This took me to the Abbey Stadium, Cambridge United's student-averse home. Giles and I only went there twice, as far as I recall. It was the John Beck era and Cambridge had no need of midfielders. They just hoofed the ball from defence to attack. The fans seemed to love it. From those hostile home terraces we were able to admire Dion Dublin leading the line, soon to be replaced by a young, and seemingly highly popular, scurrying striker with his socks rolled down and no shin pads. Later that particular evening, I remember our friend Sean saying he'd spotted Steve Claridge in one of the city's less salubrious night clubs.

Football continued to play an important role in my life – the avoidance of reality. The most pressing issue in my actual life was my finals. In order to avoid thinking about them, I spent my life consuming football reports. On one occasion, I missed an essay deadline by a country mile, having chosen to spend the night before the writing was due lying in bed listening to BBC Cambridgeshire's commentary on Southend United playing Cambridge United at the top end of the second division. Two teams I didn't support. I hung on the commentator's every word. 'Pressure building now at Roots Hall.'

*****

After climbing over the gates of the Senate House at midnight to discover on a notice board that I was to graduate with a 2:2, I spent a summer in Wimbledon with Giles watching lots and lots more football and working in a shop and a pub. Having no cogent plan for how to spend the whole of the rest of my life, I simply retraced my steps and returned to Hamburg to try and figure out what to do. Or rather, how to do it.

I wanted to become an actor. I had expected the city to throw up its arms in surrender in the face of my comic talent. After all, this was, alongside Berlin, the home of the German *Kabarett* tradition, of which the Schmidt Theater on the Reeperbahn was the unofficial national headquarters and whose managing director, Corny Littmann, one of Germany's best known comedians, would go on to become St Pauli's president.

It didn't turn out to be quite as easy as that. I struggled for work, occasionally getting gigs playing totally incidental German characters for low-rent British TV shows, or British characters for low-rent German crime dramas. Sometimes I dubbed cartoons. For two summers I toured primary schools dressed up as a sad tiger. Once, in the best paid gig I ever got, I helped launch the latest Airbus plane model (which was assembled near Hamburg) dressed as one of the Montgolfier brothers, the 18th-century hot air balloon pioneers, in front of an audience that included Helmut Kohl and Michael Heseltine. Once I even attempted some stand-up comedy in the Schmidt Theater itself and still get flashbacks to this day of gazing out at a mostly empty venue and absolutely no laughter.

So, I had time on my hands. More than that, I had a total aversion to thinking deeply about the course of my life. I was heading rapidly towards my mid-20s and didn't want to admit that I had achieved nothing. Self-reflection was my kryptonite. In this regard an obsessive interest in football was perfectly suited. My sudden and deep infatuation might have stemmed, in part at least, from the fact that I was living in exile, a long way from friends, family and accountability.

Rather than consider too deeply how to emerge from this gathering crisis, it was easier to rush to the newspaper stand to pick up the local paper and lose myself in all the latest rumour-mongering about who Pauli might sign. Imagine my delight when they announced they'd landed the prized signature of the reasonably talented Marcus Marin, who'd scored nine whole goals in the actual Bundesliga for Kaiserslautern. Of course, I was among the small clutch of fans who made their way to the very modest ground of a local amateur club to see Marin make his debut in a hastily arranged friendly. 'Olé!', we sang, to the tune of *Go West!* '*Olé, Marcus Marin is da!*'

More than anything during those years in exile, I lived for Saturdays. The previous six days were simply an irritating prelude. If Pauli were at home, I was there. Always. My place was in the Nordkurve, just to the right of the goal, halfway up the stand. I always gravitated to that same spot, where I would stand next to the same moustachioed and befuddled jesters with denim jackets bedecked with sew-on patches and scarves tied around both wrists. We'd nod at each other. There was a confused lady of advanced years who wore nothing, even in the depths of winter, but a sleeveless Pauli T-shirt, a very small pair of Pauli shorts and a pair of wellies. The stand kept her fed on a diet of *Bockwurst* and *Brötchen* (sausage in a roll). It was a community, of sorts. My affiliation to Pauli would last for many years. I watched closely as the team became clearer to me, as familiar in the end as a family in a much-loved sitcom.

There was Bernd Hollerbach, a ridiculously bandy-legged and short-arsed winger who was just about Pauli's only genuinely exciting player. He possessed the occasional ability to dribble uncontrollably, in a style that meant he teetered on the brink of total ignominy, as if he were trying to play Jenga on a unicycle. Receiving the ball wide on the right, with a bit of space in front of him, the crowd would roar with sudden anticipation. Moments later they'd be groaning in unison, then swearing, then laughing. '*Hollerbach! Du Vollidiot!*'

Once I saw him lose control of the ball as he bore down on the keeper in the pouring rain, fall over, continue to slide at the same pace as the ball, reach out a hand, and gently guide the ball around the advancing goalie and over the line to score a rare, but legally questionable, goal. Hollerbach was sent off. Millerntor shook with laughter and outrage.

Then there was the masterly Peter Knäbel, who ran the midfield like a reasonably high-functioning warehouse manager. The appropriately handsome team captain used to point a lot, and stroke passes as if he were Matthäus and as if the team had a plan that necessitated pointing anywhere other than just wildly upfield. There would come a point towards the middle of the second half when, tiring, he'd invariably horribly mistime a tackle, bringing down some unfortunate opponent so violently that his cries would be heard above the din coming from the fairground, the police helicopter and the loose chatter of 17,000 fans slowly giving up on the game. Wonderfully, Knäbel never quite gave up on the idea that he was any good.

Klaus Ottens was blonder than snow and slower than a falling flake. He hailed from Herzlake, a tiny village in the Emsland, a region characterised by flat ploughed fields, a unique variant of the German language and a terrifyingly strong juniper-based spirit. He was supposed to put the ball (known in German football slang as *das Ding* – the thing) in the bloody net ('*das Nezt, Ottens!*'). He didn't manage to do this very often. But when he did, the crowd erupted into one of those disbelieving cries of delight and simultaneous hilarity. Every club, I subsequently learned, has an Ottens. Heartwarmingly, he was also a shocking goal-hanger. He 'played off the shoulder of the last defender' but didn't turn them with a drop of the shoulder as much as simply run through them, trampling them underfoot as he advanced on goal in an unswervingly straight line to the sound of thousands of inebriated anarchists screaming '*Oddi-oddi-oddi-oddi!*'

And then there was Leonardo Manzi. Signed by Pauli in July 1989, when they were hanging onto a place in the top division by the skin of their nicotine-stained teeth, he was quickly described first by *Bild Zeitung* as 'Pauli's Pelé', and not long later by *Die Welt* as being 'the only Brazilian, seemingly, who can't play football.' We loved him, more than he loved himself, which was, in fairness, quite a lot. And once or twice I saw him score, though I can remember nothing of those vanishingly rare occasions since seconds later I'd always be jostled to the ground and covered in sweet German mustard, beer and half-eaten preztels.

At the end of whatever defeat I'd just witnessed, I'd rush home to my violently sordid shared flat and tune in to the Bundesliga highlights show that began, amazingly at 6.30, just over half an hour after the end of the matches. *Ran!* was presented by Reinhold Beckmann, an estate agent in a turquoise blazer, and filmed in front of a studio audience. In other words, it did all those things that received TV wisdom tell us cannot work for a British audience, as has been proven time and time again when broadcasters attempt to deviate from the straight and narrow of three blokes and a couch.

Thus, did four years of my life pass.

Any sense of personal development might have been put on hold, my football journey was only just beginning. I watched Germany fail in '92, beaten hilariously by Denmark, and Carlton Palmer's England fade into total insignificance, just as my non-starting career was threatening to do. At a time when more precocious friends from Cambridge were already completing PhDs and others were already embarked on trajectories that would turn them into household names, editors of the biggest papers in the country and internationally celebrated playwrights, I was sitting in my pants almost penniless in my unfurnished Hamburg rented room entering a TV prize draw to win a Germany '94 kit (which, rather impressively, I won).

My most notable achievement came about the day before my 24th birthday, just as I witnessed Germany being eliminated from USA '94 by Bulgaria – the winner being scored by SV Hamburg's completely bald Yordan Letchkov. Writing on a typewriter from my attic room in Hamburg's least glamorous red-light district, I composed a letter to *The Guardian's* Notes & Queries section. The question I was answering was about which British footballers could speak foreign languages. Kevin Keegan, I told the world. Keegan spoke passable German. On the day of publication, I rushed to the international press stand and bought the paper, stopping dead in my tracks when I saw that my letter had actually been published. I looked up at the old clock on the tower of the *Hauptbahnhof*. The minute hand juddered on and then stopped again.

If only, I thought, there was a way to carry on loving football, but also become an adult.

5

Football Factory

ENGLAND 1–1 GERMANY (GERMANY WIN
6–5 ON PENALTIES).
26 June, 1996. Wembley Stadium, London.

In which illusions fall away.

I returned to London in 1995. Hamburg had been a rewarding adventure in every sense of the word except for the ones that tangibly matter. I was now 26 and totally bereft of a plan. Plagued by the creeping realisation that my 20s were flashing by, I was painfully aware that all I had to show for them was a smoker's cough, a rucksack full of dirty clothes and an in-depth understanding of the strengths of Werder Bremen's attacking options under the charismatic leadership of opera buff and Socialist renaissance man, Otto Rehhagel. This seemed an inadequate CV for life. I also had nowhere to stay, nor money to spend.

My sister, Emily, rescued me. As luck would have it, she was a more convincing human than I was. Having completed a theatre studies degree and having lived with a couple of actors who had no income, she took the business of being an adult very seriously, which meant getting a job, then a mortgage, then a career, then an actual house. Through a friend, she'd managed to get some work in TV – sports TV, to be precise. It might not have been her first choice, but it was a job. And she was good at it.

She did so at a time when there was a sudden and deregulated boom in the market, as the monopoly held by the BBC and ITV came crashing to the ground. Brave new broadcast horizons were opening up across the landscape. Some of them were a bit rubbish (the 'Squariel' of British Satellite Broadcasting fame), but one of them was a bit less rubbish: Sky was being born, with Monday Night Football, cheerleaders, Richard Keys, wooshing graphics and all.

Emily swiftly rose to be a producer at Sky Sports during those early years, exhibiting a willingness and ability to learn and, perhaps most significantly, get the best out of people. And before too long, as their portfolio of programmes expanded to match their ambitious purchase of live Premier League rights, she went on to become producer of *Soccer AM*, working at first with the highly talented, quirky Helen Chamberlain. She, in turn, was paired with Gary Stevens, who had perhaps a little less of those admirable qualities, but had played for Spurs and England, which Helen hadn't. To cut a long, nepotistic story short, to save me from eating all her food and not ever leaving her house, my sister managed to smuggle me into her place of work to do a Saturday job, the TV equivalent of a paper round.

It was that autumn of 1995 that I got my first job in telly. I was paid £50 a day to make tea and run errands behind the scenes at *Sports Saturday*, the very wonky forerunner of the cult *Soccer Saturday*, hosted by a roster of different presenters, one of whom was Jeff Stelling.

Back then, *Sports Saturday* was actually the fiefdom of a brilliant, fiercely intelligent presenter called Paul Dempsey, with Stelling still very much 'Plan B'. The show was a kind of low-rent *Grandstand*, with a smattering of horse racing, extended round-ups of whatever golfery had been going on overnight in some manicured and probably racist part of the United States. With Dempsey at the helm though, whatever the event was, it elicited the utmost intensity. Dark and brooding, he was a man who took his sport extremely seriously. He was very much in keeping with the house style of Sky Sports, for whom the word 'sport' meant everything: it was an absolute value, a virtue, a beacon, a natural law, a religion. The way Dempsey referred to an 'eagle putt from Ernie Els' or a 'late fitness test for Jamie Redknapp' left you in no doubt that these were the issues of the day, and, as such, needed to be dealt with as if he were reporting the outbreak of hostilities on the Western Front. There would come a time when I would be called onto the studio floor during a commercial break, to stand in front of him while he told me my work was 'useless', which, to be fair to Dempsey, it was.

When Dempsey was called away (boxing, or 'pugilism' to be more accurate, was a big love of his and the only sport that's not a metaphor for combat), the Sky Sports bosses would reluctantly promote the light-hearted Jeff Stelling to the *Sports Saturday* hot seat. Jeff's remit was usually restricted to the numberless 'other' sports with which Sky packed their schedules – minority pastimes that bordered on hobbies. Sky Sports worked under the not-unmeritorious proposition that it didn't matter what the sport was, so long as it was live people would tune in.

So, Jeff would move from greyhound racing and darts to football, where he felt most at home. At three o'clock, he came into his own when *Sports Saturday* turned into an elastically extended version of *Final Score*. This is where he would effortlessly woo the audience, daring to express, with a fan's outrage, the crueller twists of fate, not resisting the temptation to find humour at every turn, and not taking either himself, his pundits nor the game with quite the po-faced seriousness that set the tone on the channel's primary output. Jeff would play a huge part in my education in TV, encouraging me to take risks, to enjoy it, to find the absurdity and look for the unusual angle in everything. He taught me to respect the game, but to mock the pomposity that surrounded it. He set me on my way.

But all that was some way off. For now, *Sports Saturday* was mostly Paul Dempsey and Julian Waters pretending to be interested in domestic basketball, or occasionally, as I recall, demonstrating some new family game live in the studio. On one occasion, this involved Stelling trying to catch fluffy balls on a Velcro cap strapped to his head. Sky was an emergent project, back then.

*****

On my first day, I arrived at Sky Sports' prosaic headquarters in an industrial estate round the back of the Gillette factory in Osterley, west London, pinned my laminated name pass to my tatty denim jacket and entered the rest of my life. I cannot adequately express the wonder I felt at what I saw when I first crossed the threshold and went into the beating heart of a TV network. Familiarity may now have inured me to the belt and braces reality of what goes on behind the scenes at a TV station, but not back then. Terrified, out of my depth, and made overwhelmed to the point of muteness by the sheer *competence* on display, I embarked on a day spent surrounded by industry professionals, fierce sports broadcasters, technical experts and producers who seemed to know absolutely everything about every footballer who'd ever played a game of football in football boots, ever.

Sky Sports back then was very different to the slick corporate behemoth it has since become. It was the new kid on the block, whose very existence was precarious and predicated on a massive punt that football would be the battering ram with which to launch a new media assault on people's living rooms. It was institutionally ballsy; brash, noisy, yellow and red, shiny, punchy. It was also tiny. Operating out of a couple of hideously ugly office units where you'd expect to see Ricky Gervais in a swivel chair round every corner, it was staffed by a few dozen young folk who were determined to make their way in the world, fast.

These men and women in turn were marshalled by some more grizzly all-male executives drawn from across the TV landscape to join this brave new world. Tiny partition office doors slammed shut then flew open as blokes in shirts and ties strode out with a 'We'll have to fucking see about that!' Things sometimes flew across the open plan offices. Tapes spilled over desks in seemingly endless disorder. There was a lot of testosterone, mostly emanating from the after-shave-splattered chins of early middle-aged white men in chinos and loafers exhibiting extremely high levels of self-confidence. Add to that mix the physical presence of Richard Keys and Andy Gray, and you might get a sense of the sheer concentration of football pheromones being pumped through the air conditioning and permeating the air we all breathed. It was heady stuff.

It was also pretty horrifying. I shrank inwardly from human contact, found it difficult to justify my presence and floundered for week after week. But, and this was the point, there was football. Lots and lots of it. Having developed, over half a decade, an almost insatiable thirst for consuming football on the telly, in real life and on the printed page, I now almost choked on the sudden profusion in which I was immersed. This building could barely contain the sheer volume of football it housed. It spilled out from every corner. There was an insane, unprecedented, overwhelming amount of football, delivered from every square inch of space, at all times, in superabundance and in an entirely naked, unexpected way.

Screen after screen after screen. Some small, some giant, others linked together side by side and one on top of the other. Screens on desks, balanced on stacks of books, in hallways, offices, edit suites and canteens. All of them flickering with flashes of Ian Rush, glimpses of Steve Bruce, patches of Tony Adams. All these images framed against the blurred Jackson Pollock of a terrace of faces, or seen from the gantry cameras embedded into the green, green grass of the homes of the still newly minted FA Carling Premier League.

The place was always 'On Air'. Big match broadcasts were either in progress ('Live and Exclusive!') or highlights were churning away, with other studio programmes and endless discussion panels previewing the football, reviewing the football, chewing over and spitting out the football being prepared. Never, not for a second, was it possible to escape the roar and reach of the nation's favourite game. This was the heart of the revolution that was about to grip the game and drag it into the 21st century. I walked around, agog, in ill-fitting slacks, trying to fit in.

On the dimly-lit ground floor, underneath the office space, was the engine room. Sometimes, on some only partially understood errand, tape in hand (just as I had walked the corridors of Kings College Hospital in operating greens carrying blood bags) I would find myself walking past the rows of windowless editing suites. These mysterious edit suites, buzzing with dozens of tiny fans whirring away to keep the machinery cool, were located in the bowels of this most soulless of buildings.

Inside each cell there were people sitting in front of banks of controls and light switches that wouldn't have looked out of place in the cockpit of a transatlantic airliner. Here, in the flickering semi-darkness, people were crafting, from odd little snippets of hitherto un-broadcast footage, the newly re-vamped genre of musical montages of footballers kicking balls and celebrating. Gone was the old slapdash vernacular of simply grafting a bit of Pavarotti onto Totò Schillaci. Now football and footballers were being re-invented as the stars of music videos and the game throbbed to Britpop's happy grind, live and exclusive.

I would watch as piles of heavy tapes were loaded and unloaded by producers, younger than me already and way more qualified. The tapes would spit out from, and then disappear into, big industrial decks, which would then spool at breakneck speed back through a match, only to come thundering to a halt at the precise frame, $1/24^{th}$ of a second, when Teddy Sheringham's right hand reached out for and touched the golden mane of Jürgen Klinsmann mid-flight. And all this, with pinpoint accuracy, to hit the drop as Fatboy Slim insisted it had to be 'right here, right now!' Sky were spawning a genre, right there and then. And, arguably, TV sport would never recover its sense of proportion.

One of my first jobs on a Saturday afternoon was breathtakingly simple. It was my responsibility to dictate the names of players to a graphics typist. As three o'clock on a Saturday drew closer, a number of us sat in front of rudimentary green and white monitors, not connected to anything like the internet back then, but somehow mysteriously linked to the whirring super-computer deep underground. Flickering across these devices, team news would be delivered, phoned in by Press Association reporters from the various grounds up and down the country, and then relayed across the world. These bulletins were known, for some reason, as 'snaps'.

My job, on reading a snap from, say, Anfield, was to filter the names of the starting XI, and those who were on the bench, and pick out the headlines. Then, I had to dictate the newsworthy changes or notable absences to a hard-pressed graphics operator who then typed them hurriedly onto a template which scrolled across the screen.

'McManaman starts. Fowler drops to bench as Collymore returns.' That kind of thing. 'Babb sidelined with groin.' You get the idea.

It was probably the most stressful job I have ever done, which may not say much for me, but says plenty about the job. For a product of such extraordinary triviality, the emotional investment and sheer anxiety that swirled around behind the scenes were entirely disproportionate. A delay of even 20 seconds getting the news on Le Tissier's return to the starting line up onto the nation's screens could have far reaching consequences. Worse still, a misspelt name could end a career there and then. The team news from Old Trafford was fraught with danger, especially when Andrei Kanchelskis returned from international duty. But it was thrilling.

At the end of the day's work, I'd walk to the bus stop with a faint sense of euphoria. I'd spent the day, at least partially, in the company of Rodney Marsh and Frank McLintock, whose bonhomie, Brat Pack good looks and booming voice extended beyond the boundaries of normal office interaction and into the urinals, where he'd often, quite volubly, continue his analysis of Nigel Winterburn's positional play, as well as croon a tune or two in the style of a central defending Glaswegian Nat King Cole. You had no choice but to listen when McLintock weed and sang.

These were things people, as a rule, don't get to do. I was able to talk to these great names from the past of the game as if they were normal humans, which in theory they were. Later on in my spiritual journey, moving the magnifying glass ever closer to football's skin, I realised they weren't actually normal people. And it would be much later still before I realised that perhaps, after all, they *were* normal people. All that philosophical confusion was still to come.

For now, I was blissfully content with what I'd got and where I'd landed. I made tea for Clive Allen, I thought to myself with pride. From time to time I'd have a drink after work with Mark Lawrenson, and then try to remember, on the way home, whether or not he had a moustache.

The 1995–96 season came to a close. It hadn't mattered how much Kevin Keegan, watery eyed and slightly too short for the camera angle, finger-jabbingly insisted that he'd love it if Newcastle won. Because they didn't. Instead, and by four points, Manchester United started their empire-building stranglehold on the English game. And with Dennis Irwin and Peter Schmeichel punching the air, Sky effectively shut down till August. It might have been the summer of Euro '96, but since satellite channels didn't have the rights to show the football, they effectively stuck a finger in either ear and went 'la la la' for the months of June and July.

This meant I'd lost my Saturday work and my sense of purpose. I spent the summer of 1996 stuck in a job in a bookies. More than ever, I started to worry about my future viability as a person. To cope with the worry, I retreated into only caring about England, which seemed simpler than caring about either me or my partner Kath who was working as a newly qualified nurse and with whom I was, hoping to start a life. I am not exaggerating. For a month, England was all I cared about; through the relief of Gazza and Scotland to the shocked delight of the game against Holland (watched alone at home, screaming along with Shearer as he waited in the middle for Sheringham to square it) to the agony of the quarter-final against Spain. When Pyscho did his shouty thing I did the same, and so did everyone else in that hot and crowded pub in East Putney.

As England marched semi-convincingly on, something incredible happened: Frank Skinner and David Baddiel discovered that it was possible to make all sorts of people laugh about football, a hitherto hidden association that blew the minds of a certain section of the population who had never realised that it was OK to poke fun at a thing that routinely made people so angry. The co-authors of the magnificent *Football's Coming Home* anthem (which I still struggle to sing without welling up when it gets to the bit about Nobby dancing) encouraged the rapid growth of the *Guardian*-reading, middle-class, university-educated football culture that grafted itself noisily onto the mass of the actual game.

I was a living, breathing, shouting cliché of the new football fan. I ticked every single stereotypical box of the Johnny-come-latelies of the '90s in my earnest desire to find a home within the rabbit warren of the English game. My German education in football, under the brown-and-white clad anarcho-syndicalists of St Pauli, had taught me much, but it had decidedly not given me a guide on how to get along in the tribal affair that English football will forever be. I didn't even have a team to claim I supported, the very lowest of the entry level criteria, an inadequacy that would dog my entire footballing life.

I did, though, have a country. Supporting England has never been a choice for me. It has simply been an impulse, the only means I had of replicating the curiously uplifting and hideously downcasting process of coupling your emotional well-being to the talent and ambition of 11 men you've never met and a hard-to-control ball they're not allowed to touch with their hands. England it was, then: unquestioningly, loyally. Hard to understand maybe, but there it is. All those years in Germany, I had wondered about where my home was and now I knew. It was among these people, drunken, happy and delighted by this team in their blue-collared Umbro kit. Venables on the touchline, McManaman all willowy, and Gazza bottle-blond and brilliant. It was a new start and it was intoxicating. Their success, and the *manner* of their play, mattered to me in ways I find hard to express. They had the power to make my mood soar and they could, and did, crush my spirit entirely in the very instant one small, white ball was struck high and wide and into the Wembley night sky.

I watched that semi-final in a pub on Lower Marsh, just around the back of Waterloo. It had been a warm day. During the long afternoon, in unbearable readiness for kick-off and convinced that things were going to end well, cocooned as I was in the bubble of that summer of football love, I had rifled through my belongings and found what I was looking for. It was the prize I had won in 1994, watching the World Cup from my Hamburg bedsit; a Germany football shirt; the really nasty one from '94 that will forever speak to the world of Thomas Häßler, Stefan Effenberg and Jürgen Klinsmann. It was three sizes too big and made of such statically charged nylon that it damn near exploded every time I pulled it over my head, sending sharp forks of lightning deep into my ears.

It was that shirt, with its *schwarz, rot und gold* chevrons, that I pulled on before making my way to the pub that evening in London.

I thought, in my naivety and euphoria, that this special summer had moved the great populations of these two rival countries into a fraternal embrace. I thought I felt that the last dim echoes of post-war dissension were dissolving into the darkening evening sky, despite the *Daily Mirror* front page 'Achtung! Surrender!' Euro '96 had changed everything, and, on a personal note, it had knitted these two sides of my lived experience together. Finally, through celebrating the game, for the sake of the game, I could resolve my love for Germany with the passion for the country of my birth.

What I hadn't realised was that for this alchemy to materialise, England would need to actually win the match.

Leaving the pub, as it emptied within seconds of Venables holding Gareth Southgate's crestfallen features in both hands, Giles, my old friend from university, turned to me and said, 'You're not going to wear that on the way home, are you?' I was still in my Germany kit. I pulled on a jacket I'd taken with me and, zipping it up, made my way home. I don't know what I did with that Germany top, but I never wore it again and now I don't know where it is.

By pure chance, about three days after England had lost in the semi-final, one morning, I saw Tony Adams on a street in south London. He was a bit dishevelled, wearing a suit with the tie barely knotted, swaying across the road towards me. As he passed me, I caught his eye, very briefly. In that instant I was seized with an impulse to tell him, right there and then, on the pavement, what it had taken me over 20 years to digest.

But of course I didn't. Years later, interviewing him for TV, during a stint in which he was coaching in the Netherlands, I did indeed try to tell him, to sum it up; the walk to the pub, the Germany shirt, what it had meant to me. But since it is a complex knot of feelings I can barely articulate to myself, I made a hash of it. He'd just looked bemused, as I recall.

The summer of '96 was over. But I was finally getting started.

6

First Dance

LIVERPOOL 3–0 ASTON VILLA.
18 January, 1997. Anfield, Liverpool.

In which a debut is made.

In 1997, just as I was beginning to think I'd never be able to leave the branch of Ladbrokes where I idled away my minimum-wage hours behind the cash desk watching the racing from Carlisle and the dogs from Sheffield, I was offered a full-time job by Sky Sports. For around £10,000 per annum, I became a production junior, at the distinctly non-junior age of 28. I was inordinately proud of myself, and yet we still depended on Kath's meagre nurse's income to pay the rent and make ends meet.

In my new role, and despite my best efforts to disappoint in almost every task I was allotted, I started quite quickly to move through the gears at Sky. My unique ability to not be terribly good at anything in particular meant that I was moved around so much I couldn't be exposed for long in any specific mediocrity.

I failed at admin, spectacularly so. On my first day of having a proper job, sitting proudly at my new desk with a four-digit extension number I remember so well it is still the PIN code for absolutely every card I have ever owned, I was charged with answering the phone and allocating reporters to go to all the matches we needed covering for the coming weekend. By now, *Sports Saturday* had become *Soccer Saturday* and a much more serious proposition. Every Saturday dozens of freelance reporters were sent out for a fee of £75 to phone in from the press box and describe the goals on

43

air, as they went in. I, a newly 'qualified' production junior, got to decide who went where.

On my first morning, at 9.30, the phone rang. The show's producer, sitting opposite me, looked up.

'You'd better answer it,' he said. 'But if that's Brian Beard, tell him he's sacked.'

I picked up the phone. 'Hello, *Soccer Saturday*?'

'Hello,' said a cheery voice on the other end. 'It's Brian Beard, here.'

I sacked him. Within minutes of starting my new job, I had terminated the career of a loyal local reporter. Then I hung up and started to shuffle papers around my desk, efficiently.

The producer, who'd been listening, looked aghast. 'What did you do that for?'

'Well, you…'

'I was joking.' He'd gone pale with shock. 'I didn't *actually* mean you were supposed to sack him. Jesus.'

There followed a long silence, during which time he simply shook his head and I stared at the desk in front of me. 'You'd better ring him back.'

I rang Brian Beard back and sheepishly un-fired him. As far as I am aware, he still reports from football grounds of a Saturday afternoon.

After that, my skills as a video producer, working on the various features, were tested out. I was charged, during my first winter in TV, with preparing the supposed-to-be-hilarious Christmas bloopers film for our Boxing Day show. I worked day after day on the project, finally finishing it late on Christmas Eve, taking my task extremely seriously. Perhaps that was the problem, because when I came to show it to the boss on the morning of the show, he watched the whole tape through in grim silence.

When it finished, there was an awkward pause. 'Ned,' he began, 'the problem is that it's not funny.' The film was never broadcast. No one ever referred to it again.

I was shunted onto other aspects of the production, where I could do less damage. One of these involved 'logging' interviews as they arrived. These interviews would be recorded and then played back, on a delay. Central to how this works in a live TV studio show is knowing two things: the exact duration of the interview and the 'out words', the cue for the vision and sound mixers in the control gallery to cut back to the presenter, so that he (it's usually still a 'he') can say something like, 'Interesting to hear the thoughts of Lee Hendrie there, reflecting on another frustrating afternoon at Villa Park.'

With a stopwatch and a note pad, I'd listen to the interviews and then supply the information to the director's assistant in charge of timings. For example: 1 minute 23. Out words: 'delighted with the three points'.

Mostly this worked, except when, unforgettably, Jamie Carragher was interviewed for the first time in his life, having made his first start for Liverpool and scored. Having struggled, initially, to recognise him at all, I could work out the duration of his interview, but could not, for the life of me, come even close to deciphering the out words. Delivered at a youthfully exaggerated version of Carragher's famous high pitch, whatever it was that he was articulating had been lost completely somewhere between the Bootle streets of his childhood and the geo-stationary satellite hardware against which they were being bounced in space for redistribution across the football world.

'Jamie Carragher. Two minutes 11,' I wrote down, with confidence. 'Out words… something in scouse,' was the best I could do.

*****

Mine was a career like a new-born giraffe.

'What shall we do with that new lad, Boulting?'

'Get him out of the office.'

One Sunday morning, they did just that.

I was trying to enjoy a lie-in in a damp, ground floor front bedroom in Tooting as a stream of London buses ground their gear boxes just feet from our shrouded bay window, when my phone rang. It rang three times. Then a fourth. Then, reluctantly, I pushed the duvet aside and got out of bed, and slouched towards the kitchen, where the cordless phone was chirruping away next to the kettle.

I got to the phone just in time. 'Hello?'

'Nedski.' My producer had a nickname for me that was well-intended. But every time he used the term, I felt as if my hair was being metaphorically ruffled by an affectionate uncle who was almost exactly my age. 'What are you doing today?'

'Er, nothing.' I should have lied, but nothing sprang to mind. It was Sunday. Working for *Soccer Saturday*, it was only natural that I had Sundays off. In my mind's eye, I had already envisaged an hour or so trying and failing to complete the crossword in the Sunday papers, before maybe meeting up with friends for a walk, and then a trip to the pub to watch Richard Keys host *Super Sunday* in which Faustino Asprilla would look like he was about to fall over and Kevin Keegan would probably say something emotional. That was my plan for Sunday and it didn't involve work.

'Why?' I asked, hesitantly.

'Well, we've got a shoot lined up for early this afternoon. But Dickie's sick and can't make it.' Dickie Davis was *Soccer Saturday*'s senior reporter. He shared a name with the other, more famous, Dickie Davis, but was shorter, didn't have any kind of iconic moustache and drove a clapped-out green people carrier. 'I thought you might like to have a go at doing a report.' I remained silent, squinting at the tiny patch of autumnal morning sky that was gradually filling our poky little kitchen with milky light.

Despite my impressively resolute silence, the patient voice on the other end persisted. 'It's at Earls Court. You'd have to get there for about 12.30 to meet the cameraman.' Silence. 'Ian Wright's there. It's a fashion show.' More silence. 'With Prince Naseem Hamed, for some reason.'

'The thing is,' I mounted my defence hesitantly. 'I'm on a day off. So…'

'Are you saying you don't want to do it?' I could hear the barely supressed frustration. 'It's a great opportunity for you, Nedski. Who knows what it might lead to.' There was a certain edge to his use of my nickname that had now moved from hair-ruffling to mock-throttling.

'I'm all right, thanks.'

After he'd hung up, I sloped back to the still-dark bedroom. Kath, who'd come off a night-shift in the hospital, had been woken by the phone call. 'What was that about?' she asked, half asleep.

'Oh, nothing.' I contemplated feigning instant sleep, but I realised that my answer hadn't quite convinced her. 'They just wanted to send me to film a report with Ian Wright at a fashion show.' I left that hanging. 'With Prince Naseem Hamed for some reason.'

Then came one word, from under the duvet, that changed the course of my life.

'Go.'

I ran to the kitchen, made the necessary humiliating phone call, rushed to the shower, got dressed and was out of the front door within ten minutes of having declined the opportunity to become a football reporter.

*****

Ian Wright was someone who I had only seen by sitting in the pub, gazing up at a TV at his tiny, animated red-and-white figure darting across the pitch, constantly agitated. Or more commonly, in close-up, grinning, exasperated, imploring. His Arsenal team was one season away from winning the title with Arsène Wenger and, in tandem with Dennis Bergkamp, Wright was at his quicksilver best. These were the greatest years of his footballing life. Irrepressible, versatile, with an ability to cut in off the wing, roll away from the last defender, volley one in from the edge of the area, or stick away a tap-in. He was capable of just about everything and his south London joie-de-vivre, coupled with Bergkamp's dispassionate sang-froid, was a joy to behold. And I was on my way to meet him.

Laden down with all the right access passes from a fashion show that was milking Wright's presence for all the PR value it could harvest, we filmed him sashaying up and down the catwalk, flinging open his blazer and kicking out his winkle-pickers and letting his contagious smile catch in the flashbulbs. And then we filmed him some more, backstage in some huge changing room area, messing around with tweedy jackets, big ruched, puffy shirts and baggy caps. And then, before I knew it, I was standing in front of the actual Ian Wright. His image was one thing, but this was another. Here he was in flesh and blood, looking for all the world exactly like the actual Ian Wright that he really was. It felt disconnected; an encounter that stepped outside of the normal time and space of a dank Sunday lunchtime in November.

'Ian, do you like clothes?' was the brilliant opener to my journalistic career I chose from all the many things I could have asked him.

There was a momentary pause, during which he almost managed to look hurt by the inanity of my first ever line of questioning. Then he launched into a reply so effusive, naturally good-natured and charismatic, that the feature was instantly guaranteed to succeed. Although my eyes were out on stalks and my breath caught short, it was the easiest possible way of starting out. All I had to do was point the microphone the cameraman had handed to me in the right direction. Though remembering to draw it back and forth in time with my questions and his answers was surprisingly challenging and felt at first like being asked to pat your stomach and rub your head. Such technicalities. And when I changed the subject from clothing to football, Wright had the good grace to deliver perfectly succinct TV-friendly soundbites that held within them the requisite optimism and passion for Arsenal Football Club – traits that will likewise forever endear him in the collective memory of gunners.

We just had time to grab a few seconds of footage of a very young and shy looking David Beckham in the company of Posh Spice, who I had not really heard of, on one of their first public appearances together. I would have missed that entirely, had their presence not been pointed out to me by my all-seeing, all-knowing cameraman. Then, we were gone. In the car park at the back of Earls Court, I was handed a couple of half-hour tapes of the 'rushes' and that was that. I scribbled 'Ian Wright – Fashion Shoot' on the boxes and made my way to the District Line, where I sat down wondering what had just happened.

For so long I had seen players from afar, either on the infinitely self-replicating screens at Sky or as distant figures separated by yards of grass, an advertising hoarding, a few rows of terrace, and, in the case of St Pauli's Millerntor ground, a swathe of netting to prevent beer glasses being thrown at the opposition goalkeeper. Players were actors in a high farce, paid performers who strutted and fretted their hour and a half on stage, and then were heard or seen no more. They existed for that time and that time only, and then simply disappeared back into some imagined life. Ian Wright was just such a character, someone who couldn't possibly exist in the real world.

But now I had proof that he did, it seemed, live in the same three dimensions as me and breathed the same air.

This inconsequential little football feature was the first 'film' I'd ever made. Though, even that is stretching a point since almost none of the editing process had anything to do with me. I'd simply chosen, with thunderous predictability, the music that accompanied shots of Wright twirling around on the runway ('I'm too sexy for my shirt'), and I'd recorded a ponderous and cliché-laden pun-fest of a voice-over to narrate it. I didn't know any better.

Thus, my first report was broadcast on *Soccer Saturday*. I had my hands over my eyes and ears, so I can't remember how it went down in the studio. Jeff Stelling had linked into it, with a twinkle in his eye, and probably reading some auto-cued line like, 'Ian Wright swapping the player's tunnel for the catwalk, as our new reporter Ned Boulting found out.' And, after they had cut back to the panel of pundits, I would imagine that Rodney Marsh would have had a laugh about Wright's fashion sense, only for George Best to have said something cutting about Marsh's sartorial tastes, and Frank McLintock to punctuate the discussion by saying something earnest about how Arsenal needed to continue to shore up their defensive midfield options.

What was to all intents and purposes the smallest imaginable contribution to the betterment of humankind via the medium of televised football content was, for me, an occasion of the utmost significance. From that shrinkingly tiny starting point, I struck out on a new path, one that would take me to a completely unknowable destination.

And I did so in a tiny Italian car.

*****

49

Unable to drive for the first 28 years of my life, I belatedly took it upon myself to pass my test and get a car. Emily, who had by now embarked on a long period of work overseas, lent me the car she'd left behind. It was not just a Fiat Panda, but a white Fiat Panda *Dance*, with the word *Dance* jauntily emblazoned across the side of its tinny flank. The seats, which were more like camping chairs than actual car seats, also featured this textured exhortation to dance. When started, and revved to its maximum capacity, its risible little engine sounded like a reasonably powerful hairdryer at full throttle. I nicknamed it 'Clairol' and took to the middle lane of the M1 with carefree abandon, forming a tiny white obstacle which BMW and Audi drivers could get very close to and flash their lights at. This Fiat Panda released my potential, as only a Fiat Panda could.

Unleashed now across the full panoply of Premier League training grounds, I started to rack up the miles, interviewing player after player, manager after manager. On reaching my top-flight destination, I would park the crap little car next to the rows of gleaming sports machines that were starting to populate the Premier League. I began to spend my life at the vibrating wheel of this ridiculous vehicle, ruining it with each passing mile, before eventually returning it to my sister, quite broken.

The season flew by. At the beginning of the week, we'd sit down in a *Soccer Saturday* production meeting and discuss the half a dozen features that our team of three reporters would have to produce for the coming Saturday, to preview the weekend's fixtures.

In the early weeks and months of my new-found status, I rarely ventured an opinion and waited to be told where I would be sent. Given that we were a London-based operation, with all the associated bias one might imagine, and I was the most junior recruit on the reporting team, I was repeatedly sent to cover the northern clubs, for some reason specialising in those whose names began with 'B'.

I must have been to Barnsley a dozen times during their exciting spell in the Premier League. Likewise, I visited Bolton over and over again and still never managed to get Colin Todd to say anything that wasn't like listening to a metalwork teacher talk about rivets. At

Blackburn I became acquainted with their idiosyncratic and almost unknown manager Roy Hodgson, as he patrolled their training facilities in the grounds of a decommissioned Victorian asylum. That particular encounter was mitigated by a bizarre conversation I had with him about Josef Škvorecký's *The Mournful Demeanour of Lieutenant Boruvka* during which he used the philosophical term *a priori* as he previewed their upcoming clash with Coventry City. Rodney Marsh thought that was hilarious, I recall.

Slowly, as my confidence grew, I'd feel more and more able to offer up a suggestion during meetings. 'Gianfranco Zola's really good,' would be one of my standard offerings. Or maybe I'd risk an 'Alan Shearer?' But these big names were the sole preserve of reporters with many footballing years on the clock and seniority on their side. Hence my presence at Leicester City, where Steve Guppy was having a good year, and Emile Heskey had just broken through. Mart Poom at Derby was deemed worthy of my attention, as was Ken Monkou.

With our 'wish list' of possible interviewees drawn up, it was back to our desks to type up on headed note paper a formal request which we'd then send through to the relevant press office. If I was contacting a club for the first time, I'd have to leaf through the *Rothmans Yearbook* to get the relevant fax number and hope that the receiving club didn't just have one machine sitting in some forgotten corner of the ticket office spewing paper onto the floor to be thrown directly into the bin.

Chelsea Football Club, which was still pre-Abramovich but nonetheless impossibly glamorous, had no press office at all to speak of. Instead, requests to interview players normally went through either the ever-patient Theresa (whose surname I never knew, but whose job description mostly revolved around putting out the sandwiches on a match day for the journalists), or Gwyn Williams, Chelsea's chief scout and assistant manager. On more than one occasion I remember sending a carefully worded letter requesting a short interview with Jon Harley or Gianluca Vialli, only to get the exact fax sent straight back to me on the same headed notepaper, but this time embellished with a capitalised 'NO' written by Williams in a big fat marker pen.

Presumably the same marker he'd just used to draw arrows on the whiteboard detailing where everyone, especially Tore André Flo, had to stand for corners.

On the other hand, perhaps for the very reason that football hadn't yet fully embraced the concept of PR, there were still opportunities to be had. Access was still possible, even that kind of unfettered, spontaneous, unaffected access that used to proliferate during the 1980s, the kind of FA Cup Final fly-on-the-wall/players-in-their-kitchens stuff that we once took for granted. In fact, there could still be a touching naivety about some players' first encounters with the media.

My colleague Dickie Davis was down at West Ham's gloriously humdrum training ground just off the long, increasingly gloomy road to Romford and beyond. It was at the zenith of the Harry Redknapp era, when the Hammers suddenly produced a welter of young talent, some of whom were related to the manager, and many of whom went on to make their mark at the biggest clubs in the land, as well as representing their country. From Frank Lampard and Joe Cole to Michael Carrick, they all excelled. But the first of the lot to break through into the West Ham first team had been Rio Ferdinand. Dickie was hanging around the training ground in order to position himself first in line to interview a teenage talent he rightly identified, even back then, would go on to captain England (a role Ferdinand eventually took over from John Terry in 2010 with a sumptuous malapropism, when he declared himself honoured to be 'assuming the mantlepiece').

All that success lay ahead of young Rio, who'd gone to school barely half a mile from Dickie's house in south-east London. Back in 1997, though, shortly before he earned his first cap for England at just 19 (a record young age for a defender), Dickie approached Ferdinand as he came off the training ground.

'Rio,' said Dickie in a voice that Dick van Dyck would never have been able to emulate. 'Dickie Davis,' he announced, with an outstretched hand of greeting. 'Sky Sports,' he added, unnecessarily, since he was wearing a jacket with *Sky Sports* written on it in big, bold letters.

Ferdinand, too young to have mistaken Dickie Davis for Dickie Davies, simply took him at face value and shook his hand.

'Just wondering if I could arrange a time to interview you for *Soccer Saturday*, Rio,' the opportunistic reporter in the branded clothing continued, shamelessly.

'OK, that'd be all right,' said Rio, answering instantly and in the affirmative for possibly the last time in his career.

'Great,' continued Dickie, trying to mask his amazement at the ease with which he'd clinched the deal. 'I was wondering though, if I could get you to come away from the training ground to do the interview at home maybe?' Now he really was chancing his luck.

'Sure,' said Rio. Then, to Dickie's further astonishment, Ferdinand asked him, 'Where do you live?' Rio was clearly suggesting that *he* would make the trip to *Dickie's* place and, not vice versa. This was a very unexpected turn of events.

'No, I meant…' Dickie began. Then, quick as a flash, he simply told Ferdinand his address in Greenwich. And a couple of days later, the future England captain rang on Dickie's doorbell and spent an hour or two talking football and posing for photos on Dickie's couch with every combination of his family alongside him.

The photos that Dickie took live on as proof that from time to time the conventions and mores of football PR could be usurped, quite gloriously so. And there is nothing funnier than seeing Rio Ferdinand's perplexed smile, as he sits in Dickie's living room, slowly figuring out that he may have misunderstood the terms of the negotiation. But Ferdinand was simply a teenager with an inestimably rich future ahead of him and a commendably down-to-earth attitude. Indeed, so laid-back and 'normal' was he that I remember seeing him a couple of years later in a traffic jam near Upton Park about an hour before kick-off on a Saturday afternoon. I was in the same solid line of cars, slowly getting anxious that I would miss the start of the match, when I saw the passenger door of a Ford Escort about two cars in front of me open and Rio Ferdinand get out, his boots slung over his shoulder. Breaking into a jog, he set off up the pavement towards West Ham's stadium, where, a little while later, I witnessed Ferdinand line up alongside Carrick, Lampard and Cole and beat Bradford City 5–4 in one of the most ridiculously open games I've ever witnessed.

Like Dickie, I also found that West Ham had a certain welcoming ethos and a distinct lack of a functioning press office, which yielded results. For a week, I went on a long-form assignment, something that would now doubtless classify as a deep dive. It involved filming a big background piece in two parts on the rise of the child prodigy Joe Cole, who was already tipped to be one of the greatest players the country would ever produce, before he'd even made a first team appearance.

I'd spent a few days already, hunting down friends and influences from his barely finished childhood, stalking the estates and boxing clubs of Camden and beyond in search of the background story; proper door-to-door stuff.

There was an understandable reluctance from some to be seen talking about young Joe, to be seen taking the credit perhaps, a hesitancy made all the more understandable when I got a mildly threatening phone call one evening from his dad George, wanting to know who I was and what, exactly, my game was. Having done my stuttering best to outline my name, at least, and some semblance of 'what my game was', I managed to assuage Cole senior to the extent that he even fixed up a meeting with his son, arranged for the following day. In fact, he completely changed his tone.

'Do you wanna talk to Joe, then?'

'Well, yes.' I said. 'Thank you.'

The next day I found myself following Joe Cole, aged 18, in his BMW that looked, like all his clothes, at least a size and a half too big for him. In my Panda, I tailed him back to a rented town house in Romford. He then spent ages on my behalf scrabbling around under the telly looking for old VHS tapes of him playing football as a child, while his mother did the ironing. Even at the time, this felt like unusually privileged access and I almost felt uncomfortable taking advantage of their hospitality, as if I were somehow exploiting their relative innocence.

In the meantime, my life at home was beginning to settle down. Kath continued to work all possible hours in a series of hospitals in south London, while I contributed to the betterment of humankind by allowing football to fatten out into every single fold of my life. When I wasn't working on it, I was consuming it, in newspapers, on the telly (Sky had by now sorted me out with a free dish) and even on a thing called the internet, which I could just about call into life after my computer had whirred and clicked its way through 20 minutes of dial-up.

In the spring of '99 Kath became pregnant and everything would start to make some sort of glorious sense at last. When I told Dad over a hastily arranged family lunch, he simply looked at me, smiling with delight and surprise, and said two words: 'Responsibility, Ned.'

I didn't know what he was talking about, really. Life was all of a sudden gigantic fun.

7

Access Codes

SHEFFIELD UNITED 3–0 WATFORD.
6 March, 1999. Bramall Lane, Sheffield.

In which things are not as they seem.

I measured and marked out my life in summer football tournaments. The summer we moved into our first house, Michael Owen had scored against Argentina. 1998.

Owen's moment, his greatest moment, was as unexpected as it was incandescent. Even now, when I think about it, I am partially unwilling to accept its truth. The kid, with his schoolboyish short back and sides, lurched with ludicrous speed from out across the halfway line, running onto a neat little pass from Beckham, half falling as he went, with a right elbow doing what it needed to do to shake off a tackle. He jinked right, feigned left, then committed to go the long way around the keeper, the ball just about under control beneath those bandy, beetling legs.

On ITV, the great Brian Moore was on the microphone to prove it. 'He's going to worry them again…' Then with lifting, scarcely containable, excitement, 'It's a great run by Michael Owen and he might finish it off!' And, still moving fast, he actually scored. The ball hit first the roof of the net, then dropped down to settle in the corner. 'Ooohhh! It's a wonderful goal!'

He was 18. They were Argentina. Such a thing seemed far-fetched to the point of fantasy and yet, quantifiably, it had happened. I stood, open-mouthed, in the middle of our little, recently redecorated room with its quaint gas back boiler that we didn't dare turn on.

When Sol Campbell then rose to nod home what I thought to be the winner, I rushed out, through the poky little kitchen which led to our little strip of a garden at the back of which there was a rickety shed, on whose walls I thumped both fists, and yelled, 'Fucking get in!' to the night sky that looked down on the back of our garden and the darkened cemetery that lay beyond. England were going to beat Argentina. They were actually going to win the match and then probably the World Cup. It was happening!

It was only when I returned to the living room and saw that the score line on the TV hadn't changed that I sensed it might not be happening after all.

'What's happening?' I remember asking Kath, with a hollow voice. 'What happened to the goal?'

She was lying across the length of the couch. She looked up from her Jane Austen. 'What goal?'

'He's disallowed it, Brian,' a mournful Kevin Keegan was telling millions in just the same state of bewilderment as me. 'I couldn't see anything wrong with it.'

When I think of our first house, the house where our oldest kid was born, this is one of the things that I remember. I continued to stare at the screen, aghast. There were still things I couldn't explain, even to myself.

*****

1998 became 1999. The world moved on.

From time to time I would make the journey up to Liverpool to be confronted with the actual Michael Owen, 10 years younger than me and 20 years more serious-minded.

The club's iconic Melwood training ground, rather touchingly, was still in the same district of suburban Liverpool that it had always been. It was surrounded on four sides by homely 1930s housing, the typical semi-detached and terraced homes of the Liverpool suburbs. The streets were made up of alternately well-kept and neglected houses. Some were lived in by the city's army of older residents whose collective memory stretches back through decades of change and who have never expressed a desire to leave. And others had fallen into the hands of the new buy-to-let generation, becoming empty brick boxes to extract capital. These were the ones that gazed across the concrete fencing that surrounded Melwood, their shuttered windows blind and guttering half-cocked and overrunning.

In the winter of '99, I visited these streets for the first time. Back then, the entrance to the training ground was at the far end of the rectangle of grass, hemmed in by tall concrete walls through which kids would still sneak a glimpse via the little peep holes that had been hacked and etched down the years. The club still made do with the kind of changing rooms and canteen that would not have looked out of place at an averagely funded grammar school.

Liverpool's manager, Gérard Houllier, unleashed from the odd shackles of co-managership with Roy Evans, was, like the teacher he had once been, a watchful and stern presence at the ground. Not much escaped the attention of the bespectacled Frenchman with his propensity to redden in the face and widen his eyes when under pressure. When I was first sent to Melwood to interview him, I had been warned of his occasionally overbearing tendencies. Like many a manager of that era (or any other probably, going back as far as Brian Clough and Don Revie), he disliked the media but was simultaneously drawn to it. When 'between jobs', he was more than ever drawn to it, popping up in TV studios across the land.

In common with most training grounds, even to this day, little thought was given to the practical needs of the many camera crews that would arrive on a daily basis from these shores and overseas, to interview players and other staff. Great ingenuity was needed by camera operators to make something (anything!) look interesting or even pleasing to the eye in the background of an interview. More often than not, there was only a small room at our disposal, with a plain white wall and a couple of plastic chairs. It's for that reason that so many pre-recorded interviews with footballers you see before matches are shot against a black background. Every cameraman carries with them a few black drapes which are used as a regular emergency measure simply to erase the ugliness of the real surroundings in which the interview is actually taking place. The mundane reality of the training ground is a long way from the aspirational drama with which the interviews are dripping once they are fully edited and colour corrected. Essentially, these puff pieces, these promotional masterpieces, are filmed in portacabins.

Melwood was no exception. Once, to our relief and delight, there was an actual object in the room we'd been ushered into. It was a magnetic whiteboard, marked out with the lines of a football pitch. This represented a wealth of visual possibilities. So, while Pete the cameraman was busy setting up the microphones and the lights, I artfully arranged eleven red magnetic counters in an approximation of a Liverpool formation under Gérard Houllier, pairing Sam Hyypiä and Stéphane Henchoz at the back, with Steve McManaman trying to get the ball in to Robbie Fowler and Michael Owen 'running the channels'. This tactical and aesthetic masterpiece was lit, dramatically, with a slash of red and a few shards of daylight. At which point, the Liverpool manager walked in.

Houllier strolled across the room, loosening his jacket as he went, in the manner that only people who are intimately familiar with the process of being filmed for television know. After a cursory nod, handshake and trademark, lightly French-accented 'hello', he sat down and took ownership of feeding the clip mic up his shirt without any help.

It was at that point he noticed the whiteboard in the background, with my formation of red dots. He stopped, head and torso craned around to see what was displayed, and, after a long few seconds in which I thought he might be sizing up the efficacy of my full-backs' positioning for set pieces, he sat back round again.

'Very fucking original,' he said, surprisingly swearily. Managers could be ludicrously unpredictable.

One of the first managers in football I got to know on my own terms was the characterful, if combustible, manager of Wimbledon, who were flying high in the late '90s. Joe Kinnear, their Irish, cockney, full-girthed manager had moulded a very cogent team out of a base of south London kids and more experienced seniors, who had almost boundless self-belief. With Kinnear, sporting collar-length hair that fell in waves down his neck in a coiffure that seemed to sit squarely between the twin poles of Kevin Keegan and Gerry Francis, barking at them from the echoing confines of his plastic dugout in the Selhurst Park Main Stand, they brimmed with organised resilience.

Joe Kinnear's uniquely roguish approach to running the team was complemented by his extrovert Lebanese boss, Sam Hamman, whose practices and personal ethics, like with so many football chairmen at the time, wavered between charmingly eccentric and downright controversial. Hamman was a force of nature. Years later, when I got to know Robbie Earle, who at the time was the ineffably resourceful club captain, I was told how Earle, who'd been offered a place at Norwich City, was summoned at the last minute to Hamman's north London flat. On entering the premises, Hamman let him in, locked the door behind him, and then dropped his keys down his own pants.

'There are two ways out of here,' he told Earle. 'Either you sign for me today and I'll let you go. Or, you have to reach in and get the keys from my pants to let yourself out.'

Kinnear and Hamman made quite a team. They actively sought the limelight, turning it to shine to their advantage. If they had an agenda (which they invariably did), then they knew with immediacy and cunning that Sky Sports could be useful fools. And in me, only beginning to grapple with the nuances of journalism, they had a very willing fool.

From time to time, they would slip up. On one occasion, Kinnear spoke frankly about how tempted he might be if he were ever approached to manage Tottenham (the club for which he had played with some distinction and which was looking to appoint a new manager). Later that afternoon, once I had returned to Sky and was just about to edit the interview, which was to air the following day, Kinnear had clearly thought better of what he had said and had somehow got hold of my office number.

'Ned?' he asked, using my first name for the first time. 'I need you to scrap what I said to you. Sam'll fucking murder me.'

'Right…' I answered, unsure of how to proceed.

'I tell you what,' he offered. 'Come down to the training ground next week. I'll have something good for you.'

The following week, I duly made my way down there again, wondering what scoop awaited me. In fact, Kinnear's idea of paying me back for helping him out was to conduct an entire interview in a rubber Prince Charles mask. At least, I think it was Prince Charles.

Time and time again I'd volunteer to head down to Wimbledon's modest base in Roehampton. Some daft scheme or other was in a perpetual state of being hatched. When rumours were flying around that Hamman was on the brink of creating the Premier League's first overseas franchise, I was shown advanced architect's plans to build a stadium near Dublin airport and relocate to Ireland. I remember watching on in amazement as Kinnear even unfolded some drawings he had in his office and showed me on the plan where his house was going to be. 'Five bedrooms, all en suite', he suggested.

Whole days of my life would pass waiting in the drizzle with a cameraman outside the changing rooms at Wimbledon's training ground, just for Kinnear to emerge and tell me that Chris Perry and Dean Blackwell were the best pair of central defenders in the Premier League and that anyone who couldn't see that didn't understand anything about football. Such landmark interviews done, I'd make my way back through the puddles to where I'd sheepishly parked my tiny white car, among the Jaguars and Porsches.

Wimbledon's training ground used to be on a patch of land the rascal club rented, just off the A3. Its car park fed directly onto this major arterial road; a fast-flowing, permanently busy dual carriageway that bore London's traffic away from the city and down towards Surrey and Hampshire. For a newly qualified driver in a grotesquely underpowered car, spotting a gap in the flow of traffic and pulling out into the road was a terrifying proposition. I must have already been sat there for four or five minutes, anxiously glancing to my right at the oncoming cars, with my clutch foot now twitching on the pedal through fatigue and my left hand sweatily clasping the handbrake, when I felt the car start inexplicably to slide forward. Looking through my rear-view mirror, I suddenly realised that a huge car had pulled up behind me and was nudging my little Panda out into the traffic. Behind the wheel of the Range Rover, marked, as far as I can recall, VJ 100, sat Vinnie Jones, roaring with laughter, as we both slid onto the A3 and away from Wimbledon Football Club.

Work was slightly homicidal fun, but fun nonetheless. The sense of football being a game was never far beneath the surface. When Everton surprised everyone by drawing at home to Arsenal in 1997, they fielded two teenagers in their starting line-up: Danny Cadamarteri, a talented midfielder, was just 17, and Michael Ball, their left-back, who would go on to play for Scotland and Glasgow Rangers, had only recently turned 18. Somehow, I managed to persuade them that it'd be a laugh to film an interview at the Pumphouse pub down on Liverpool's Albert Dock, but make the still underage Cadamarteri sit outside, while I chatted to Ball over a pint on the inside. Both the young Everton stars played along with it gamely, Cadamarteri hamming up his part, and looking suitably alone and dejected while we sat in the warmth, waving at him occasionally through the window.

On my next visit to Everton's humble training ground, I met Walter Smith, their famously no-nonsense Glaswegian manager. At first, hilariously, I believed he'd wanted to congratulate me on the wonderfully entertaining vignette I'd produced. This wasn't quite the case.

Talking to me in a slow, measured, headmasterly tone from within his office at the training ground, from whose windows he could oversee the various different pitches, he made his feelings known to me that he'd hated what he'd seen. There'd be no more of that kind of thing. 'It's not a circus, son,' was the gist of his point. There might have been an expletive thrown in.

He was right, of course. It wasn't a fucking circus. I was just slow on the uptake. Perhaps it was because my introduction to football had come late, and I'd 'never played the game', that I'd failed to grasp its seriousness. I had no idea that, to many of those within the game, it was addictive, incalculably pressurised and mostly devoid of entertainment. It palpably wasn't the giant, often joyful, sometimes painful, occasionally hilarious pantomime that I took it for. This came as a revelation.

Often, I'd be surprised by the dissonance between the public face of a player or manager and their actual attitude when confronted with them face to face. This cut both ways, of course. The former Everton player Graham Stuart, who I was unaccountably nervous of meeting, turned out to be the epitome of charm and humility, and to this day, the only Premier League player I ever met who offered to carry a camera tripod after we'd been filming in a greasy spoon near The Valley. At times like that, the rarified world in which I operated felt gloriously normal again, but special at the same time. Normal and special were the two conflicting strands woven into my understanding of the game.

I once shared a car ride with Sunderland's archetypally normal and special Kevin Phillips from their training ground down to the wild, deserted seafront at Roker, during which his phone rang.

'Kevin?'

'Yup?'

'It's Kevin.'

The former warehouse stacker turned irrepressible striker pulled his car over to the side of the North Sea and gazed out over the grey waves rolling onto the long, windswept strand. 'Kevin Keegan here.' Phillipps was being called up by the England manager to his first squad. For the rest of the afternoon, we filmed with him as he absorbed the magnitude of the phone call he had just received. After we left the beach behind us, we filmed in a branch of Dixons and he recreated for the cameras the job he'd been doing before he joined Watford and it all began. It was affecting to be face to face with this grown-up boy who'd just fulfilled a dream: things that seem and sound unreal actually seeding in someone's real life, in real time, in front of my very eyes.

Later that year, Phillips scored a goal at St James's Park in torrential rain, which I watched, soaked to the skin, wearing an entirely ineffective Newcastle United poncho that had been handed free of charge to us all in the press box. It was the infamous evening on which Ruud Gullit had benched Alan Shearer, inviting the city's population to rise around him in revolt. With their favourite son watching powerlessly from the side lines, and with the skies dumping incessant heavy, cold rain on the pitch until the ball would no longer roll, the very worst that could happen to Gullit's management on the Tyne, happened. Sunderland beat them 2–1.

I had woken the next morning in a hotel near the ground wondering how I could possibly complete the Gullit profile that my editor wanted for Saturday's show and give it a new twist. A fitful night's sleep had produced the happy side-effect of incessant dreaming. In one of my half-asleep hallucinations, I hit upon the idea of talking to Frank Rijkaard, Gullit's Holland and AC Milan teammate. Rijkaard, long since retired, was now managing the Netherlands national team. In my dream, it had been simple; I would just ring him up and arrange an interview.

By now fully awake and stirring a cup of Holiday Inn tea, I gazed at the telephone in the room. Before too much longer, I picked it up. And shortly after that, I was connected to the Royal Dutch Football Association headquarters in Zeist.

'Good morning,' I opened the conversation. 'Do you speak English?' A ridiculous question.

'Sure, I can just about get by,' came the fluent reply. 'How can I be of assistance?'

'I'm calling from Sky Sports in the UK.' Perhaps I hadn't expected it to be that easy, because I wasn't ready with an answer. 'Could I please speak to Frank Rijkaard?' was about the only thing I could think of to ask, because it was the only thing I wanted to do.

'Just a moment please.' I sat on the end of my bed in the Newcastle hotel in my pants and stared at my dim, shadowy reflection in the polished glass surface of the TV. Then a click and another voice.

'Hello, Rijkaard?' It was clearly Frank Rijkaard or someone doing a very good impression of him. I explained what I wanted. 'Can you be here by lunchtime?'

About five hours later I'd flown over the North Sea and was, by some miracle, sitting in Rijkaard's office near Amsterdam, watching him drink black coffee and chain smoke, while he told me that he was sure 'Ruud would be a great manager'. Then, when the cameras stopped rolling, he flatly contradicted himself. 'Ruud likes clothes, you see.' Rijkaard stubbed out a cigarette and then asked me all about Wimbledon, for some reason.

But this astonishing window of access had been closing fast, even if the Dutch were still not prepared to draw down the shutters. TV cameras were by now prevented from getting beyond the outer perimeter of a Premier League training ground without being marshalled with the same degree of life-sapping control familiar to anyone who has flown with Ryanair. Even by the end of the 1998–99 season, the year of the Manchester United treble, it had probably passed the point of no return.

The forgotten middle-eight of that treble success was the FA Cup victory. It was the first cup final I had ever covered and my work started early. Posted outside a five-star country hotel somewhere in Hertfordshire, I had been charged with contributing live reports to an epic eight-hour cup final build-up.

Standing in the car park in front of Newcastle United's luxury accommodation, I had my first 'on air' encounter with Sky's anchor, Richard Keys.

'What's their schedule, Nick?' inquired a tinny, but unmistakable, voice in my earpiece, using a name that wasn't actually my name. 'How long before they get in the bus and start to make their way to Wembley?'

I had no way of knowing. Newcastle's press officer had not replied to any of my requests for information and security wouldn't let us close to the front door. All I had experienced that endless morning was some light rain and a mostly empty car park.

'Well, they've had breakfast,' I offered, in the hope this might assuage Keys' voracious journalistic appetite. Then Andy Gray chipped in, unhelpfully.

'What was on the menu?'

I froze.

'I'm not sure,' I said, in a tone of self-loathing.

How different it was from how I'd imagined it to be. I remembered outrageous FA Cup-day features from the Jim Rosenthal era in which the ITV reporter got a massage from Glenn Hoddle and Chris Waddle before a Tottenham final, and they all sang 'Ozzy's on his way to Wembley' on the bus. I breezed into it as if it were all a bit of fun, a game. I thought football was a game.

And, at the centre of this self-perpetuating vortex of change, sat Manchester United, with its manager whose all-consuming drive to crush the opposition and bend the world to fit his will was setting the template for everything which has followed. Alex Ferguson was kicking football so hard up the arse that it reached the 21st century long before the millennium had actually come and gone.

It was never my duty, in those early days, to go to Old Trafford. Such was Manchester United's special status in the football eco-system that only a select few, more senior, reporters were ever charged with going there. Though there was a degree of symbiosis between the Sky Sports project and the growing dominance of Manchester United on the pitch, the relationship always felt uneven to the foot soldiers of Sky's empire who had to do the work on the ground. Sky's representatives were treated with the same unspoken dismissiveness as plenty of others were during the years of Ferguson's tenure. This was an attitude that persisted and sowed itself in the DNA of almost every professional football club in the land.

My first oblique brush with Ferguson came during an international break in 1999. Since there were no Premier League games to focus on, *Soccer Saturday* made a rare foray into the Football League. To that end, I was sent to Preston North End where two ex-United players, Michael Appleton and Jon Macken, were enjoying something of a purple patch.

On tape, and for want of anything else to talk about, I encouraged them to recount their years at Manchester United's academy, where they would occasionally encounter Ferguson. With a smile, they told of 'the Gaffer's' propensity for sudden bouts of anger, including one occasion where Appleton had been dragged out of the canteen 'by his sideburns'. None of this was recalled with anything like malice or grievance and the interview duly aired one Saturday afternoon. I thought nothing more of it, clocked off for the week, and went home to my pregnant partner, our tiny new house and the rest of my increasingly grown-up-seeming life.

But early on Sunday morning, my phone rang.

'Ned, have you seen it?' The voice belonged to Pete Caine, the hugely experienced cameraman, who had filmed the interview for me. 'Oh. My. God.'

He went on to explain how the back page of the *Sunday Mirror* featured a huge headline that ran: 'UNITED KIDS LIFT LID ON FERGIE'S REIGN OF TERROR.' All of the quotes from the piece had been taken from the interview that I had done with Appleton and Macken, but spun by the paper in such a way that the levity of the edited item had been stripped away and all that remained were the cold, hard facts, none of which looked anything other than damning of Ferguson when printed in black and white.

I ran to the newsagents. As I walked slowly back, reading my interview re-hashed in this manner, my phone rang again. It was the agent of one of the players I'd interviewed.

'I know it wasn't your intention,' he explained as if he were talking about the leaking of some nuclear codes, 'but it's out there now. The Gaffer's fully aware. He may want to call you. I've passed on your number. Just so you're warned.'

I stopped dead on the pavement, the paper hanging loosely at my side. Traffic rolled by as it would do on any normal Sunday. For days, I knew no peace. This hadn't been why I'd got into this job, to find myself sandwiched between the rutting antlers of two stags – the tabloid press and football. And yet, here I was. Ferguson never did call me, but the sense that he might had already done the trick. Shock and awe.

My first appearance at the Manchester United training ground came about some four years later, when I'd been sent (by ITV, now) to interview Ruud van Nistelrooy and David Beckham ahead of the League Cup Final. Ushered into our allotted place and told to wait by United's press officer, Di Law (daughter of Denis), she asked me if I had ever fallen foul of 'the Manager'.

'I don't think so,' I replied, with half-truth and a sudden empty feeling. 'Why?'

'Strange,' she replied. 'When I showed him the list of reporters on site today, he picked your name out. Said you used to be at Sky.'

'I was.' I said, by now fully unsettled. Ferguson did not miss a beat back then.

This fear of upsetting the powers that be was one of the aspects of the job that I started to wrestle with. But there were day-to-day hurdles to overcome all the time. I always dreaded the moment of arrival at training grounds I was visiting for the first time, as any lack of familiarity and assuredness exposed a weakness that could be exploited. To this day, I cannot recall the experience of driving up to George Graham's Leeds United to interview his assistant David O'Leary with anything other than visceral fear.

Arriving at their training ground at Thorp Arch, close to Wealstun Prison, I drove slowly up the leafy approach road. As I drew close to a small gardener's hut to the right of the driveway, the little door flew open and a middle-aged man flew out. With a kind of deranged, limping gait, he rushed as best he could towards my car, which I had brought to a sudden halt. He was screaming abuse at me, asking at the top of his voice if I was 'taking the fucking piss'. I told him, most earnestly, that I wasn't. He told me that I 'fucking was' and that in fact I was a 'fucking piss-taker'.

'Now go and park up with them other wankers over there and don't fucking move until I tell you to.'

I glanced over my shoulder to see a line of cars I'd just driven past. At the wheel of each and every one sat a solitary local journalist wanker laughing at me. Meekly, and feeling scrutinised by all the established reporters whose patch I was on, as well as the madman from the potting shed who was watching, still barely able to control his rage, I executed a ponderous three-point turn and eventually parked up at the back of the queue of journalists all awaiting admission to the training ground.

Seemingly I had just met Jack from Leeds United, custodian of the training ground and, in a crowded field, one of the most incandescently furious men I ever met in football. In the ensuing years, I would never lose my anxiety at having to confront Jack in his tiny wooden shack, and ask him to tick off my name on his clipboard and issue me with a laminated pass on which he'd hand-printed my name with scarcely concealed rage.

Later that afternoon, after our allotted interview, the effusive David O'Leary would ask me, 'I've not seen you before. Is this your first visit to Leeds?'

'It is.'

'Did you meet Jack at the gate?'

'I did.'

'Jesus, I'm sorry.'

Some grounds were more welcoming than others. Fulham, that Archibald Leitch-designed masterpiece of inoffensive gentility on the Thames, was probably the least threatening environment. They were an interesting club to visit back then, a year or so into their march up through the divisions under the eccentric stewardship of Mohamed Al-Fayed, a fragile fusion of ego, kitsch and Kevin Keegan that culminated in their promotion, relegation and erection of a truly terrible statue of Michael Jackson unveiled outside the ground on Stevenage Road.

Some time prior to that, I was sent there to cover Fulham versus Hartlepool in some early round of the FA Cup. It was a misty, fuggy, November-ish day, one of the first truly dank winter afternoons of the year. I was just plugging in my kit in the press box, one of the first journalists to arrive, when I noticed a pair of old men in hats walking a little unsteadily straight across the pitch, towards where I sat, in an otherwise almost entirely empty stand.

When the shorter of these two figures reached the side of the pitch, he stopped. His companion lurched beside him to a slightly unsteady halt, as well. Then, from underneath a Stetson, the voice of Mohamed Al-Fayed emerged, loud and clear.

'Ladies and gentlemen of the British press!' I glanced across at the only other bloke there, some wiry chap from Hayters Press Agency. Al-Fayed continued, unabashed. 'It is with great pleasure that I introduce to you my great friend, Mr Tony Curtis!'

It was at that moment that Tony Curtis, one of the greatest names in the history of American cinema, lifted his hat and, with an almost imperceptible nod of the head, bowed briefly at me and the wiry bloke from Hayters. There was an awkward silence, during which I think I bowed my head back at them. Then, with no more words being exchanged, or rather shouted into the rafters of Craven Cottage, the star of *Some Like It Hot* and the owner of Harrods turned on their heels and started the long, slow walk back to the other side of the ground, to resume whatever it was they'd been doing before Al-Fayed had suggested it would be a good idea to come and say hello to me and the bloke from Hayters.

Sometimes I would simply be sent on a Saturday to a ground solely in order to interview a manager before kick-off, and then head home. This was a strange and mind-bendingly simple way to earn a living. Absurdly, during Dave Bassett's tenure at Nottingham Forest, I drove all the way from south London to the County Ground and back home again, having asked the voluble gaffer one almost-question: 'Dave, your thoughts ahead of the game?'

About three minutes later, Bassett had covered every single issue at stake, including Pierre van Hooijdonk's refusal to play for the team he'd helped get promoted, which controversy had been the real reason for my having been despatched to Nottingham. So, at the end of the longest uninterrupted stream of consciousness in televised football history, I simply said, 'Thanks Dave', got back in the car and drove home. I had travelled over 200 miles to say nine words.

In common with anyone who has ever embarked on a new, or different, challenge, I was inclined to indulge a feeling of rank under-qualification and inadequacy. Nowhere was this more apparent than in the often-rickety construction at a football ground in which football's motley selection of journalists would be housed when a match was in progress.

To arrive at Selhurst Park or Vicarage Road and stand mutely in the corner of the shoddily carpeted 'lounge' clutching a cup of remarkably hot and watery tea while all around you grizzled local football writers griped about various unknowable grievances, casting disdainful glances to where I stood, ridiculous in my Sky Sports-branded wax jacket, was the stuff of nightmares. In stark contrast to their carefully constructed careers in sports journalism, starting by working on matchday programmes and then graduating through to the local paper, I had breezed into the trade on a wave of nothing much more than enthusiasm. It didn't feel fair, because it wasn't. And no amount of fancy-dan free clothing from a satellite broadcaster was going to endear me to this band of brothers, the freemasons of the press box.

Often, I'd stay at the ground to provide updates on the action as it unfolded. Once the match got underway, the true horror would come at the moment that Tommy Smith (for example), latching onto a lofted pass from midfield, would skip past the full-back and drive a low-angled shot past the keeper. On seeing the net billowing, I'd have to lift the phone in front of me and dial the *Soccer Saturday* studio as quickly as possible. If the Watford goal came at a quiet moment in the afternoon's proceedings and there was no queue of other goals from Dunfermline or Plymouth Argyle, I'd be on air within seconds.

'Back to Vicarage Road now, where Watford were being held by Cardiff,' Jeff Stelling would chime in with impeccably calibrated enthusiasm. 'The deadlock's been broken. Here's Ned Boulting.'

Hearing the cue come crackling through, I'd launch into my unscripted verbal replay of what I'd just seen, through the steamed-up glass of the wooden shed tacked together at the back of the main stand: the ball somehow chipped forward by Micah Hyde, the roar of expectation as Smith controlled it, a lunge from a defender, or perhaps two, and then a right-footed shot, sharp and perfect. With my eyes closed and at the top of my voice, to reflect the thrill of the moment, I'd describe it as best I could: '...past the despairing dive of the keeper!' and, with a flourish to round it off, 'So it's Watford 1, Cardiff City 0.'

And with that, I'd gently replace the receiver of the phone. The press box, meanwhile, would have fallen silent. All around me football reporters would have been listening intently to the words coming out of my newcomer's mouth, scrutinising them for inaccuracies, discrepancies or other sundry objections. Now, amid the light clatter of keyboards, the hubbub of crowd noise from outside the box in the stands and the occasional slurp of tea, the first whispered complaints would seep across the awkward space between me and the established football reporting world.

'You hear that?' A conspiratorial glance.

'Wasn't Hyde's pass.' A shake of the head.

A year or two into my tenure on *Soccer Saturday*, stranded up on the gantry at an enormous height in the eaves of the South Stand at Bramall Lane, I was reporting on Watford's attempts to come away from Sheffield United with three points. With the visitors already 3–0 down, a momentary lapse in concentration by the ruggedly configured Chris Morgan in the heart of the Blades' defence allowed Watford to nick a goal and peg the score back to 3–1.

The goal was greeted with a complete lack of interest. Vanishingly few Watford fans had bothered to make the onerous trip up the cone-laden M1 to the match, so there was no cheer as the goal went in and nor was I expecting one. My head down, I dialled into the *Soccer Saturday* studio and before a minute had elapsed, I was informing the viewers with the appropriate degree of melodrama that Watford had pulled one back and that an unlikely comeback was being mounted.

Twenty minutes later, my phone rang. The show's statistician, a tireless miner of football facts, was on the other end. 'Ned, can you just double check the details of that Watford goal?' He sounded stressed. But not as stressed as I was about to become. 'It's just that no one else seems to have reported it.'

I shot a glance at the scoreboard. With a shudder, I saw that it read 'Sheff Utd 3–0 Watford'. There had been no Watford goal. It must have been disallowed and the game must have restarted while I had my head down, dialling the number for the studio.

In that moment, my football world collapsed and reached a black point of singular failure that threatened to suck everything into its gravity: me, my career, my love of the game, the game itself, Bramall Lane, Sheffield, The World. With my stomach in a quiver of fear, my thoughts caught like a wounded bird in a shuttered space, I was thrown back on air to explain myself.

Jeff Stelling clearly thought the whole thing was hilarious. 'Watford fans!' he chirruped. 'If you thought you were having a tough afternoon in Yorkshire, it just got a whole lot worse. Here's Ned Boulting again to explain.'

'Yes, Jeff…' I began, before going on to explain the error of my ways.

Later that afternoon I drove down the M1 in a Fiat Panda that was close to collapse, water occasionally spraying up at my feet from a rust patch underneath which afforded a glimpse of the motorway passing by at 70 mph. I stopped, as I recall, for a burger at Leicester Forest services, which is, on any given Saturday afternoon, a nexus for travelling fans, a kind of watering hole for migrating herds. Avoiding eye contact with anyone and without my ludicrous Sky Sports wax jacket, I hurried back out of the services with my head bowed. Once back inside the tinny safety of my sister's little car, I sat staring out of the windscreen at the drizzle, occasionally lifting a chip to my mouth. I felt very alone.

8

Best

CHELSEA 0–2 MANCHESTER UNITED.
30 September, 1964. Stamford Bridge, London.

In which you need to see the whole picture.

My mother was recovering from an operation.

Her medical insurance had paid out to place her in the Cromwell Hospital in west London; a modern, private institution with mirrored windows that gazed down on the four lanes of nose-to-bumper traffic on the main road from Knightsbridge to Heathrow Airport. It was strange to me that Mum was in London, the city I had now made my own. In my imagination, her restful, supporting presence belonged in Bedford, where my childhood memories were still housed. So it confused me that she now lay in a hospital bed on the main road I travelled most days on my way to and from Sky Sports.

Armed with a bag of clichéd food supplies, I made my way down the ghostly quiet carpeted corridors of the hospital and knocked on the door of Mum's private room.

'There's a lot of excitement among the staff here, you know,' she told me, as I placed the grapes on her bedside table.

'Why's that?' I asked.

'We've got a celebrity patient at the end of the corridor.'

'Who?' I took a grape.

'It's George Best,' she said. 'I don't think he's very well.'

*****

It seems extraordinary now, but George Best was one of the first people I worked with when I started in TV. The world has moved on so fast, and the passage of life has rattled by with such breathless speed, that simply to invoke his name is to bridge a sudden rift in time. His name and his age are already long, long gone. Was he really there? Was I, too? He was a regular panellist on *Soccer Saturday*. Softly spoken, sometimes a bit shambolic, shy; he was just George Best. But there it is. I remember him.

Even now the mention of his name is enough to elicit a certain inward sigh. His stardom evoked class, for all his obvious shortcomings. Where Sky's repackaging of the game had involved cheerleaders, whooshing graphics and proud boasts made on behalf of football, the Best era already seemed like velvet-lined nostalgia – a time of technicolour, tight shorts and aviator shades in which everything looked like it might have been shot on a cine camera.

The man in the middle of his own personal maelstrom was enjoying it less, I suspect, by the time necessity and a certain tailing off in his income stream led him to *Soccer Saturday*'s door. And for as much as he was suffering, others in his entourage and family suffered more at his hands as a result of his lack of control. He often avoided eye contact and could sometimes be taciturn to the point of seeming rude. Mostly, I suspect, this was because he was feeling terribly, routinely sick, as his puffy face and sallow complexion revealed on a weekly basis. The best make-up artists that Sky could bring to the studios struggled to make George look anything other than simply heavily patched-up; as if there were no natural look left to enhance.

Yet, even then, covered as he was in whatever cosmetic shade they had chosen to mask his actual state, there were times when he shone and a sparkle of wit lit up the show. A quiet yet forthright presence on the set alongside the noise and volume brought to proceedings by his old friend Rodney Marsh, the towering McLintock and the total effervescence of Phil Thompson, Best had a way of playing his key cards to devastating effect.

At times self-effacing to the point of ridiculousness, he would occasionally, always unforgettably, remind the viewing public that sitting in that moulded plastic chair in a TV studio somewhere in west London, trapped in the fated body of a man consigned to ruining it, lay the ghost of genius. Sometimes, Best couldn't help but remind us of who he was and why he was still a class apart. David Beckham? No pace, doesn't score enough, can't dribble, but apart from that he's OK. It was hard not to laugh along and not, deep down, to agree.

Soccer Saturday would send a car every Saturday morning, not often to Best's house, but to pick him up from the Phene Arms, the Chelsea pub just off Cheyne Walk where he used to drink and very near to where my mum, as a young woman, had shared a room while she taught in Hackney.

When the car arrived, Best didn't always show up and the driver, by now familiar with the routine, would phone in the news to the show's producer. Once it was established that this given Saturday was another Best-less weekend, which it was at least 50 per cent of the time, it would fall to one of our production assistants to phone the ever-willing Clive Allen, who would always be available to come off the bench for Best.

'Sorry to bother you, Clive…'

'George?' the former Tottenham striker would ask.

'Thanks, Clive.'

'I'm on my way.'

There were other times when, even though Best had made it as far as getting in the car and being driven to the studios, he still couldn't quite bring himself to take the final step and commit to the appearance, opting instead to head for the club bar of a very low-key rugby club that bordered the industrial estate in which Sky was located. Once there, he subjected himself to continuing his much-loathed, much-loved diet of white wine. The staff there got to know their extraordinary, illustrious, solitary guest, and added their number to the long, long list of well-meaning people who came into George's orbit and were powerless or unwilling to do anything other than smile and give him what he wanted.

For that was exactly the case with George. He had a distinct effect on people. From time to time, I'd be sent out on some filming assignment with him, which was never an easy affair. But what was striking was to witness the world he had been consigned to: wherever he went, he'd be stopped and greeted by complete strangers who thought they knew him well, tricked by the brightness and warmth of his story into a false chimera of intimacy. They had never met him and yet they were sure that they knew him like a fabulous errant brother. In those much-missed pre-selfie days, the accidental meeters and greeters in shops or on pavements, car-park attendants or simple passers-by, would turn a head, exclaim, retrace their steps at a jog and demand his attention.

'George?' He'd turn to face them, a trace of weariness visible to me as I came to read his expressions more closely.

'George. Just to say, George. You were the greatest. The greatest player I've ever seen.'

'Thanks.' Not so much impatience, as a controlled patience, and acceptance in his quiet acknowledgment, and a slight shift of balance where he stood to suggest he was moving on. But not just yet.

'May I shake your hand.' And Best would, of course, oblige. 'You're a legend.'

And then, always, always, the sting in the tail, 'You take care of yourself George.' They knew. He knew they knew and that made it all the worse.

*****

One time I found myself high, high up on the television gantry suspended under the roof of Chelsea's East Stand, directly above where my father would have sat a lifetime ago. George and I were gazing down on the floodlit pitch far below. It was an early autumn night and Chelsea were in action against some mid-table opposition. In a bid to get him more involved in the programme and to keep him busy, *Soccer Saturday*'s producer had suggested sending him along to film a 'scouting report' on the Blues' new prestige signing Brian Laudrup, whose first few weeks for Chelsea had hardly impressed. With a camera trained on him and a microphone thrust in his hand, George Best was providing a blow-by-blow assessment of the Dane as he lumbered his way through another underwhelming performance.

My job had simply been to pick Best up from Cheyne Walk, navigate his path through the hordes of well-wishers, help him up the steps that led to the gantry and make sure that the filming went off as we had envisaged it. Most of the time, this meant reminding George to actually talk, since his default setting was silence, as if he had forgotten that it wasn't obvious to the world what he thought of Laudrup simply by judging the intensity of his frown.

Halfway through the first half as I sat alongside Best swaddled up in a puffer jacket, my mobile phone rang. This was something of a novelty, of course. I'd only had the thing a matter of a weeks and still thought it was slightly thrilling that I could be called when I wasn't sitting inside a building. Dad was on the end of the line.

'What are you up to?' he wanted to know. I pictured him, sitting on a comfortable armchair in the living room of the house they'd moved to in a leafier part of Bedford, as soon as my sister and I had fled the nest.

'Well,' I replied. 'You'll never guess where I am.' I looked down at Stamford Bridge, the grass already worn in both goalmouths, the mud glistening under floodlights that seemed to drain it of colour. It had been many years since Dad had attended a match there; years that had seen the old ground chipped away as the new one took shape, all-seater, of course, and filled with chatter rather than singing. These were the days that followed on from the arrival of Gullit, Vialli and Zola; the prelude to the Abramovich cash-bomb that was about to detonate in west London. Holding my Nokia to my ear, I told Dad that I was gazing down at the same patch of Chelsea turf that had held him entranced as a kid.

'You're not!' Dad was still grappling with the notion that I was being paid to attend football matches. 'You lucky sod.'

'And guess who I'm with...' This was going to be good. 'George Best.'

The line went quiet, while Dad absorbed this information and composed his thoughts. Something perhaps had surfaced, some memory was wriggling up from the depths and there was nothing that could be done to stop it.

'Christ,' he said. 'I remember seeing him take us apart. He ran the game. He was everywhere.'

I had heard this before from others. But this was the first time that Dad was testifying to the same unanswerable genius so many hundreds of thousands had been able to witness. George Best exists, for the most part, in celebrated clips, seconds long and fleeting: chipped goals, dropped shoulders, socks down, mazy runs, muddy pitches, wheeling away from goal in celebration. Or long-haired, with broad collars open to reveal his tanned chest, leaving airport terminals in baking sunshine, showing up at night clubs, getting out of fast cars and filling up champagne flutes. To the generation that never witnessed him play, nor took their place in the stands to see how he ran, ball at feet, how he moved unobserved into lethal empty space, this is all we can ever know of Best. These fragments to line up alongside the famous quotes about his sun-kissed, charmed, failed, couldn't-give-a-toss, wastrel life. The sum total of a life only half understood.

But Dad had seen him play. Dad had seen how he glided around the pitch; quicksilver and, idling, placing himself in unexpected pockets of the pitch, or wriggling free Houdini-like from the opponent's chains, appearing with quantum ease in several places at once. And as Dad spoke about the man sitting alongside me, hunched against the biting wind whipping up the stand and swirling toward the roof of the gantry, something from which I was excluded crackled down the line. When he had finished, Dad summed his feelings up in two words: 'George Best,' he said. And that was that.

After the call I sat in silence for a while, as George continued impassively to watch the game below. Then I spoke.

'That was my father, George.' He turned to look at me, with watery eyes. 'He said he'd seen you here when you beat Chelsea.' Then I lied. 'He said you were quite good.'

George Best smiled at me. 'I was half decent.'

I grinned back at him, and then returned my gaze to the huffing and puffing on the pitch below, as Brian Laudrup was being substituted for Tore André Flo.

Somewhere in my imagination, a slight, impish figure in a plain red jersey with a white collar was dancing between defenders, bringing Stamford Bridge to its feet in appreciation. Lighting up the dark night.

9

The End of the Day

KIDDERMINSTER 1–1 MANSFIELD.
1 September, 2001. Aggborough Stadium,
Kidderminster.

In which an uncertain future lies.

Towards the end of the 20th century an invisibly spreading fear of originality had started to seep into the public utterances and articulations of every player in the land. A default vocabulary entered the lexicon and took seed. There was a gradual but widespread proliferation of the phrase 'taking each game as it comes'. After that came its ironically framed, yet equally stultifying, successor, 'I know it's a cliché, but I'm just taking each game as it comes.'

My producer at the time, a laid-back north Londoner with a vintage Mercedes and a love for Tottenham Hotspur, recognised the difficulty of extracting blood from stones. But still, he felt we had to try, since we received a monthly salary to do just that. I used to dread returning late to the office on a Friday afternoon from some interview or other that had left me non-plussed and facing the same question from him, each and every time.

'How was the interview?'

I'd either not reply at all or reply evasively. Then he'd ask the dread question: 'What was the top line?'

The 'top line' is a journalistic stock in trade. Without one, you haven't really got a story. More often than not, as I mentally replayed the interview that was embedded onto the tape sitting in my bag, I could not discern a top line.

'Oh, you know,' I'd buy myself a bit of time. 'I think he was just saying that they've got to keep working hard on the training ground, stick to their own game and the results will come.'

We used to draw straws to avoid being sent to the Reebok Stadium, an archetype of new football blandness, surrounded by the spiritual torpor of the out-of-town shopping centre and its adjacent, always-windy car park. I am sure this environment forced the prevailing mood of bleak functionality that seemed to filter down into the bare-minimum utterances of the bluff manager Colin Todd's playing staff.

Once, in sheer desperation, and in the gathering sense that I had been filming already for 10 minutes and had not one usable quote, I remember asking Bolton's Danish midfielder Per Frandsen what he ate for breakfast.

'Cornflakes.'

Stumped by the blandness of his one-word answer, I followed it up with a question I was certain would elicit some mirth. 'What's Danish for cornflakes?'

'Cornflakes,' he told me.

On the long drive back to London, I questioned everything about my life choices.

*****

It wasn't all bland. As a counterpoint to Bolton, I used to love visiting Oakwell during Barnsley's brief stay in the Premier League, under the classy stewardship of the affable Danny Wilson. This had coincided with my first season on the road as a reporter and would constitute an eternal high tide mark in the history of a football club that seemed to fit genuinely and snugly at the heart of a community.

I remember inviting their plain-speaking, square-jawed captain Neil Redfearn to drive up and away to the outskirts of town, to perch on a fence with the blackened brick-and-steel skeleton of No.3 shaft from the disused main colliery behind him. Redfearn spoke at length about the gift of a season in which the *glitterati* of world football would be guests in this gnarled old town.

Besides, Barnsley FC actually had an official poet. A little-known local writer called Ian McMillan, a lifelong supporter of the club, had started to compose poems about their season. I became aware of this and, before long, arrived in Barnsley with a camera crew to film him performing a poem he had specially composed just for *Soccer Saturday*. We filmed the cheerful McMillan walking soulfully around the surrounding hillsides, looking down on his beloved ground. We shot footage of him stalking the side of the pitch, delivering a fast-paced sequence of words that brought back to life the trauma of Ruud Gullit's impossibly glamorous Chelsea coming to visit and putting six past them. And, after that, in the evening, we filmed him in the stands, as he watched his team scrap their way to a one-all draw against the not especially charismatic Bolton Wanderers.

These little films, set to music, and with Ian McMillan's mellifluous Yorkshire tones woven through them, satisfied a desire within me to do something different with the way that football was presented, appreciated and consumed. I wanted to be able to tap into the secondary texture of the game, how it had the power to evoke a whole landscape of emotion; feelings that were indeed complicated and nuanced, like hope, anguish, anger, pride, dread, boredom, humour, shame, love. Because they were all things that were present in the heart of every fan, even if they were too often constrained within the rectangle of play itself. It seemed not enough to me simply to set goals to pumping soundtracks, the common currency of the early Sky Sports years.

Feeling like I'd hit upon something new, some weeks later I unearthed a couple of poets in Liverpool, after making a few phone calls to local libraries and arts centres ('You don't know any poets who like football, do you?'). It was Merseyside derby time and I commissioned a poem that was going to be split down the middle – red and blue.

Representing Everton was a bald livewire called Terry Caffrey who'd go on to become the poet in residence at the National Football Museum. He'd written something choppy and aggressive which featured an ill-advised line about Dietmar Hamann 'bombing our grandad's chippy'. He stomped and snarled his way around Stanley

Park and the backstreets of Goodison, declaiming his portion of the lines to camera in the style of Alexei Sayle. 'Head it, Dunc! A derby goal and Reds are sunk!'

The Liverpool poet's contribution was altogether more cerebral, but just as stuffed with passion. He was a smooth, verbally adroit and very funny bloke from Birkenhead called Keith Wilson whose greatest claim to fame prior to his sudden rise to prominence in the world of TV sport was the fact that he'd played guitar on Toni Basil's 1980's hit *Mickey*. His subtlety, wit and unexpected turn of phrase brought the little film to life.

We filmed both parts separately, at Goodison and at Anfield. Then the two characters met, Western-style, in Stanley Park as if to duel. Inevitably, they clapped each other on the back, and sauntered off in friendly conversation, playing lazily to the soft-focus notion that the Merseyside derby is a family affair and that no ill feelings abide; a convenient TV myth.

Yet, even though the ending to this piece was a gelatinous cliché, the meat in the middle of the pie had been decent. It had worked, primarily because of the words that Keith had brought to the script. He had a knack of applying to football a terminology he'd appropriated from other walks of life; and they fitted like a glove:

And though consistent inconsistency
Recuts and reshuffles the pack,
The word in the bars and the signs in the stars,
Never stray from the beaten track.

*****

I often think about those days, many of which I spent in a blur of bewilderment at the course my life had taken, as if an invisible hand had grabbed the wheel of my Fiat Panda and was pointing it resolutely at the heart of football. But the closer I got to what really went on behind the walls of the training grounds and in the tunnels of the great stadia, the harder it became to transmit that; to do it justice. The more the target honed into the view, the more it blurred.

And times were changing too. These years invisibly marked the beginning of something that was about to change forever in the national game. A year or so later, Manchester United would somehow wrestle the fates in Barcelona to win that treble that cemented forever and a day the legend of the Ferguson era. Henceforth, he, they, were untouchable.

Their achievement towered above the rest, and on the back of its insurmountable edifice the game started its rapid mutation into something that would transform lives, tear down venerable old buildings, give rise to new cathedrals of football and make thousands upon thousands of millionaires when the billionaires pitched up. It would still take time, but the end game of English football was begun. Twenty years later, a centre-half would be sold for more than the entire British Steel industry. And Saudi Arabia would own Newcastle United.

In the late summer of '99, I'd been speaking to Charlton's manager, Alan Curbishley, at their homely training ground in a drab south-east London suburb. Before we got the interview underway, I'd asked him for his agreement that I might leave my mobile switched on. Kath, enduring a horrible two-week wait to go into labour, had been feeling contractions for some days. I had barely got into the part of the interview where I could talk to Curbishley about how to replace Clive Mendonca up front, when the phone call came. I interrupted the manager, mid flow.

'Alan, I'm really sorry…'

He grinned. 'Go. Go!'

I went. And in an instant, all thoughts about the viability of Charlton Athletic's second season in the top-flight vanished, as I raced over to Lewisham hospital in a small car.

*****

A few months after that, in a farmhouse in Normandy, a long way from work and a long way from the rolling drama of a football season with its slumps, blips, sackings, drubbings and spankings, and in the company of my extended family, we saw in the damp, windy Millennium. We woke the next morning, much the same people, but a thousand years older.

Over breakfast I stared at the three month-old baby who now counted herself among our number and watched her flopping in her high-chair, good naturedly mashing food into her face. She was a kid of late '99. I'd been born in '69. We were both destined to age forever to the tic of the turning decades. I was suddenly 30.

A decade on from having discovered it, football still occupied most of my waking life. I could, and did, spend long drifts of time thinking about Leeds United and their sudden rise, or Manchester City's tortured nosedive. Football filled out certain dreams. Even now I get them; unreal settings in which I play for England and don't entirely disgrace myself, presenting the manager with an unexpected selection dilemma, before I wake up and slope off in search of breakfast.

Football naturally roars into lives to fill those long interludes when not much is going on in our personal narratives. When Saturday flows unopposed through to the following Saturday it's simply because of the lack of friction in the vacuum of the universe. If you think too deeply about this spinning blue globe, lit and darkened in turn as it faces and hides from the sun, then you probably need to recalibrate and focus instead on Derby County's recruitment policy or the state of Scottish football. It's easier that way; football being a kind of ersatz life, a proxy philosophy to hide the darkness, a placebo.

And yet I found I could no longer fully acquiesce to the absolute seriousness of sport. Perhaps I'd never been able to. This slight standoffishness was not a virtue, but felt more and more like a shortcoming. It might, in part, have been explained by my neutral upbringing, without a club to call my own. Not Dad's Chelsea. Not Norwich, nor Celtic. Not even, if I am honest, St Pauli, which was slowly beginning to fade from memory with every year that passed. Millerntor was receding. I noticed I had stopped looking for their results and that made me question how I could ever possibly have been as obsessed as I palpably had been.

A tribal part of me was missing. I often had to sit out swathes of conversation in the office during which a couple of Arsenal- and Spurs-supporting colleagues genuinely found each other unforgivable. Unforgivable that is until they briefly embarked on an ill-fated office romance; perhaps the only and worst way of settling their differences.

Without knowing it, I had found myself uncomfortable with the tone set by my employers. There had been, ever since their inception, an unforgiving edge to much of what Sky did. Approaching the Millennium, its workers were the natural inheritors of a company ethos that had seeped into the very breeze blocks in which it was housed in that industrial park in Osterley. I found Sky quite frightening, if truth be told.

I swallowed down the bitter French supermarket coffee, rubbed my eyes and stared at my daughter, who grinned gummily back. 'It's not their fault,' I wanted to tell her. 'It's mine.'

*****

One Tuesday, in the *Soccer Saturday* production office, I waited for everyone to go home, so that I had the place to myself. Then I picked up the receiver. Looking furtively around the empty desks as I did so, and with my heart pounding and blood pumping in my ears, I dialled the number of the newly-installed head of Channel 4 Sport, Mark Sharman.

Sharman had only recently left Sky Sports, where he'd been Deputy Head, and had been responsible for my promotion. He'd also thrown me an opportunity, in the summer of 1998, to either fail spectacularly, or to succeed, when he'd asked me to make an hour-long documentary entitled *Dennis Bergkamp; Dutch Master*. 'I've dropped a bollock,' he'd told me. 'I've put in it in the schedules to be shown in three weeks' time. The problem is, it doesn't exist. And we've not got any money to make it.' He'd nodded at me, before adding, 'Good luck.'

Thankfully, with the help of the excellent journalist and Arsenal expert Amy Lawrence, we managed to cobble a film together in record time, which just about passed muster, featuring, as it did, extensive interviews with such luminaries as Sheffield Wednesday's Wim Jonk and Leicester City's Matt Elliott (whose job was to tell us how daft he'd felt when Bergkamp turned him inside out, twice in a row). The film had made its allotted transmission time by a matter of minutes, as we put the final touches to it. I still felt I was in his good books.

The conversation, when eventually I was put through, was no more and no less than a thinly veiled 'come and get me' plea, though I naively believed I was being extremely subtle. In fact, I was simply wasting time with pleasantries and was cut short by a typically blunt intervention from a characteristically to-the-point TV executive. 'You want to get out, don't you?'

'I'd like to offer you a job,' he went on, before adding less encouragingly, 'Except, I don't really have one. You see Channel 4 haven't really got any sport,' said the Head of Sport at Channel 4 by way of explanation. I saw his point.

Then, a new thing came along, with impeccable timing. Like a flummoxed and newly hatched ostrich, a clumsy-looking flightless bird called ITV Digital was trying to get off the ground. Everyone in television was staring at it, flapping around, wondering what it would become.

Two senior producers from the nascent Sky Sports News, who'd spent a number of years producing the Friday night football news show, *Sports Centre*, had been head-hunted by ITV Digital to launch their ambitious new venture, the ITV Sports Channel. Nick Atkins was a Leicester City fan, dry as a bone and yet wickedly funny. Together with his best friend in the industry, an extremely excitable Ulsterman called Shane Stitt, whose surname provided huge potential for rhyming slang, he was charged with recruiting a team of producers, commentators and presenters for the new channel, which was going to stake its future on acquiring the broadcast rights to the Football League.

This deal would prove to be the single worst decision in the long history of broadcasters writing out absurdly large cheques and overpaying football's governing bodies for their product. But no one knew this at the time. Or at least people assumed that they must know that they were doing. In order to put the matches on the screen they also signed up, among others, Matt Smith from the BBC, who'd go on to have a long career with both ITV and subsequently BT Sport. Then they added a very credible roster of pundits, such as Garry Nelson, Robbie Earle and Graham Taylor.

Atkins phoned me, as I stood in the Sky Sports' car park, pacing up and down among the cars, glancing guiltily up at the CCTV cameras. 'Come in and see me. I'd like to have a chat with you.'

'Thanks, Nick. I'd love to.' This felt like a scene from a TV drama and not real life.

Their offices were in a brand-new building on Battersea Bridge, premises that they shared with the QVC Shopping Channel. Already this felt different, like light entertainment – almost. Not so straight-jacketedly sporty. I made my way there one Wednesday morning.

'We can offer you this much,' said Atkins, probably knowing that he was behaving like Peter Ridsdale hiring Seth Johnson. I glanced at the figure, which was more than double what I was currently earning at Sky. Much later, and with hindsight, I began to understand the financial folly of the entire ITV Digital enterprise.

'In that case, I should probably…' I remembered the one bit of advice I'd been given about accepting job offers, '…think about it.' I had been told that you should always go back to your current employers to see how they react to the prospect of losing you; you never know.

'Well, we can't offer you any more,' said my besuited boss at Sky from behind his desk. 'So, good luck.' I was waiting for the friendly handshake. Instead, I got a rather chilling final word from the head of the channel that had rescued me from unemployment and given me my break.

'I hope it's not a decision you regret. It won't be possible to come back.'

From now on, my livelihood, and that of my young family, would depend on how many people tuned in to watch Kidderminster Harriers v Mansfield Town. That seemed like a very good idea.

10

Monkey Business

ROCHDALE 5–4 YORK CITY.
5 February, 2002. Spotland Stadium, Rochdale.

In which nothing would be this good again.

I paused and looked around me. To my left was a tall, grey stone-built wall, rounded at the very top. It rose some 20 feet above street level and ran the length of the road. To my right was a bay window, recessed behind a tidy front garden with a few shivering potted geraniums straining for a glimpse of sunlight.

It was mid-morning in Swansea, in one of the narrow, terraced streets that flank the old prison, not far from Swansea's venerable old tumbledown ground, the Vetch Field. I was being filmed as a swan chased me. To be more exact, Cyril the Swan, a humanoid flightless mascot that had clashed repeatedly with other mascots, collided with Norwich City's manager and been sanctioned for kicking the ball at Millwall players. Cyril was the bastard of football mascots.

It was 12 September, 2001. I know that much because the previous day I had been sitting at my desk on the 19th floor of the ITV Digital Studios tower on the South Bank, preparing for the following day's comedic swan-based filming. It was some time during the afternoon that the Twin Towers were struck in New York. Shortly afterwards we had been evacuated from our tower block, as were many other workers from across London. Not knowing what else to do with ourselves, we all drifted off and followed the anguish of the day from the safety of our homes. Very early the following morning, I had driven to Swansea, my mind still partly stuffed with images of the previous day, but equally distracted by the morning's filming that lay before me, as I set about shooting the opening sequence to that week's *Football Third* programme, featuring Swansea City.

Now here I was, sitting on a wall, unwrapping a bacon sandwich and prizing the plastic lid from a polystyrene cup of tea. Alongside me, with his head detached and placed on the wall to his left, sat Eddie Donne, Swansea City's groundsman and the man inside the darkly violent, nine-foot bird. Eddie, it turned out, was a lovely bloke. As we ate and drank our tea, looking out over the The Mumbles, he was in a contemplative mood.

'Terrible, what happened in New York yesterday,' he ventured, thoughtfully.

There was a long pause, as I gazed at the waters of the Bristol Channel and tried to think what possible response to make.

'Yes,' I said, eventually. 'Terrible.'

There was another wordless passage of time, before Eddie, having finished his lunch, hauled himself upright again and stood in front of me; his large, downy tail, grown slightly grubby, and his feathery wing-arms hanging limply at his sides. Then he stooped to pick up his vast swan's head, and, thoughtfully placing it once again on his shoulders, turned to look directly at me. From somewhere within the hollow interior of his colossal neck cavity, I heard Eddie's all too human voice, with its gentle South Wales lilt.

'We've just got to carry on as normal, really.' I nodded. 'Otherwise, they've won.'

*****

In many ways, this extraordinary morning summed up my experience of the months in which the ITV Sport Channel briefly sparked into life, glowed with a peculiar intensity, and then burnt itself out. It was a year of almost complete absurdity, in both the best and the worst possible ways.

Of course, with the benefit of hindsight, it was entirely obvious that ITV Digital's financial 'model', if such a thing even existed, had been drawn up on the back of a matchday programme. In an almost unparalleled act of collective corporate bravado, ITV Digital, known at the time as On Digital, signed off on a deal worth £315 million for three years of Football League broadcasting rights. The Football League, hardly able to contain their surprise and delight at this ridiculous windfall, leapt into the arms of their remarkably undiligent patrons. They threw open their collective coffers in anticipation of the riches to come.

It was fun until midway through the season, when the first rumours started to circulate that ITV Digital could no longer afford to pay their bills. The speed with which it all unravelled was breathtaking. Rarely in the corporate world has so much bluster been followed so quickly by such a collapse. By the winter, stories started to appear in the press suggesting that some live games on the channel were attracting so few viewers that it would have been cheaper for ITV Digital to send a limousine to each viewer's home, drive them to the game, give them a three-course dinner and then run them home. This was no empty hyperbole – at the height of its massive miscalculation, it was said that the company was losing £1 million per day.

But what was worse was the fact that they stopped paying their dues to the League, who in turn were left without the promised funds to distribute across the clubs. And it was these clubs to which we, the unwilling representatives of ITV Digital's disaster economics, had to address ourselves, week in, week out.

Interviewing fans outside the stadium as the discontent spread was at first fraught, then dangerous, then against company policy on the grounds of health and safety. The anger among the fans of Football League clubs was palpable and understandable. I was in no mood to defend my employers too vigorously, since I faced almost certain redundancy within a few short months of leaving my old job to sail off into this bright new tomorrow. Perhaps I should have been alerted to the prospects of glittering success when Johnny Vegas and a stuffed monkey were hired to be the faces of the marketing campaign. I still have the monkey somewhere, with his punchable face and useless arms, a symbol of overreaching fecklessness.

And yet, in terms of coverage, the Football League had never had it so good. I greatly enjoyed the work, which marked a welcome and complete change in the way I related to football.

No longer was I confronted with the sheer cliff face of money that was rearing up in front of us all, that invisible drawbridge being hoisted between pitch and terrace, the forcefield that kept the top clubs distant from their supporters, separated by the width of a living room, from the new-fangled widescreen HD TV to the couch.

A strain was pulling at the game. Football was still being wrenched free of its roots.

*****

Over the last few years of the 20th century, we'd felt it changing, almost weekly. Even pre-Abramovich, Chelsea seemed to be a honey pot of stories. Marcel Desailly, for example, freshly arrived from Marseille, was rumoured to have forgotten where he'd parked his club-issue Mercedes. Days later, Chelsea seemingly received a call from the police pound, which had traced it back to the club. The club, so the story went, duly notified Desailly that his car had been located. 'What car?' he'd apparently replied, confused. The Frenchman, it seemed, had simply given up looking for the old one and bought a new one. Whatever the veracity of this story, it seemed delightfully plausible.

At the same time, Desailly's teammate, Frank Lebouef, had also returned from France as a newly-minted World Cup winner. That year, he became one of the very first Premier League players to earn more than £50,000 per week.

Days after signing his new contract, I interviewed him for *Soccer Saturday* at a café of his choosing on the King's Road. He turned up on time, was very polite, accepted the coffee I bought him, and then shortly before we set the cameras rolling, turned to me and said, 'We have not spoken about a fee for the interview.'

Somewhat surprised by this (the only other player to have gone down this route had been another ex-Chelsea player, Dennis Wise), I explained that it was not Sky's policy to pay for interviews from players still earning from the game, a point Leboeuf seemed to accept.

It was only at the end, when we'd finished recording the interview, that I asked him how much he might have wanted for his time.

'Oh, I don't know,' he demurred. 'Maybe £200?'

Towards the end of my time at Sky, the BBC screened an expensively produced documentary fronted by Alan Hansen in full black polo neck existentialist sociology lecturer mode, called *The Football Millionaires*. Hansen, an unsmiling, haunting presence whose outward appearance veered between poet and undertaker, patrolled the carefully manicured training grounds of the superclubs and examined the increasingly unreal wealth of the millennial generation of players at Liverpool, Manchester United and Chelsea. It was only years later that I discovered from a TV agent that Hansen was supposedly being paid £1.5 million by the BBC – £40,000 per edition of *Match of the Day*. What that amounted to, per word uttered, remains uncalculated.

As a riposte, I had made a short film called *Football's Not Quite Millionaires*. The low-rent counterpoint film that *Soccer Saturday* commissioned, on my urging, might feasibly have cost them several hundred pounds by the time I handed in my petrol receipts.

Making it took me all the way to Hull, where I spent a day filming the club captain fitting toilets on a building site after training to make ends meet. At Rotherham, I featured a scouse kid who commuted from his gran's terraced house near Goodison Park every day to go training. And at Exeter City, a recently retired midfield club legend, awaiting his testimonial, welcomed me to the club and then told me he had no idea what he was going to do next to earn a crust.

It was like throwing open a window. Unearthed, unadorned and nakedly revealed for scrutiny was a whole parallel version of the game, played more or less to the same rules, but in an entirely different social context, with a real relationship to the lived-world experience of those whose actual cash pushed the turnstiles. It was like drinking real ale after years of being force fed Carling.

This little film had been one of my last contributions before leaving Sky.

*****

Before the season had even got started and ITV Sport Channel had come on air with its first live match from Maine Road, I had already visited all 72 clubs in the Football League. Keith Wilson had penned an epic poem about every single club in the land. Over a week in midsummer, we toured the country and filmed a little line or two at every ground, sometimes bumping into managers as we went.

Neil Warnock was there at Bramall Lane, wearing shorts and football boots in his office. Kevin Ratcliffe and Keith almost came to blows over some outwardly lame Liverpool–Everton banter by the side of the pitch at Gay Meadow, and Barry Fry did his cockney geezer schtick at Peterborough United. ''Ere's my mate Keef, all der way from Scouseland. Watch awt for ya 'ub caps. 'E'll 'ave 'em off ya car!'

But it was at Oxford United's new three-sided stadium, named after its chairman, that Keith's penchant for convoluted allusion and subtle wit came to the fore. Standing by a roundabout, with the stadium behind him, Keith mimicked the famous Bob Dylan video, with *Oxford United, To Be Continued...* written on cards which he let fall, one by one. Over that, he added the line:

Now hear this, Robert Zimmerman, I stole this line for you,
No flash cars, just flash cards, the Suburban Homesick Blues.

Even now, many years on, I only half understand it, with its sly David Bowie reference, but it struck a subliminal nostalgic note that I liked. The Kassam Stadium was an architectural low point in the rush for clubs to sell up from their town-centre ancestral homes, leverage their value to persuade a council to develop a new site and whack up a retail park with a football club attached – an unlovely home with a mortgaged soul. Character was voided from the architect's budget-first drawings. The culture and heart had all simply been designed out.

A few days before Oxford United's opening match in their new ground, I filmed an extended interview with the man who had taken over the club, brokered the deal and named the stadium in his own honour. Firoz Kassam was a tall, suited man who had made millions in London buying up hostels and filling them with homeless people, a course of action that led to him being dubbed a 'merchant of misery' in sections of the press. Strolling through yet another unfinished function room in this eponymous breeze block and cement homage, I had a question for him. The cameras rolled as we dodged electric cables hanging from the ceiling. 'How did you come up with the name for the ground, Mr Kassam?'

'Well,' he appeared temporarily flummoxed, before recovering the quick-witted equilibrium that had helped him to stake a place just outside the top 300 richest men in Britain. 'It wasn't my idea.' I remember beaming at him, until, unsettled by my odd smile, he spotted something else he wanted to show me. 'Look, here's our ticket office.'

Of course, Oxford, like so many other clubs, would rue the day they ever shook hands with anyone from the ITV Sport Channel. A few months of financial honeymoon remained for us, before we realised that our mutual paymasters were skint. The ritual abuse from fans, staff and chairmen alike would come, but it was some way off still.

There was something intensely immediate about our dealings with the Football League. I found a repeating pattern of dedication and strange obsession in each and every club, however often its purer path was diverted by shady chairmen or rotten managers. Rochdale, for example, welcomed us with open arms and a huge Spotland pie, filled with melt-in-your-mouth chunks of steak and rich gravy made by a large man whose passion for pies was matched only by his passion for joviality. Rochdale, home to Gracie Fields and the cooperative movement, was football heaven as far as I could make out; an entity that existed almost without any genuine hope, but wrapped itself up in the embrace of a community that followed every meandering step of its deeply important, pointless way.

For our highlights programme, we followed Rochdale's teenage Victorian urchin of a striker, Kevin Townson, through a match day. I was delighted to see him score two first-half goals in a ridiculously exciting 5–4 victory over York City. Completely swept up in the moment, I rushed to the tunnel at the end of the match and found myself uninvitedly ruffling his hair as he departed the pitch, walking backwards and clapping with his arms above his head. In that instant,

I cared more about the 17-year-old Liverpudlian I'd only just met than I did about almost anything else in my life and I dived headlong into the wonderful silliness of my occupation.

In this manner, I began the process of leaving memories all over the map of England and Wales, just as we now drop pins on Google Maps. Affection for places I had scarcely known, hidden away localities and oddly obsessive characters: such things pooled in the pitchside puddles in tumbledown old grounds from Southend to Carlisle.

Swansea would be a place to which I returned throughout those brief winter months on the road for ITV Digital. I found myself drawn back over and over again into the bleak gravitational pull of Swansea City, who were having an *annus horribilis* of their own. I visited again and again those houses clustered together for comfort, behind whose pebble-dash walls memories were kept alive of John Toshack, a long-limbed colossus, gobbling up yard after yard of Vetch Field mud and grass, his long locks wet in the white floodlit evening – back when Swansea had status and success.

The problem was that the club, and those who dedicated themselves to it, was on its knees. Wages eventually dried up, both for the backroom and the playing staff, and the club's very existence became a voluntary act of faith. The old stadium was a sight for sore eyes, a bizarre Mr Potato Head of a ground, with odd bits of structure accessorising its Edwardian skeleton, reminders of brief moments when there was a few quid knocking around. The floodlights were a mismatch, drawn from across the history of industrial infrastructure through the decades. As a result, during night games, the light seemed to limp across the pitch, collecting in slightly different coloured patches ranging from yellow to white. One of the stands only ran along two-thirds of one of the ends.

Apart from history, they had sod all. And they had in Mike Lewis, a chairman who was hell-bent on extracting even that from them. A tall man, with a face that was easy to redden, and grey, thinning hair, he strode around the place like he owned it, which awkwardly, he did. He was typical of the kind of businessman who seemed drawn to struggling clubs. Guided tours were his thing, especially if there was a TV camera in range. On one occasion, he allowed our cameras to travel with him in a Rolls Royce to the club. His PR tone deafness was almost admirable.

Wherever I pointed the dented bonnet of my underwhelming car I discovered a seemingly endless procession of local businessmen with brittle egos and shaky financial plans that seemed to unravel at the merest hint of pressure, leaving them exposed to the ire of the newly mobilised online fan forums of the early noughties.

There was the Oyston family at Blackpool, whose father, Owen, was locked up after a rape conviction and whose son and heir, Karl, once treated me to lunch at the ground during which he protested the family's good name, without drawing breath.

In Gillingham, there was Paul Scally, a Dubai-based ex-photocopier magnate. Scally redeveloped the Priestfield (which he makes no secret of wanting to leave) to such an extent that, as early as the noughties, it boasted the inevitable profit-generating conference facilities and a huge marble ball that gently rotated, supported by a flow of water from a subterranean pump.

'What do you think it cost me?' he invited me to guess.

'I don't know'

'Go on, guess!'

'A hundred thousand pounds?'

'You fucking joking?! Way off, son. Way off!' He looked aggrieved. 'Fifteen grand.'

Reading chairman John Madejski, who also had a penchant for having things named after himself, showed me around his home, as well as his club. After some perfunctory negotiation, he even allowed our cameras into his underground exercise room. Flicking a switch, Madejski had revealed a glass wall at one end behind which a clutch of supercars suddenly became visible, trapped in some kind of garage/ aquarium.

'Wow', I'd said, with only mildly contrived admiration. 'How do you get them out?'

'Oh, they're just there to look at really,' Madejski, a close friend of Cilla Black's, answered unapologetically.

And then there was Darlington. It was a curious and wonderful ground, Feethams, complete with scaled-down, old Wembley-style twin towers and adjacent cricket pitch. It had been acquired in some predictably depressing way by a local man called George Reynolds. Reynolds already had numerous convictions and multiple prison sentences for theft, smuggling, burglary, safe-cracking and handling explosives. On the up side, he'd made a fortune selling kitchen work surfaces, so that meant he was a fit and proper person to acquire Darlington, get rid of their lovely old stadium and build a breeze block palace on the ring road, which he duly named after himself.

With almost comical predictability Reynolds led Darlington into insolvency in 2004. In 2005 he was sentenced to three more years in prison after he was found with half a million pounds in the boot of his car. The Reynolds Arena subsequently became the Northern Echo Arena, named after the newspaper whose pages would often fill with the ex-chairman's latest misdemeanours, right up until his death in April 2021.

And then there was Albert Scardino, who was a bit different. The first time I met him (in fact, the only time I met him) was in his London penthouse, opposite the Victoria and Albert Museum. It was a grand corner house with a glass turret that looked down the length of Knightsbridge towards Harrods and beyond. He had a grand piano in his flat, on top of which stood a framed photograph of him and his wife, Marjorie, with Bill and Hillary Clinton. Scardino, a Pulitzer Prize-winning, former *New York Times* journalist presented himself as a welcoming figure and made coffee for us all on the ITV Sport Channel film crew, which had descended on his elegant peace. He seemed fairly bemused that he was the centre of our attention. He also seemed bemused that he was the Notts County chairman.

This oldest and most unassuming of professional football clubs just happened to be (guess what?) almost completely broke. Scardino approached the job with humility, great interest and probably not the faintest idea what a thankless task it would prove to be. Indeed, within a year or two he left the club as it fell into administration, proceeding along a thoroughly familiar-sounding path to insolvency.

Scardino had ill-advisedly wrested control of a venerable old club and, like some hopelessly under-powered version of the Glazer family, had clearly no idea how to turn a loss-making club like Notts County into anything other than a loss-making club like Notts County.

The last I heard of Scardino he was back in the States, raging about Donald Trump's mental health and Brexit, and he rarely mentions the months he spent learning football's most idiosyncratic song, which they lustily bellow from the sombre black stands at Meadow Lane:

I had a wheelbarrow,
The wheel came off.
I had a wheelbarrow,
The wheel came off.

No one knows exactly what this song means. But everyone knows exactly why they sing this song.

Such drama played out in the realm of living, breathing humans, whether they were battering along the wing to get on the end of the full-back's lofted, speculative pass, or sitting sweaty-palmed in the directors' box, avoiding eye contact. And to all those thousands in the stands, stamping feet and blowing on chicken tikka pies, this was the intoxicating mix that brought them back every week. It was a happy time for a journalist interested in the whole of football and not just the bit that happens on the pitch, which could sometimes pass into muddy incoherence.

*****

It was a good year's work. Despite the embarrassment with which it subsided, we enjoyed a curious kinship with the men and women we encountered along the way. Hopes were high, intentions were estimable and through a rather touching combination of naivety, desperation and good faith, the clubs variously granted us quite unfettered access to their workings; to the kitchens, the kit rooms, the boardroom and the training ground. We pinned microphones on managers, hid cameras in all sorts of nooks and crannies, and strolled around the areas of clubs which are usually out of bounds with a certain entitled swagger.

No one seemed to mind too much, whether it was at Plymouth Argyle, under the canny stewardship of Paul Sturrock, a jovial Scot with a furious temper, or Cheltenham Town, whose slightly manic, excessively wiry, manager Steve Cotterill would regale us with expletive-strewn West Country-accented motivational speeches, as if we were about to line up in midfield for him.

But the romance could not last forever. The goodwill started to run out as rumours started to abound that ITV Digital were about to welch on their arrangement. By and large, neither the managers nor the players seemed overly irritated by our being there; the presence of a camera at a training ground, especially at clubs whose work often goes unrecorded, can lend a certain sense of importance to the occasion, and a televised match is the best shop window for players from the lower leagues. Yet the fans knew who we were and often let their feelings be known.

At the best of times, TV crews and their accompanying reporters, often wearing branded clothing, are unwelcome guests at the party and for perfectly understandable reasons. Even when I had been at Sky, I did my best to disguise the fact when I was working in plain sight of the general footballing public milling outside Ewood Park or Bramall Lane.

'You from Sky, mate?'

'Er, yup.' There was no hiding the blue-and-red logo on my standard-issue jacket.

'Well Sky can fuck off.'

'OK.' I'd normally leave at that point. 'Thanks.'

But if Sky had simply been generally not very popular, by March 2002 ITV Digital's presence at football grounds had virtually become an incitement to riot.

To be perfectly honest, those supporters might have guessed what would happen the moment they'd picked up one of the specially manufactured ITV Digital remote controls. Its tacky build, lightweight feel and silly shape were like a parody of the Sky one. ITV Digital was an idea whose time had not come. It went wobbling off into the history books like a Sinclair C5, with a bunch of creditors chasing it down the road.

As the very final weekend of Football League action reared its head, instruction was sent out via the channel's leadership that no specific references should be made at any point during the broadcasts, either live or pre-recorded, to the fact that the whole project had gone spectacularly, publicly wrong; not just wrong, but nationally, historically wrong.

It was difficult to adhere with total compliance to this edict, as we all sat pitch-side during various defining moments of another football season, contemplating our imminent redundancies, regaled by sporadic chants exhorting us to stick various things up our arses.

Of course, while it would be wrong to say I was not pre-occupied by my own job prospects, it was also true that we felt deeply ashamed and guilty by association. This was made all the worse by having enjoyed so much of my 10-month deep dive into the English Football League. I felt wedded to the project, so implicated in the broken promises.

I also felt distinctly unemployed, in my early 30s, with a second child on the way.

11

Gap Year

ENGLAND 1–2 BRAZIL.
21 June, 2002. Shizuoka, Japan.

In which there is no bang and barely a whimper.

Football broadcasters can be very tribal. In my formative years at Sky, we'd collectively act as if summer international football didn't happen, owing to the fact that the satellite broadcaster owned none of it. As FIFA kicked off, we clocked off. The most that Sky Sports News would do in reference to the major event that was captivating the rest of the world was to speculate which Swedish midfielder Martin O'Neill might be interested in signing in order to bolster his Leicester City squad.

Such had been our total news blackout that during France '98, for instance, instead of mentioning the World Cup, I'd spent June presenting a series of inner city five-a-side tournaments. Instead of being sent anywhere near Marseille for England's fractious opener against Tunisia, I was dispatched to careworn patches of astroturf in places like Byker, Holbeck and White City to film a load of children's teams actually enjoying the game and only occasionally breaking into fights. Misguidedly, in my new presenting role, I'd bought a white linen jacket and strode around these very urban settings like Martin Bell in a war zone. Children more or less openly sniggered as I exited the Fiat Panda. Sometimes their parents would join in.

But four years later, things had moved on for me. Or they should have done. June 2002 should have seen me getting onto a really big aeroplane and heading to Japan and South Korea as part of the ITV

Sport Channel's World Cup team. The prospect of being sent a long way away to watch the unimaginably glamorous Argentina, Italy, Brazil and France knock a ball around seemed completely fanciful. And, as it happened, it turned out to be actually fanciful. I watched the afterburners of my imagined jumbo jet to Tokyo dip over the horizon and disappear.

As redundancy negotiations ground on and ITV Digital was officially wound up, I counted my coins into my bank account and spent the summer of 2002 watching the telly, painfully reminded of what I was missing out on. Kath was pregnant again and very sick with it, and our almost-three-year-old daughter was still a ferociously early riser. During those early morning kick-offs she became my companion, sitting alongside me on the couch with a sippy cup of milk for when Des Lynam, weirdly cheapened by being compelled to throw to commercial breaks, greeted a bleary-eyed nation with a version of his trademark arid charm that never quite hit the heights of Des in his BBC pomp.

'Shouldn't you be at work?'

The irony of his famous opener from four years previously was not lost on me. In fact, my joblessness nagged at me all the while I watched Paul Gascoigne uncomfortably clowning around for ITV Sport with England fans in Trafalgar Square, and Gary Neville, whose turn it was to 'have a metatarsal', making his TV studio punditry debut with an assuredness and clarity that came as a complete surprise to those of us who simply, mistakenly, thought he was just Gary Neville.

I took whatever work I could. Touting myself out as a kind of generalised hired hand, I snapped up scraps of employment here and there. From time to time, I ended up producing work for RTÉ Sport in Dublin, whose attitude to broadcasting the World Cup was thrillingly close to descending into a pub brawl every time they went on air. Eamon Dunphy was the chief difference between the sobriety of a BBC or ITV studio and the Irish version. The shock-jock and general controversialist, who memorably gave his name to a fictional sausage in Roddy Doyle's *The Van* because the sausage 'looked like a prick', was the width of a hair away from getting escorted out of the studio by security, at any given moment. Dunphy insisted on wearing a tie that reflected the colours of whoever it was the Republic were playing that day, in protest and solidarity with Roy Keane, who'd exited the cup before it had even begun. It was brilliantly different.

More odd jobs piled up around me, as I tried to fill in the gap between the previous bit of my life and the completely unknowable future bit which had not yet taken shape. Quite unexpectedly, and through the mediation of a mutual contact, I resumed my relationship with Rodney Marsh, with whom I had worked at *Soccer Saturday*.

The closest Marsh and I had got during my couple of years at Sky was when I had walked at his side to the centre circle at Valley Parade on the opening home game of the 2000–01 season. Marsh had declared, at the beginning of Bradford City's first Premier League campaign the previous summer, that he'd shave his head if they managed to stay up. They managed to stay up and their publicity-savvy chairman, Geoffrey Richmond, held Marsh to account, insisting that the former QPR and Man City talisman sacrificed his unusually blond, still faintly mulletted, locks in front of a capacity crowd. There is a colour plate in Marsh's archetypal footballer's autobiography *Priceless* (it cost £17.99) that depicts me, in a baggy brown suit, leaning towards Marsh as he sits on a chair in the middle of the pitch, good-humouredly allowing a barber to clip off his trademark barnet.

I liked Marsh, though I had been wary of him at first. I was fascinated by his slightly avuncular/older brother relationship with George Best, to whom, unlike almost everyone else in Best's sphere, he expressed no deference, only fondness and concern. Marsh, who loved to play the fool on camera, was actually an intriguing character, with a natural curiosity and a set of opinions and values that were hard to predict. He took himself seriously, had an odd sense of humour, but a genuine warmth. And when he approached me to produce a series of interviews for a new venture he was involved in, I was flattered and grateful.

During those pioneering days of start-up channels, the Professional Footballers' Association itself tried to launch its own platform, in association with a few other stakeholders. The Footballers' Football

Channel never flickered across anyone's screens in the end, widescreen, HD or plain old cathode-ray. A cursory Google search almost 20 years later reveals only a single thread on the Digital Spy platform in which a few bewildered posters swapped rumours about its imminent launch, and then were heard no more. That was in 2002, a good year to fail, it seemed. But that's not to say that money was not spent on the project in the first instance.

In this manner, Marsh was hired to conduct a series of interviews with an assortment of his high-profile mates from sport and showbiz, in which they discussed their love of football. I produced three long interviews that were never broadcast. One was with Henry Cooper in the Thomas à Becket boxing gym on the Old Kent Road, in which the old champ charmed and amused us all for hours with tales of greatness on the world stage and collecting lost golf balls in the south London suburbs of his childhood. Cooper even helped to carry the kit down the fire escape at the end of filming and dropped an enormous tip in the hands of the cleaner who had to sweep up after us.

After that we relocated to Switzerland, where Marsh had persuaded Phil Collins to meet us and talk us through the slightly convoluted story of his football fandom (was it Spurs, Chelsea or QPR? I never did figure it out as his allegiances seemed to oscillate). The afternoon's filming with Collins was memorable mostly for Marsh taking a lead from Mrs Merton and asking the ex-Genesis drummer what had attracted him to the tax haven Switzerland? Somewhat surprisingly, Collins didn't seem to mind that and later invited us all to watch Leeds United play in the Champions League around at his house. That was odd, sitting on a couch, drinking a Becks, alongside Phil Collins and Rodney Marsh. I didn't say much.

Then it was the turn of Elton John to get the Marsh treatment. We filmed the encounter at the singer's Berkshire residence, where he kept us waiting for hours. But when at last he arrived, and under gentle, well-prepared and surprisingly sensitive questioning by Marsh, he talked candidly about his early days as a football chairman – in particular, his first trip with Watford to an away match, on which he took his mother. When taking his seat in the stands outside the director's box, a little too early for the beginning of the second half, the crowd spotted him and started singing, to the tune of *My Old Man Said Follow The Van*, 'Don't sit down while Elton's around... or you'll get a penis up the arse.'

Elton John roared with laughter, echoed by Rodney Marsh. 'Mum turned to me and said, "What are they singing?"'

Again, I was left wondering how I'd ended up in that room.

And all this time the World Cup rumbled on. It was on a flight back from working in Ireland that I landed in Stansted to news that England had beaten Argentina and Sven-Göran Eriksson's team had somehow scrambled through to the knockout phase. Here they met Denmark. I sat in a Welsh pub, watching Emile Heskey rampage through a World Cup defence. I remembered, as I stuffed my face with crisps and tried to disguise any hint of my nationality, having interviewed Heskey during his late teenage years at Leicester City. He'd been perched on an item of gym equipment, exuding explosive strength, yet timid and cautious to a disarming degree, and totally at odds with how you might otherwise perceive him. He'd told me that one of his middle names was 'Ivanhoe', which I never could push to the back of my mind when I watched him play. Now here he was, doing this. I started to feel the bewildering swoosh of passing time through my career. Also, I was drinking lager in the late morning, largely unemployed, heading towards my mid-30s.

I was in Wales for a reason. That evening I was due to be a guest of honour at my brother-in-law's village football club annual dinner near Aberystwyth. This brother-in-law was in fact Sean, the self-same intellectual centre-forward from the university college football team. Some years previously I'd introduced him to my sister and, not for the first time in his life, he had rather overplayed his hand. And now, overplaying another hand, he'd convinced me to come along to his village football club's annual dinner on the understanding that I was 'something of a celebrity'. I was, it goes without saying, nothing of the sort.

Rather awkwardly, the real guest of honour was Tomi Morgan, manager of Camarthen Town FC. Morgan was a resolutely dignified and somewhat shy man, well known to everyone in the hall. He was doing great things with the local semi-professional team and had spent half a lifetime in the game. Yet, ridiculously, Morgan deferred to my completely non-existent public profile and sat down after speaking for only a few minutes saying, 'I don't want to keep you now, as I know you've come here to hear from the real star from Sky Sports, Nick Bolton.'

People craned their necks to figure out who this Nick Bolton might be. They continued to crane. Then I stood up, at which point they simply looked puzzled. Having nothing to say, and to no laughter or applause, I filled a horrifyingly blank couple of minutes in a rural Welsh village hall with sound, before making some ill-judged remark about John Hartson not being worth £7.5 million and immediately thereafter sat down again.

A week or so later, back home in England, I woke early for the Brazil quarter-final, my child patiently arranging and rearranging her three dolls on the couch alongside us. It should have been more exciting than it was, but the early hour and the totally predictable outcome robbed it somehow of a sense of occasion. It was a curiously bloodless game, epitomised by Gareth Southgate's assessment of the half-time team talk in which the England team had 'needed Churchill', but instead 'got Iain Duncan-Smith'.

In 2018, 16 years after that match, I accompanied Jeff Stelling on a charity walk along the banks of the Thames. A few dozen of us were joined the whole way by Dennis Wise, and other ex-footballers dropped by for a few miles to show their support as we followed a route from AFC Wimbledon's ground to Wembley, via Craven Cottage, Stamford Bridge and Loftus Road. To idle away the walking hours, we talked endlessly about football and, for some reason, turned to discussing that quarter-final in 2002 against Brazil. A group of us agreed that it had been a weird England line-up.

'I bet we'd find it hard to name the starting XI,' I suggested. And of course, we immediately started to try.

The names started coming: Seaman, Beckham, Scholes, Owen, um... After a few minutes of increasingly ponderous guesswork, interrupted briefly by someone punching the air with satisfaction at having plucked the name Danny Mills out of thin air, we were still two names short and showing no signs of getting the remaining players.

'No one's going to say Sinclair, then.' A voice from the back of our group of anorak-clad walkers piped up. We all turned to look at the person who'd suddenly piped up.

'I thought I did OK, to be fair,' said Trevor Sinclair.

Many years after that fated quarter-final Southgate, recently sacked by Middlesbrough, accompanied me on a long trudge through a wintry Turin. We'd set off in search of a branch of Avis, where I was to pick up a hire car in which I'd intended to drive to visit a young Chris Froome the following day (I was increasingly moving into cycling work by then). Tramping around to find a hire car depot was perhaps not where he expected to find himself and yet Southgate expounded on all sorts of issues, most memorably the peculiar bathos of Japan and Korea 2002. He told me, as we passed the afternoon before Chelsea's match against Juventus, which we'd be covering for ITV, that for him, as for us, the 2002 World Cup had ended not with a bang but with the whimper of air as the Ronaldinho-propelled spinning ball passed hopelessly beyond the reach of David Seaman. Curious to discover that sometimes the Venn diagrams of fandom and playerdom overlapped, I hung on Southgate's every word and, for the umpteenth time, imagined a different version of the past, in which England had triumphed.

2002 was a blank. The World Cup came and then went in a blaze of national and personal apathy. It had all been at the wrong time of day, anyway. And I was ready to get back to work, assuming that someone would let me.

12

A Good Out

DERBY COUNTY 4–2 NOTTINGHAM FOREST.
20 March, 2004. Pride Park, Derby.

In which, for one man, there can be no winner.

It was around about then that Mum and Dad retired from their teaching jobs in Bedford and moved to Scotland. This represented another unsettling jolt on the path to full-blown adulthood. The fact of being a parent, with officially retired parents of my own, had alarmed me. But there was a geographical dislocation, too. All throughout those early years when I'd been finding my feet and voice at Sky and then with ITV Digital, I had banked on my parents' physical presence at home in Bedford, just a half-hour's drive from junction 13 of the southbound M1. A cup of tea and a chat with them on my way back from Hartlepool or Barnsley: this was a touchstone of a value I understood only when it disappeared.

Now when I passed that junction, the motorway sign for the exit made my stomach lift.

*****

The head of ITV Sport at the time was Brian Barwick, a forthright, gregarious and slightly dishevelled Liverpudlian who had joined ITV from the equivalent role at the BBC and would go on, much to everyone's astonishment, (and possibly his own) to become the chief executive of the Football Association.

Barwick presided over the last great era of excess in ITV's history, arriving at a time when financial largesse was still the norm and leaving at a time when it wasn't. Tall, fleshy and normally seen with his feet up on a table, the crumbs from a tuna baguette catching in the red hair of his moustache, he was a highly personable big beast of an executive who enjoyed the status that went with running such an operation. It was Barwick, for example, who had settled the absurdly generous terms on which Alan Hansen and his cohort of pundits plied their trade at the BBC.

He took the same attitude of anti-austerity with him to ITV when they nicked not only the Premier League highlights rights but, much more significantly, his fellow moustache-wearing Des Lynam to go with them in what was inevitably dubbed by the redtops *Snatch of the Day*. Together they recruited a new panel of pundits, whose contract negotiations were, in the words of one broadcast agent of the time: 'Embarrassing. We'd go in with a rough idea of what to ask for and they'd offer double. It was extraordinary.'

This was the residual fiscal company ethos tacked onto the fag end of ITV's long monopoly on TV advertising revenue. During the 1980s, the channel's wealth creation was prodigious. Survivors of that era at ITV tell stupendous tales of overtime earnings and fiscal decadence. Barwick, in his understanding of the role of a TV executive, was determinedly old school. He would take his particular munificence with him again when he went to the FA and negotiated a contract in a room sitting opposite Fabio Capello.

But he also had real charisma. Barwick had an own-brand bluff humour that was hard not to like. After he'd re-signed some sports rights to ITV and had told me about it over a drink in a hotel near Teeside, I'd asked him what price he'd had to pay.

'That's for me to know, Ned,' he'd said, tapping the side of his nose. 'And for you to fuck off about.'

A passionate Liverpool fan, he was also credited with having said, on the morning flight back from Istanbul after Liverpool's Champions League win in 2005, 'I'm made up for Liverpool and I'm made up for ITV.' Then he'd added, 'But most of all, I'm made up for me.'

I liked his unapologetic chutzpah. Years later, when he'd annexed the vast desk that used to belong to Adam Crozier at the minimalist headquarters of the FA in Soho Square, I popped in with a colleague to visit him. Again, even in the sleek surroundings of the Crozier-designed corner office overlooking the streets below, Barwick insisted on putting his feet up on the otherwise completely barren table.

'So what is it you actually do here?' I asked the new FA chief exec.

'Well,' Barwick started. 'Various things.' There was a pause while he rubbed his cheeks. 'I've got Trevor down the corridor. He does my football.' And with that, the new FA supremo nodded his head in the direction of where Sir Trevor Brooking presumably sat in quiet obeisance at his desk in a separate office, diligently 'doing his football'.

*****

It was thanks in part to Brian Barwick that the beginning of the 2002–03 season saw a spattering of reporting jobs come my way, a trickle that eventually became a bit more of a stream. Presented by the pioneering Gabby Logan, who I had known, admittedly at a distance, from her early days at Sky, ITV's *On the Ball* was the early 21st-century reincarnation of an eponymous 1970s insert into the *World of Sport*, which was hosted by a combination of Brian Moore, Ian Saint John and Jimmy Greaves. This was the iconic show that eventually became known simply as *Saint and Greavsie*.

After an eight-year hiatus, following the migration to ITV of the broadcast rights to the Premier League the format returned, revamped, polished and changed forever to fit into a more sanitised age. Co-presented at first by Logan and Barry Venison (whose nickname of 'Spandau Barry' never really took off, despite my concerted efforts), *On The Ball* featured the usual soup of soundbites from training grounds, the rumble of predictions and mild to middling 'banter'. It had a pleasant lightness of touch and a quality that could be described as breezy. And Logan, who really set the tone for the very many, very talented women who followed in football, struck a perfect balance between a relaxed, welcoming style and hard-nosed knowledge.

Its producers, some of whom had moved across from Sky, approached their task wanting at least to try things differently. I was allowed a certain scope to repackage things in what I hoped was an imaginative way, even if we often had to default to listening to Gordon Strachan predict that the upcoming match against Everton would be a real test as to whether or not Southampton would be able to 'push on'. The standard football rhetoric was never much further away than a drab Thursday lunchtime at a press conference in the training ground of some mid-table club. Days of my life were swallowed whole in such surroundings.

Across the land, many of the old training facilities with their inter-war pavilions, fitted out some time in the '80s, gave way to brand new, sparkling premises that matched the stadiums the clubs now called home. One by the one the whole architectural language of the football ground was rewritten or erased. The bulldozing meant a new start, but also the end of so much; that ocular connection of the outlines of stands against scudding spring skies, the whirlwind breeze that lifts suddenly from one unlovely corner, the landscape of shared memories: Stanchions, gables, bannisters, gantries and corridors, all the texture of matchday forcibly extracted from the collective unconscious of fans and placed beyond reach into the rusting bin of time past, and the digital neverland of YouTube.

It went the same way with clubs' new training grounds, too. Behind their pine-clad, smoked-glass exteriors, a world opened up of AV suites, hydro-pools, indoor, heated, all-weather pitches, physio rooms, gyms, canteens and press conference suites, all built for the same cost as a half decent striker from Anderlecht or Ipswich. Players now swept in past clutches of celebrity-hungry fans through gates that bore signs warning against trespass and advising that players would not be stopping to sign autographs.

We lived off scraps now. Where once some clubs like West Ham and Charlton, Everton and Sunderland used to ask reporters in for tea and beans on toast, surrounded by the staff and players, muddy studded boots and all, now conversations with players only normally took place within designated areas of the training ground. And if that access failed, as it often did, the only fall-back option was the car park, where you might be afforded a critical eight seconds of semi-legitimate contact as the player scuttled from the safety of the training ground to the safety of his car.

From week-to-week I knew less clearly where I stood, save for the fact that I felt uncomfortable even trying. Even before you factor in the increasingly remote and controlling distance placed between the players and their public, there is an absurdity in the status of 'football journalist' that no amount of denial can disguise. To ask questions, even good ones, is a fatuous pursuit when placed alongside the demands and rewards the players enjoy and endure. The actual pressures and prizes of playing the game remain unknowable to us. We talk as if we are equals. We are no such thing and we never were.

Some more hard-nosed colleagues positively rejoiced in their status of shabby, unloved mutt running alongside a thoroughbred racehorse. One of my predecessors at ITV, Gary Newbon, was one such survivor, whom nothing much seemed to bother. Newbon was famous above all in the small world of televised sport for two things: persuading Alex Ferguson to stop and do a half-time interview during Champions League matches, and for flipping the coin to see whether ITV or the BBC would get first dibs at World Cup fixtures. This earned him the self-styled title, 'ITV's official tosser'. Once he walked with a young producer right in front of the Holte End shortly before a match kicked off. The Villa Park crowd, spotting him, struck up the boisterous and unmistakable chant: 'Gary Newbon, he's a wanker, he's a wanker.' Newbon, quite unfazed, turned to his young companion and said, with a beaming smile, 'You see? They know who I am!' I found this admirable.

Yet *On the Ball* gave me a platform to poke some fun at the seriousness with which the game took itself; this great funniness that lived at the heart of football, a perfectly simple social activity that had its origins in rioting in small English market towns and had somehow become a dominant human concern.

In this spirit, at the end of the 2003–04 season, the programme's producers decided that we should hand out some cobbled-together, homemade awards. The thinking didn't go much beyond that, save for the not insignificant fact that they invested a few quid in the production of around a dozen bespoke trophies, tacky fake bronze statuettes with a footballer kicking thin air at an anatomically improbable angle and the words *On The Ball Awards* badly engraved on a wobbly stand. Armed with these insultingly cheap-looking objects I set off for a couple of days in search of players to award them too.

The problem was that the season had already ended, save for Millwall and Manchester United, who were about to dispute a not very memorable FA Cup Final. As a result, a lot of players had either gone off to meet up for international duty or were simply on holiday in Dubai, already padding around the perimeters of swimming pools in flip-flops.

With this paucity of possible recipients hampering our bold ambitions, we dropped in on various training grounds. If we happened upon anyone we'd heard of, we instantaneously retrofitted an entirely made-up category to suit them, essentially creating an award from thin air. This policy led us, almost inevitably, to Jimmy Bullard. Tracking him down at Wigan Athletic, we handed the floppy-haired cheeky cockney his gong for having jumped out of the changing room behind Geoff Horsfield like Spike Milligan from a hole in the desert, during a taped interview in the winter. The sole nominee in his category, he took home the 'Best Naked Appearance by a Footballer' gong.

Back on the awards trail, which had already stopped in on Ian Holloway for some equally made-up reason, Patrick Vieira saved the day. Turning up pretty much unannounced at Arsenal's new London Colney training ground, we'd scarcely parked up before a surprisingly trusting press officer had persuaded the Arsenal captain, dressed in something expensively denim and leather, to stop walking and accept a completely bogus award.

'Patrick Vieira, Arsenal captain,' I said to him, checking the cameras were rolling. They were. Vieira, standing to one side of me, looked politely if sceptically in my direction. He resisted the temptation to shoot a glance at his watch. In my left hand I held a microphone and in my right a terrible statuette. Then, suddenly, my mind went blank.

'Please accept...' there was a long-ish pause. 'An award.'

'Thank you,' said the great Frenchman. He looked visibly shocked at the shoddy feel of the trophy as he received it. Then he smiled, as he looked back at me, immobile and grinning vacantly at him. 'Thanks for this,' he was nearly done, 'award,' he added.

Shortly after that we made our way back towards our hastily parked crew car in silence. And an Arsenal Football Club press officer walked meditatively back to his place of work, wondering what he'd just endorsed. At the same time Patrick Vieira, one of the defining talents of the early 21st century, glanced at his rear-view mirror as the cheap statuette rolled from the back seat, where he'd probably lobbed it, and almost certainly fell into the plushly upholstered footwell of his huge and powerful motor car.

*****

Towards the end of March, 2004, and because Derby County were locked in a relegation dual with Nottingham Forest, there was a possibility that one or other, or both, of these two venerable clubs that had won titles both domestically and in Europe, might be relegated to the third tier of English football. This clearly represented an unthinkable outcome for their legion fans (32,000 turned up to watch the 'A52 derby' on 24 March), but an even more shocking prospect for the man who had marshalled them both to their respective, unforgettable high tides in the 1970s – Brian Clough.

Brokered by a third-party journalist colleague in the East Midlands who knew him well, *On The Ball* managed to secure an interview with Clough. I was sent up the M1 to meet him, to walk around the County Ground with him and to sit him down to talk about his history with the two clubs.

I'd only ever seen Clough once in person. That had been from the distance of the Holmesdale End of Selhurst Park in 1993 on a rare visit home from Hamburg. I'd watched him in his green sweatshirt with its upturned white collar depart the scene of another Premier League defeat, just weeks from the end of the single most captivating career that ever passed through English football; man, player and manager.

Eleven years later, I parked up outside a ground that was mostly unaltered by the march of time, its 'megastore' a portacabin, its club offices like the brick-built headquarters of a reasonably successful light manufacturing firm in an industrial estate on the outskirts of a Midlands town. Walking into reception, feeling like salesmen clutching prospectuses for new carpets, we told the staff that we were here from ITV 'to see Mr Clough', a phrase that, as simple as it sounded, rang hollow in my ears. It was a bit like turning up at NASA's Houston headquarters and asking for Mr Armstrong.

Before long, and after having enjoyed a cup of tea on a saucer with a plain digestive, Clough appeared in front of us; older, a little whiter than I was expecting and slightly stooped.

'Good morning, and welcome to Nottingham Forest Football Club,' he said, his voice just a few notes thinner than it had been, but still precise and deliberate, as if such a seemingly casual act of extending a welcome to a group of three strangers to the football club he used to run an age ago were much more than the sum of its parts. Clough intoned those simple words as if they amounted to a ritual of some kind, one that required thorough adherence, no small gesture. He was a deliberate man.

We set about the usual, awkward rigmarole of pinning on a radio microphone to the collar of his knitwear and hiding a transmitter in the pocket of his sportsman's slacks. For people unused to such treatment, this finicky and slightly invasive procedure can often quickly degenerate into a confusion of raised arms, lifted jumpers and tangled wires. Not so with Brian Clough, whose fluency in getting his mic on must have been born of countless television appearances, going right back to the very first outbreak of punditry on the nation's screens in the 1970s.

I remembered his occasional presence on TV from my childhood, how he'd sometimes provoke a generalised rolling of the eyes from my dad, followed perhaps by an affectionate sigh of exasperation at Clough's latest stunt. 'Old Big 'Ead' had been a feature of the panel assembled by ITV for the 1974 World Cup and remained a regular guest all the way through the rest of the decade, clashing fantastically with Don Revie over his ill-fated tenure at Leeds United, eliciting a challenge to a fight from Mohammed Ali, and generally being forthright, boastful, correct, wrong and always entertaining. He knew where the microphone was and how to use it. He knew what a camera could do. He understood the language of TV, because he wrote it for the generations to come, before the script was adapted for the 21st century by the likes of Robbie Savage and Gary Neville.

Slowly we walked the corridors of the City Ground, stopping every now and again to gaze at framed photos on the walls, those not-quite-focussed inky night time shots of brilliant red jerseys and tight white shorts, unnaturally green dew-speckled grass caught in the startling floodlight. Cups held aloft, players running along athletics tracks by the sides of pitches, arms stretched straight up in celebration.

Time and time again, Clough would raise a curved index finger and point at a face, frozen in time. 'A good player, he was. A very good player,' he'd muse, with emphasis on the word 'good'. 'He might have been more than that, but there you go.'

Or, scanning his watery eyes over the line of players in a pre-season squad photo, 'I admired them greatly, as a group of men. As they admired me.'

And every room we walked into, there was another young clerk who rose from behind a desk to acknowledge him, or another middle-aged lady who would bustle across to be embraced by Mr Clough. As our short, guided tour of the backroom offices at the City Ground came to a close, we paused.

'Which was the greater achievement, do you think? What you did here at Forest or at Derby County?'

Clough suddenly stopped where he was to answer the question I had just posed him. We were standing, blocking the way, near a photocopier and a trophy cabinet. His answer took a fraction longer to come than I was expecting, leaving me momentarily unsure whether I had somehow caused offence, or was about to get a telling-off for my impudence. But then he answered, without equivocation.

'It was, I would say, Derby County.' He started to walk on and then paused again. 'That was the best team I ever built.'

Later still, when we had sat Clough down to interview him in more depth about the comparison between the Forests and Derbys of his time, and the current versions of them, both some 60 places lower down the leagues, he started, naturally to work towards a conclusion.

'I'll tell you this. It would be a tragedy if either of these fine clubs were to fall through the bottom of the leagues. It would be nothing short of a tragedy.' This last line he delivered no longer at me, but directly to the camera.

He paused to allow the words to resonate. Then he turned back to me and, just before reaching to unclip his microphone, said with a smile, 'And that, young man, would be a good "out".'

It was as if he'd just stepped off the set of Parkinson.

Four months later, Brian Clough died. I think, although I cannot be certain, this was the last time he was ever interviewed on television. Nothing I was fortunate enough to do in many years reporting on football ever amounted to much, save for this moment, when I found myself sitting opposite this very extraordinary man; the incandescent late 20th-century talent, born for the television age, who started out in those distant almost post-war years, playing the game in black and white, then charging Mourinho-like through its every level as a club manager, before he finished off, forlornly, just as the game was about to change again and sweep him aside.

Clough's voluble brilliance and unflinching dogma may just have ignited the whole process, but he was not going to live long enough, healthily enough, to be part of it when it all took off.

There'd been plenty to ponder in the car on the way back home that day, and many, many times in the intervening years when that hour of my life came back to me. In the meantime, the journey continued. The personal encounters with the men who had shaped the game, and continued to bend it to their design, piled up. They stood sentinel as my life in the game flashed, and seasons came and went.

13

Wednesday's Child

DINAMO BUCHAREST 1–2 MANCHESTER UNITED.
11 August, 2004. National Stadium, Bucharest.

In which an international incident is narrowly averted.

My career in football reporting unfolded like an A–Z map, marked here and there by spilt coffee, some towns circled with a biro. My professional days were passing by me like so many hired Vauxhall Vectras (the Panda had long since been crushed), fuel tanks filled with unleaded on a cold and prematurely darkening forecourt somewhere near Coventry.

My children grew used to it. My family became accustomed to my absences and the rhythm of a life dictated by a sudden phone call on a Thursday night and a four o'clock alarm the next morning to get to Middlesbrough in time to meet Craig Hignett. It all built towards Saturday. My life was underscored by Saturdays; row upon row of Saturdays, when I would set off for Selhurst, or Carrow Road, the County Ground or Villa Park and come home to find the evening already settling into night. Or later still, returning from the ITV Studios after recording a round-up voice-over of the games deemed unimportant by the programme's producers: 'Ned, you've got Ipswich.'

On Sunday it abated, crashed and surged back, like the most regular wave in the world. Football writer Ian Ridley referred to his late wife and fellow sports journalist, Vikki Orvice, as his 'Saturday Girl'. Football peaked on Saturdays. But the opposite of Saturday afternoons were Wednesday nights.

Wednesdays were wildly different, rare and exotic. When I was at Sky we were eaten up with envy at Wednesday nights, able only to watch on with a feeling of distant longing while the giant black-and-white globe-sized footballs of the Champions League logo swooped across TV screens to the strains of that majestically silly anthem: 'The Champ-ions!' Sometimes, as if to make the experiential gulf still more extreme, we'd be sent out to film an early round of the League Cup on a Wednesday night, aware that somewhere warm and very far away, Arsenal were already two-nil down.

Wednesdays were ITV's domain, with ratings in the tens of millions, rather than hundreds of thousands. They were exotic theatre: warm evenings in Seville, misty nights in Turin, torrid backdrops in Turkey and greyed-out scenes from Minsk, Prague and Moscow. They took over our living rooms and Clive Tyldesley, that reedy-voiced high priest of the Champions League, welcomed us to join him in Milan, Bucharest or Athens. The Champions League seemed to operate at a higher physical and metaphysical level, and held clunky old English football under its spell.

The English game might have started to pull in names like Tony Yeboah, Jürgen Klinsmann, Gianfranco Zola and Dennis Bergkamp, but these were isolated jewels of glittery exoticism in team sheets that were still heavily populated by blokes called Mark and Andy. When David Batty and Graeme Le Saux started fighting each other in Moscow, the fact was laid bare that English football was still a preponderance of huff and puff over finesse.

When occasionally it excelled it was so often thrillingly last-gasp desperate stuff or fragile, forever teetering on the very ragged edge of viability. English players ran into blind alleys. They could not hide their nerves. Even if the English game was slowly heading towards a more winning future, it often didn't feel like that.

Even before the Champions League Final of 1999, I was conscious that the hopes of Manchester United were pitted not just against Bayern Munich, but also against this undertow of awed negativity that clung to the hull of the English game as it set sail for a distant horizon, battling history.

On 26 May, the date of the final, I was in Leeds to do some filming on another project. I stayed at my friend Paul's house in Headingley whenever I was in town. Paul was a Derby County-supporting professor of linguistics with an incomprehensible obsession for horse racing and racehorse breeding. No one was allowed to touch his *Racing Post*, which lay every morning on the doormat, before he'd come downstairs to claim it and retreat to the toilet with it under his arm.

That evening we settled down with a terrible curry and a couple of cans of Stella balanced on the couch to watch the Champions League Final. For most of the match we discussed our generalised antipathy towards Manchester United; their perceived brattishness, their unshakable grip on the domestic game and their sheer Manchester Unitedness. As the game ground its way to an inevitable victory for the superior European footballing technocrats, I told Paul about the time I interviewed Jesper Blomqvist, and he pretended to be interested.

But then to our astonishment, when the final, improbable double salvo of goals from Sheringham and Solskjaer went in, we found ourselves leaping in the air with that staged, technical jump that ensures no spilling of curry. We celebrated the victory as if we actually supported the club that had just wrestled the European Cup back to these insecure islands.

We marvelled delightedly at the sight of poor Sammy Kuffour dropping to his knees, as if we were invested somehow in the story, which I guess, indisputably, we were. Maybe that alchemy was the genuine miracle of Barcelona; getting people who had no reason to, to like Manchester United. Even if just for a few minutes, on a Wednesday night in May.

*****

These evenings remained trapped in the prism of the TV in the corner of the room, until suddenly, they became real. In 2004, I found myself for the first time added to the roster of ITV's presenting and reporting team for the coming Champions League season. This very fact astonished me.

A decade began of packing my bags and heading for Gatwick Airport (it was always Gatwick Airport for some reason) to join beery choirs of Chelsea and Arsenal fans, Liverpool and Rangers, even, occasionally Manchester United supporters, on their travels overseas. I had spent years watching the top four teams face those self-same, impossibly remote opponents who I had marvelled at from afar. Now I was about to smell the air they breathed and visit their mythical homes, one by one: Napoli, Kiev, Marseille. I inhaled as deeply as I could.

My job, on nights when ITV were showing the Champions League across two channels, was to be the pitch-side presence overseas. Often, our main presenter would be in a studio in London, flanked by pundits. The team who actually went to the matches was sometimes small, especially in the opening group stage. I would often be paired with a commentary team of Peter Drury and the ex-Liverpool full-back Jim Beglin, with whom I formed a firm friendship and enduring working relationship. They would focus on the 90 minutes of the match. My job was to provide snippets of content, occasionally during the action, but mostly for the pre- and post-match show.

My first trip was nearly my last. It began with Manchester United. Suffering the indignity of having to go through a qualifying round to enter the group stage, they visited the Romanian capital Bucharest to play Dinamo in the late summer of 2004. Alex Ferguson's team had this tiresome hurdle to overcome. I was sent to cover the match.

United's visit was a big deal for Romania. Arriving at the press conference and training session at Dinamo's archetypal ex-Eastern-bloc, shallow-bowled, athletics-tracked stadium, the team of United stars and their manager, still at the absolute height of his powers, were greeted by a phalanx of charmingly unruly and very persistent local TV crews and journalists, for whom Manchester United had only ever seemed like a distant chimera. Now, here they were: Scholes, Giggs, Beckham and all, in flesh and blood, standing unreally, right on their patch.

United came, trained, kicked the press out of the stadium after the UEFA-prescribed statutory 15 minutes, trained some more, showered, changed, and then filed out of the dressing room area and onto their luxury bus that would take them to the Athenee Palace Hilton Bucharest. However, in order to reach the sanctuary of their transport, they first had to cross a few feet of crumbling concreted walkway, on which the entirety of Romania's sporting media and local press had gathered, all of whom wanted an exclusive with David Beckham.

From a distance, I watched on with wearied familiarity as, one by one, all the United players simply ignored the press, as if they weren't there, and strode poker-faced through the open door of the coach, at which point they disappeared behind the tinted glass. I watched them go. When the last of them had vanished, and on the sudden realisation that not one of the English team had stopped to talk to them, the Romanian press pack visibly drooped. Microphone arms fell at their sides, cameras were unshouldered, recorders lowered. Then one of them, a radio reporter, approached me.

'Excuse me,' she said. 'Why did the players not talk to us?'

'Oh, it's a certain kind of attitude, I suppose,' I ventured, feeling somehow responsible.

'But is this normal?' enquired another reporter, with a hint more urgency. I turned to look and, within a very few seconds, I suddenly found myself at the epicentre of a minor media storm. In their understandable hunger for anyone speaking English, I had become the last chance soundbite for the entire media pack.

'Do they not like the press?'

'Not really.'

'Do they like Romania?'

'They probably don't really care.'

'Are they unhappy to be here?'

'I suspect so.'

'Do the players respect Romanians?'

'I don't imagine they've thought about it.'

I answered as honestly as I could, caught out by the deluge of questions and not wanting to run away from them as I'd just seen my countrymen do. But already I was starting to feel uneasy.

It was only a few hours later, unlocking the door to my absurdly ornate and expensive hotel room, just a couple of floors beneath the corridor occupied by Manchester United, that I turned on the TV out of idle curiosity, only to find that I was on the telly, subtitled in Romanian, but clearly telling the world what I thought of the behaviour and attitude of the Premier League stars who were here as VIP guests in the Romanian capital. I changed channels, where another bout of sports news was being introduced on another local channel. Again, my moving mouth was the centrepiece of their report, too. Over the next anxiety-ridden hour or so, I saw myself at least four times, on various different channels.

That night I couldn't sleep for the notion that, maybe a few doors along from me, Ferguson, suffering perhaps from insomnia, sitting on the end of his bed in his embroidered Man Utd pyjamas, was flicking through the TV channels and lighting upon ITV's inexperienced pitch-side reporter, who he dimly remembered from some incident a few years previously, disrespecting his precious squad on the eve of a match.

Such things still haunt me.

*****

I would always shoot some sort of feature on the day before the game. Normally the English team would make available one of their players and the manager, since they were obliged under UEFA's own regulations to do this. This was often an arduous negotiation which could result in some ridiculously literal games of hide and seek in the unfamiliar surroundings of football grounds far from home.

We'd set up our camera equipment wherever we could, in kit rooms, empty hospitality boxes, medical facilities, referees' changing rooms, and then hope that we could persuade the reluctant player who had drawn the short straw of being on media duty to make the short walk to whichever cubby hole we'd be hiding in. The patience of players and managers, even a day and a half before kick-off, was next to zero.

The slightest deviation or delay that they could attribute to TV inconveniencing them would often provoke a series of dismissive gestures, walk-outs or simple no-shows. Such a reaction could be followed by a stern rebuke from the club's press attaché, who would be caught between a slightly porous rock (us) and a very, very hard place (the manager of the football club). That rebuke would often lead to more disappointed censure aimed at us from the UEFA media liaison officers, expressing dismay but powerless to do anything about it.

If things went to plan, we got five minutes on tape, which we then had to edit. A few words from Wenger/Benitez/Mourinho/Ferguson, intercut with the sparingly expressed thoughts of a young player who had been forced to sit down in front of our cameras ('There are no easy games in the Champions League'). That was about all we could bank on. It was a consistent frustration of mine, over many, many years, that I could rarely turn these few precious and expensive minutes of television into anything particularly watchable.

Even as I reviewed the footage or sat in the edit suite as the final cuts were being made, and sometimes when I was actually filming them, I became acutely aware that these were the bits of telly that no one cared about in the slightest. In pubs, where football was still being watched, people glanced up as the team news was announced, but returned to pints and chat for the rest of the build-up. And if people were watching at home, the interview with the player, moodily lit against a black backcloth, provided an opportunity to go and boil the kettle, or rootle around in the fridge for a can of lager and a left-over chicken wing. These interviews, as far as I could tell, were a necessary irrelevance. But the reason they were considered essential had been long since forgotten. Like cigarette lighters in cars, they simply were.

There were rare occasions when I managed to create something watchable, but mostly when I was allowed to develop my interest in the exotic opposition, rather than the British team. I was sometimes able to give expression to my natural curiosity about the new environment I found myself in, whether this meant filming among the cypress trees and cigarette smoke of Benfica's faded grandeur, the frozen, crumbling austerity of CSKA Moscow or the cacophony and complexity of Galatasary and its seething, beautiful surrounds. From time to time I made a little film to be proud of.

But other times, as I did on a visit to Amsterdam for the visit of Arsenal, I massively overreached. Inspired by the notion of Johan Cruyff, still very much a living legend who seemed to stand for an attitude to life which I deeply admired, I had spent much of the day before the match dreaming up a wholly unnecessary philosophical reverie about the metaphysical meaning of Cruyff.

With our film crew, I had visited the Betondorp, Amsterdam's fascinating, architecturally significant, model suburb, built futuristically in the 1920s from concrete, in which Cruyff had grown up, just across the road from the old Ajax training ground. After that, and thinking I was Simon Schama, I embarked on a hugely ambitious exploration of the nature of modernism and total football; its intellectual incorporation of the twin impulses of libertarianism and conservatism, made flesh by Cruyff and his continuing legacy, as reflected in the political and sociological development of post-war Netherlands. Then I made the grave mistake of committing this sixth form diatribe to film, when what I really should have been focussing on was Ajax v Arsenal and Adebayor's hamstring.

It was a wildly inappropriate nonsense of pretension. Once it had actually been broadcast, the then Head of Sport at ITV was prompted to comment, 'I didn't understand that piece at all.' He looked at me, caught somewhere between amusement, exasperation and fury. 'I think our viewers just wanted to know about the football.' It was a reasonable point.

Sometimes, often, the football did indisputably demand and claim centre stage. My first visit to the iconic, growling box of a stadium, San Siro, was for a Champions League quarter-final between the two Milan clubs. Having reported from the side of the pitch before the match on how the occasion felt like a cage fight, I then took my seat in the press box next to the commentary team.

The game, played in a frenzy of terrible intensity, was barely two minutes old when my attention had wandered just far enough from the movement of the ball to find myself idly watching Andriy Shevchenko drifting around the centre circle as Inter pressed for a goal. The great AC Milan striker found he was being paid very close attention by Marco Materazzi, Inter's tremendously easy-to-dislike central defender.

Materazzi appeared to whisper something in Shevchenko's ear. The Ukrainian visibly flinched, and then spun around and head-butted the Italian, who reeled away clutching his head like he'd been shot. The referee didn't see it and nor, seemingly, did many others, save for the tens of thousands of Inter fans who howled their outrage.

That tumultuous match was later abandoned, with the score at three-nil to Milan, when Inter fans started to hurl dozens and dozens of lit flares onto the pitch, one of which struck the Milan keeper, Dida. Up in the stands, barely able to believe what I was seeing, I wondered if this was simply the norm for matches at San Siro. It was one of the most astonishing sights I have ever witnessed at a football match.

In Silvio Berlusconi's scandalous version of Italy, at his very own club, perhaps this was just to be expected. After the game, down in the claustrophobic tunnel area where media interviews are conducted, the Italian president breezed past me, a tiny figure, absurdly heavily made up. In a pre-Trumpian era, he was the prototype.

Twice I had tried to get Berlusconi to talk to me at football matches. This was the first attempt, which landed me with nothing more than a light blow to the solar plexus from one of his security detail. The second time was as he arrived at the Atatürk Stadium for Milan's ill-fated attempt to win the 2005 final. 'Silvio!' I'd yelled at him sufficiently loudly to get his attention. 'Silvio! A word for ITV?'

'No.'

I wasn't a political journalist, then. That much had become clear, but it had felt fun trying. In fact, the whole of the Champions League experience felt heightened, almost magical, as if the hype matched the reality and got under my skin. Wednesday nights felt important in ways that suddenly relegated the weekend to a distant second best.

I was never more fulfilled. What had always seemed impossibly remote had come brilliantly close. The draw for each successive season of Champions League fixtures threw up a glittering itinerary of venues to drop in on; Napoli, Schalke, Porto. I took my seat at the side of the great pitches of the world and could see with eyes that had once squinted at a badly tuned TV in a Hamburg bedsit the magnified reality of lives that seemed illusory. The flight of a free kick, the arc of a save, the switch and flick, nod and thunder of the best in the world, played across a real distance between touchline to touchline, goal to goal, from city to city.

The Champions League was a real thing after all. And I had been invited in to see it for myself.

14

Championship Form

READING 3–1 WEST HAM.
12 March, 2005. Madejski Stadium, Reading.

In which stuff gets real.

Though the Champions League sat incandescent at the heart of my footballing life, there was still proper Saturday work to be done. ITV's coverage of the Championship had returned and cast a lengthening autumnal shadow across our weekends once more. As the sole inheritors of the Football League highlights contract, which had somehow migrated back to ITV with its fiscal tail between its legs after the debacle of the ITV Sport Channel, ITV used to put out an hour-long highlights show on a Sunday morning.

Since it concentrated mainly on the Championship, it went by the name of *The Championship*. It was a kind of low-rent *Match of the Day*, with more goals and no studio pundits, because there was no studio to sit them in. In fact, it was open to the vagaries of an English and Welsh winter.

Every other week I was sent out on the road to a match, in order to make a scaled-down feature around a game. Sometimes we'd select a club in crisis, which would inevitably require the extensive use of the gloriously irritating TV format, the vox pop. But more often than not we ended up following the fortunes of a striker in good form, or a team with a long unbeaten run, that kind of thing. The striker would fail to score, obviously, and the unbeaten team would get beaten.

These could be long days of work, full of driving up motorways, waiting around for hours until the moment came when Darren Bent, or someone about as good as Darren Bent, would disembark from the team bus at somewhere like Portman Road and we'd have to try and cajole him into talking to us before disappearing into the dressing room, shamefully hobbling along after him, imploringly saying his name ever louder.

Matt Smith was the regular host of the programme and presented the show from whichever fixture had been deemed to be the best match of the day. Often this involved West Brom, or one of the Sheffields. From time to time, when he was unavailable, I'd be one of the 'B team' of presenters who'd be called upon to deputise. This had the effect of sending me into a tailspin of anxiety the night before the shoot. It had to do with clothes. Dressing for telly on *The Championship* presented fierce complications. And while Matt Smith effortlessly managed to look both smart and down to earth, urbane and a man of the people, I simply looked a mess, often by trying to pair an impulsively purchased puffy jacket (it was *always* freezing on *The Championship*) with some slightly too skinny jeans and big clumping boots. No amount of offsetting this with a natty little scarf could rescue the sheer disjointedness of the image.

And then there was the dispiritingly long list of short 'links' that had to be shot:

'Welcome back', after a break.

'Let's hear from the managers', before the interviews.

'Your commentator at Loftus Road is Peter Brackley', for a round-up of QPR's match.

'After the break we'll have the best...' (pause) '...and the worst...' (quirky intonation as we show someone on loan from Stoke missing an open goal at the Bescot Stadium) '...of the remaining games in the Championship'. Etc.

Getting these myriad links filmed was a drain on your emotional life force. The need to change location each and every time, and set up somewhere 'new', was psychologically sapping. Given that most football grounds, though differing subtly in style, feature the same selection of facilities in a variety of constellations and colour schemes, there was an inevitability that the locations chosen for these links would get tiresomely repeated, week after week. There was the nonchalant 'lean-against-the-goalpost' with arms folded, the 'stride-along-the-middle-of-a-terraced-street', which was almost exclusively the preserve of Yorkshire or Lancashire clubs plus Gillingham, the 'start-on-a-shot-of-the-onions-being-loaded-into-the-burger-bun' interactive snack bar link, which often ended in some 'spontaneous' interaction with the cheery soul behind the fryer.

Filming the last of these variants almost inevitably ended in the following conversation, as we tried to take our leave of the location having filmed it:

'Is this live?'

'No, we've just recorded it.'

'When's it going out?'

'Tomorrow morning.'

'I'd better switch my Sky on then.'

'It's on ITV.'

'Is it on *Match of the Day*, then?'

'No,' followed by a pause. 'It's on ITV.'

'Will I be on it?'

'Yes, I reckon so.'

'I'd better get Sky on then.' And so on.

Then you'd have to dash off to the players' tunnel where you'd have to wrangle for the right to stand at the side of the pitch with a series of successively more and more finickity matchday stewards. The closer to the inner sanctum, the bigger the club, and the more years they might have spent in the Premier League, the more fanatical to the cause of not letting anyone near the players they were. Then, after an entire Frost-Nixon of negotiation, you'd have to hold yourself in front of the camera in grinning readiness just to the left of where the players ran out.

Isolated on this spot, in full view of the fans as the PA system blasted out whatever bombastic, odd or charming musical nonsense the teams usually ran out to, you'd have one chance, and only one chance, to get quite a long link recorded.

'Well, with one defeat in eight, Norwich are certainly the team in form. But West Brom have a point to prove and haven't lost here in nearly 10 years' (I'm totally making this up, but it sounds convincing enough). 'Which way's this one going to go? Let's find out in the company of your match commentator, Jon Champion.'

If you stumbled, or otherwise screwed up, there was no chance to go for a retake. Not only that, but you also had to contend with the dangers of the players behind you trying playfully to disrupt your work, or worse, being derailed by the close attentions of that particularly active and vocal kind of supporter who delights in congregating near the players' tunnel so as to impart their excellent advice, often about where you can stick your microphone.

*****

During December we'd try to bank up some pre-filmed specials, which meant we could lighten the workload slightly over the relentless holiday period. One year we decided it would be amusing to spend a whole day with Ian Holloway, following him from breakfast to dinner, and through everything he got up to. The ebullient Bristolian had washed up in Plymouth by this point of his ever-ruminant career, on the short-lived third leg of his long and occasionally quite good managerial journey which ultimately led him to Grimsby, as all things surely must in lower league footballing folklore (at the time of writing he hasn't had a managerial appointment after that).

I'd first met Holloway back in my days at Sky Sports when I'd driven down to his house to hand him the Performance of the Week award, another idea with a limited life span dreamed up by Frank Clark at the League Managers' Association (LMA). His Bristol Rovers team had done something quite impressive against some other side, which is about as much as I can remember of the detail.

What I can recall with great clarity, however, is the fact that Holloway was fluent in another language. His twin girls Eva and Chloe, who'd been born profoundly deaf, were very young at the time, and their younger sister Harriet, whose is also deaf, all communicated with their dad and each other using sign language. Never having spent long before in the company of people who sign, I found myself feeling oddly privileged to be welcomed into this house, which I thought was exceptional. The unfussiness, the straightforwardness of his signing, as well as the obvious love he bore for his family struck me. From that moment on, I followed Holloway's career with interest, and paid special attention to his achievements (there were some) and his setbacks (there were many). In short, I guess I liked him. Even when he waded unhelpfully into the Brexit debate some 20 years on, I still liked him.

So much happened from the moment he swung into the club's car park, with his windows open and Nat King Cole blaring out, until the minute we left him, dressed in a dinner jacket, at the front door of a naval commander's house, that it's hard to imagine you could pack that much human experience into one day, however much you enjoyed the close presence of the cameras, something Holloway relished.

In the morning he manhandled me across the training ground, pushing me left and right, dragging me forwards, moving me around, while all the time keeping up a completely impenetrable diatribe about 'affecting the full-backs' in order to explain some very specific point about tactics that I don't think even he understood.

After training, he spent at least 20 minutes bobbing energetically around the whitewashed and labyrinthine corridors of Home Park, jumping out from behind walls and bellowing 'GREEN ARMY!' straight into young players' faces, who shouted 'GREEN ARMY!' back. Then he'd whisper 'green army' at them until they whispered 'green army' back at him. It was a certain type of cult.

He stormed out of a press conference to berate his players, who were noisily trying to manoeuvre their SUVs out of an implausibly small car park right next to the tiny room in which he was holding court, and then, on his return, posed the simple question, 'How good is Nat King Cole by the way?'

Then, back at home, he nearly exploded with rage when he couldn't find his phone. Or his wallet. And then his keys. When he inevitably discovered them somewhere totally obvious, his relief was almost more furious than his fury. 'BACK OF THE NET! JURASSIC PARK!' he hollered in treacly Bristolian, to no one in particular, save for himself and half a million viewers on ITV's *The Championship*.

But it was his afternoon appointment as one of three celebrities charged with turning on Plymouth's Christmas lights that will live longest in my memory. Actually, I'd like to think it'll be the very last thing I ever forget, or the one memory that will suddenly come back to me at the very hour of my death. Ian Holloway, the manager of Plymouth Argyle, was paired with Linda Lusardi, the former glamour model, and Spongebob Squarepants. The trio were spellbinding.

In front of a huge crowd in the city centre, on a stage erected by the local radio station, the three celebs placed one hand each on a giant comedy switch while the DJ counted down. 'Three! Two! Come on Plymouth! One!'

Squarepants, Lusardi and Holloway flicked the switch.

A thousand people looked around them, cheering wildly as somewhere off to the left a rather ordinary looking tree, wrapped in perhaps 20 or 30 flashing clear bulbs, made its presence flickeringly known. A thousand people continued to look around for more evidence of Christmas lights, but returned their gaze to this solitary tree, the sum total, it seemed of Christmas in Plymouth.

On stage and forgetting that he was still wearing our radio microphone, which caught every word perfectly, Holloway smiled manically and clapped, inclining his head towards Linda Lusardi.

'Look at them,' he said to the former Page Three Girl. 'They're bloody loving it!' He nodded his head towards the whooping crowds, as he continued to smile and clap. 'Hope they never go to London!' Lusardi actually snorted with laughter. And they both clapped some more, with Squarepants wordlessly jigging around at their side.

*****

But if Holloway was a slightly unhinged moth to the flame of TV, other managers were less eager to indulge the whim for entertainment inside the DNA of everyone in telly. Quite early on during my long stint working on *The Championship*, I'd been sent off to vox pop (there it was again) fans outside Upton Park.

In 2004, West Ham was in a semi-mutinous frame of mind, with its new manager Alan Pardew under pressure from some of the supporters right from the beginning of a campaign that would ultimately end with their promotion. I was despatched to go and film a feature that reflected their travails.

Sighing inwardly at the thought of filming vox pops, I decided instead to reflect the same schism in the support by standing at the side of the road with a sign that said 'Honk If You Want Pardew Out'. When I edited the finished piece, and in a style familiar to anyone who has watched the news over recent years, I was scrupulously balanced in my editing, matching the number of honks with the number of non-honks. West Ham went on to win their fixture handsomely. The last line of voice-over on the report of the game ran something like, 'Crisis, what crisis? Not even a blip.'

I discovered, months later, that Pardew had been sitting at home watching the programme, simply apoplectic with rage. I also discovered that he had somehow managed to contact the programme's producers, incandescent with fury at what he saw as an act of gross disrespect. The thing was, no one told me he'd complained.

So the season trundled along and I remained in blissful ignorance. In March I was sent, still gloriously unaware of my autumnal transgression, to feature West Ham's visit to Reading, where Pardew's managerial career had begun. Obviously, further vox pop analysis was undertaken. Then the game began, Pardew's West Ham got forensically dissected and lost 3–1. Then I went down to the tunnel area to interview their manager who'd been humbled at his former home ground.

I realised that something was awry as soon as I asked him for an interview. He stared at me with extraordinary intensity, then simply walked off. Still needing the interview, I followed, and waited until he'd done some more interviews. Eventually, all the other reporters had gone, leaving only me without an interview, by now seriously sensing that I was not going to get one, but still puzzled.

'Alan?' I said, with trepidation, as he made to leave.

He stopped, walked over to me and stopped again. Then said, with a voice that betrayed considerable effort of self-control. 'You and I have got history, haven't we?'

I did not know that we had. 'Have we?'

He stared at me for a while longer. Long enough for my leg muscles to start to dissolve. Then he said, 'They haven't told you, have they?'

They hadn't, whoever *they* were. 'Who?' I asked, now with the roof of my mouth suddenly dry and my voice aquiver. 'What?'

Then it all went blank. I can't remember if he did give me an interview after all. But I remember his parting look. Pardew left me in the darkening pitch side, without a clue what I'd done and deeply unsettled.

It was only in the car, on my way back to London, hands shaking still, that I dialled the office and discovered the whole back story from my bosses, who'd taken the collective decision to leave me unaware of the offence I had caused and carry on as if nothing had happened. I didn't know whether they'd apologised on ITV's behalf to him or not. But I did know, as the lights of the landing jets at Heathrow lit up the night sky alongside the M4, that I had felt the close and actual scorn of a football manager for the first time in my life and that it had been intense.

The grudge that Alan Pardew carried against me was sustained for a surprisingly long time. I'd always imagined that the big beasts of the dugout shrugged off the slings and arrows with practised ease, as they seemed to do during matches; screaming in rage one minute, and playfully patting the back of the head of the same person they'd been viciously abusing only minutes before the next. It seemed this wasn't always the case.

Two years later I was once again sent into Pardew territory, this time the West Ham training ground, to preview their match against Palermo in the Europa League and with my eyes wide open to the dangers. There was no let-up in his hostility, though at least this time I was prepared to be massively unwelcome. There was to be no interview. With a sharp order, he took me outside the room we had set up our camera in so that, in private, against a portacabin wall, he could tell me that I was not welcome at Upton Park the following Thursday night. Then I was told to leave the training ground, although I probably didn't need for him to say that in order to figure it out.

I left that encounter, too, feeling shaken and foolish. On the one hand it was eye-opening to me quite how deeply hurt the West Ham manager had been by that flippant broadcast some two years previously. I couldn't deny that this was his truth, his genuine sense of grievance. I learned from his anger that I had underestimated the sensitivities of the football manager; and that they, too, took criticism to heart and found themselves strangely vulnerable to what others might say and write. On honest reflection, he had a point. The piece had indeed been unfunny, ill-advised and possibly disrespectful; three points I conceded to him, face to face.

What I learned about myself was more revealing. I discovered with a rush of weary lucidity that I did not want to be the guy who has to either apologise or brazenly tough it out in the face of such fury, as others might well have been inclined to do. I recalled the spat between my former colleague Rob Palmer at Sky Sports and Alex Ferguson, after Palmer had filmed a piece to camera in the empty Manchester United dressing room that for some reason involved him hanging a pair of women's pants on a hook and claiming they belonged to Posh Spice. That hadn't gone down well. Or more significantly there was the long-lasting feud between veteran journalist Pat Murphy and Ferguson that resulted in the Scotsman boycotting the BBC for years on end. I didn't really fancy being that cog in the machine: not for the price of football, a bauble, a trinket, a nothing really. A way of having fun.

Actually, I didn't want to be in that situation at all. This loss of dignity, all stemming from a throwaway bit of telly about something as supposedly harmless as a game of football, was not a price worth paying. If this was what real football looked like on the inside and these forms of behaviour were legitimised, then I should perhaps gently step aside and let others take my place who might relish the challenge or even bite back.

So, from time to time, when I was in the company of grown men with anger in their hearts, I wondered what I thought I was doing there at all. That thought had lodged itself with me now. And even though it only seldom rose to the top and found its voice, it never quite left me again. I carried on, stung.

15

The Colour Blue

CSKA MOSCOW 0–1 CHELSEA.
2 November, 2004. Lokomotiv Stadium, Moscow.

In which money talks.

Year on subsequent year I'd seen my dad withdraw that part of him that cared noisily about Chelsea to a more private spot within. I sometimes wondered if he was bothered at all any more.

Maybe I'd imagined it, but I seemed to remember in sharper relief the peaks and troughs of his rollercoaster ride, hitched to the fortunes of what was a fairly crap club, for most of his working life. Now I felt in him only a sense of perfunctory celebration when it came to Chelsea's glut of trophies. I had long suspected that he'd given up on investing emotionally in the serial successes his club had enjoyed over many years; years during which I was often pitch-side in Munich, or front of camera in Turin, reporting on his old club's travels. His home in Scotland was literally and figuratively a long way from the Chelsea of his youth.

It was a curious quirk in the folds of time and fate that I had ended up spending so much time in the press box at Stamford Bridge watching the west London crowd file into the ground in time to pick up their little Chelsea flags and wave them aloft to the tune of *Blue is the Colour*, something my dad had done 60 years before, denied his rattle, but with that blue-and-white knitted scarf. For a decade, I became something of a regular at Chelsea.

I passed through the bewilderingly exciting tenures of José Mourinho, via the gloom of Avram Grant, the curiosity of Felipe

Scolari, André Villas-Boas, Guus Hiddink, Carlo Ancelotti and the sphinx-like Roberto Di Matteo, with whom I once spent an afternoon in Madrid Airport wondering why he was wordlessly staring into the middle distance and smiling. I witnessed Di Matteo's almost accidental European Cup before my acquaintance with my father's childhood club finally dried up after a night in Amsterdam on which they added yet another trophy – the Europa League.

That was when I watched Rafael Benitez stand to one side, entirely sidelined by the last hurrah of Frank Lampard, as he collected the final club medal that was missing. That was also the night that I watched John Terry, injured, yet fully kitted out for the second successive year, waiting to pose for photographs to commemorate a victory he'd played no part in on the night. That Europa League Final was in the summer of 2013, a decade after the Russian money arrived and everything turned a bit cloak and dagger at Stamford Bridge.

For a while, until it became normal, the mystery and sudden glamour of an unstoppable wave of wealth had been something you could not take your eyes off.

*****

In 2004, I found myself charging around Moscow, from hotel to hotel, navigating solid traffic lanes with surprising recklessness in pursuit of a small fleet of blacked-out SUVs that may or may not have contained Roman Abramovich. This was the final part of a little film I'd been compiling about the Russian oligarch with the stubble and the odd little smile. It had been a bit of an epic by the standards of the match preview features that routinely get ignored by drinkers in pubs with better things to do.

I'd started filming it some days before, on the King's Road in London outside a branch of the Halifax Building Society. On the back of an envelope and based on the best available estimates of the Chelsea owner's notional wealth, I had calculated that if he stuck it all in a high interest Halifax saver's account, he'd earn interest on his money at a truly boggling rate. Standing in front of the branch, I delivered a line to camera that lasted around about 12 seconds, during which time, just out of shot, a producer had been handing me £20 notes at a rate of over one per second. This represented the money Abramovich would have earned in the time it had taken me to deliver the words. It was a tricky item to film, not least because it involved me withdrawing a few hundred actual quid from my own account so that we had some money to use as props. Once we'd finished, I paid it straight back in. And then we resumed our search for the oligarch.

Hunting Abramovich was the working title for the film, a task I knew already was pointless, but I suspected might be quite fun to attempt. Shortly after the Sibneft owner and governor of the snowbound, oil-rich province of Chukotka had taken the reins at Stamford Bridge, the football world was still under the spell of his impossible wealth. He was, with his incredibly good-looking Portuguese manager, his leather jacket and jeans, a figure of tremendous interest. Deeply unknowable and utterly unlike anything that had gone before in the game, we were all learning together about the lives of the global super-rich. Ken Bates, his unreconstructed predecessor at Stamford Bridge, might have had a Rolls Royce and a Monaco residence, but Roman Abramovich had a navy of superyachts, one of which, the *Pelorus*, had not one but two helipads on board, in case one of them was busy, I guess.

It went without saying that every single attempt to interview Abramovich, whether the request went through official channels or via some other speculative route, was rebutted almost before it was even articulated. When he first arrived at Chelsea he granted some very occasional requests and then he pretty much clammed up forever. The closest we managed to get to him was through the charismatic agency of a PR man marvellously called John A Mann II, who worked with the Russian in Moscow and had his ear. In the end we had to make do with interviewing Mann himself, with the Chelsea owner a distant dot in the background, sitting on a bench in CSKA Moscow's empty ground, watching Claude Makélélé horse around with Mikel John Obi instead of actually training. Abramovich was as mysterious as his wealth was unfathomable.

Only once, accidentally, did I ever talk to him face to face and that came right at the beginning. It was the final day of Claudio Ranieri's tenure in 2004, in the immediate and tearful aftermath of Chelsea's last-day victory over Leeds United, which everyone knew would be the Italian's last game in charge. This was clearly destined to happen, despite the fact that they'd reached the Champions League semi-finals and had finished the league season in second place to Arsenal. Abramovich had Mourinho lined up, so that was that.

The 1–0 win over Leeds had been complete for some time and I was waiting for the goalscorer, Jesper Grønkjaer, in the tiny post-match interview area directly opposite the Chelsea dressing room in the narrow confines of the tunnel area at Stamford Bridge. Ranieri, after his emotional lap of honour on the pitch, had entered the Chelsea dressing room, where cheers and chanting could be heard. Shortly afterwards the Italian had come through to give me an interview in the TV area, in which he'd understandably and rather skilfully extracted as much capital as he could from his suspended victim status. After that, and still teary-eyed, Ranieri had scooted off to well up in front of the massed media in the adjacent press conference room.

It was then that I spotted Abramovich, flanked by his security guard and his close associate, body double and former head of corporate finance at Sibneft, Eugene Tenenbaum, walking purposefully across the pitch from the West Stand where they'd been seated like Roman nobility in the Coliseum. The three men came striding up the tunnel and straight into the dressing room, at which point, once again, the door closed. This time there was no cheering to be heard and a minute later the three of them reappeared, Abramovich first.

To my great surprise, he strode across to me. With a smile and in nearly accent-free English, he simply asked me, 'Where is he?'

It took me a split second to realise Abramovich meant Claudio Ranieri. With only a slight hesitation, I pointed in the direction of the press conference.

'He went that way,' I said and straight away felt like I'd somehow snitched on the Italian.

'Thank you.' Abramovich nodded curtly at me, as if in recognition of my new status as informer, which immediately had an unsettling effect on me. Then he turned to the left, took one step in the direction in which Ranieri had disappeared, stopped, changed his mind, turned around again, and strode off wordlessly with his companions back out of the tunnel and onto the pitch. I watched him go, loping along, an implausibly powerful man in a suit, with plans for us all.

Six months later I was still fascinated by Abramovich and continued my filmed pursuit of him. I contacted various London-based Russian emigrants, most of whom were reluctant to break cover simply for a football report on ITV. In growing desperation for a talking head, I even sought out the thoughts of Ron 'Chopper' Harris on the new man at the Bridge who told me, unsurprisingly, that he thought he was 'great news for Chelsea'. Then I drove down to the low-key and decidedly average looking offices in Weybridge of his mysterious UK holding company, Milhouse Capital. We rang the bell, but no one answered. And from there we drove on to Sussex to see if I could drop in on his house.

It was only when I got to Fyning Hill, Abramovich's £12 million, 420-acre estate in Sussex, which he'd bought from Kerry Packer, the Australian media tycoon, that I realised what the reality of doorstepping a Russian oligarch might actually look like.

With the added pressure of a cameraman following my every move, I minced up to the front gate, where I failed to find any kind of bell, intercom, telephone, doorknocker or any other means of signalling my unwanted presence. But I did see enough CCTV cameras to make me mince still more purposefully back into the car, which I started and drove away at some speed.

After a brief conflab, and after my producer had stopped laughing, it was generally agreed that we should have one more attempt at the footballing scoop of the century. Touring the perimeter of the estate at a speed designed to arouse further suspicion from the cameras that were by now doubtless tracking our progress, we pulled up at another gate towards the back of the walled enclosure. This one had a buzzer. Strolling nonchalantly up to it, as if it were the most ordinary thing in the world to approach someone's house with a cameraman a few steps behind, I pressed the bell. After a couple of ring tones, someone picked up.

'Hello?'

'Hello,' I said. Not having for a moment believed that anyone would answer, I was now suddenly very unprepared for how the conversation might unfold. So I said nothing.

'Can I help you?'

'Yes,' I replied. 'I'd like to speak to Mr Abramovich please,' I asked with sudden chutzpah designed to obscure the truth, which was that I had no chutzpah.

It was at that moment that I heard the engines. Through a small gap in the gate, I could see a quad bike approaching at speed down the tarmacked driveway, carrying what appeared to be four quite large men dressed from head to toe in black.

I cannot remember much of the next few minutes, but at some point I realised I was driving up the M3, back towards London, and I was alive. The footage of my exit from the scene, when I watched it back, proved conclusively that I was not made out for investigative journalism, undercover, overcover, or otherwise. The film, that somehow escaped the attention of BAFTA, ran on ITV2, just before Chelsea's match against CSKA Moscow, in which Arjen Robben scored the only goal.

*****

That evening in Moscow was the first time I fell foul of both José Mourinho and his Chelsea PR man. Trying to film two things at once, we had not been ready with our camera to interview Mourinho the instant he arrived, so he did not wait. I was ticked off three times: first by Chelsea, then by UEFA and then by ITV, which left no one else involved in the negotiation who hadn't ticked me off. So I ticked myself off.

For three years I saw much of Mourinho and he saw more of me than he'd ever wanted to. He never knew my name, that much is certain. This is probably because he never asked my name and I certainly never told him my name, since he always looked for all the world like a man who wasn't interested in knowing my name. I found him to be distant, barely tolerant of the banality of the process of pre and post match interviews, impatient to be gone, but still somehow deeply compelling as a character.

Only once, and mystifyingly, did it go badly wrong between us because of something I said. And, even with years of hindsight, I am still not sure whether it was he who took umbrage or whether umbrage was taken on his behalf by his press officer. An away game for Chelsea at Wycombe Wanderers one Wednesday night in the semi-final of the League Cup should not have presented a flash point. But the evening ended with me being banned from talking to José Mourinho for an indefinite period of time.

On a freezing cold night in 2007, Chelsea, featuring a mix-and-match line-up of fringe players and first-team regulars, had found it surprisingly tough going trying to break down and beat a spirited, energetic and hard-working Wycombe side. In fact, they didn't beat them. Wycombe held the two-time and reigning Premier League champions to a draw, which was less of a drama than it might have been, given the home leg at Stamford Bridge was still to come. On balance, it was just a blip.

But one player who'd looked decidedly like he'd rather have been anywhere else that night was Michael Ballack. The tall, upright Germany captain, for whom I had a huge and self-explanatory soft spot given the time I'd spent in his home country, had been bullied off the ball throughout the match and had not appeared to be very happy about the whole experience. At the end of this dour encounter, I moved with great reluctance, polished shoes and a heavy heart towards the unfamiliar tunnel area in that most unprepossessing of little grounds, Adams Park.

I located the particular bit of corridor where the host club had velcroed a sponsor's logo board to a breeze block wall and waited for the arrival of Mourinho with his daemon press officer at his side, clutching his dictaphone. Even before he stepped in front of the camera, avoiding eye contact by looking anywhere rather than at me,

I could sense it was going to be a terse encounter. After the generic and open-ended opportunity for the Chelsea manager to express any frustration at the result, and to suggest with reasonable optimism that they would be able to turn the match around in a week's time, I opted to explore the detail a little more. I asked him about Ballack's performance. Would he have hoped for a little more from his captain?

'Why?' Mourinho looked appalled and, for the first time, straight at me. 'Are you anti-German?'

Then he walked away from the interview, muttering as he went, followed by the press officer who glared at me. I turned to look at my producer, who was with me. She was a veteran of many seasons of football and had seen it all, one way or another. But even she was at a loss to explain the offence that my question had caused.

Shortly afterwards, the press officer sought me out again, this time without Mourinho. He took me to one side and looked immensely serious, almost sorrowful, as if he was sad that I had let myself down so badly and that he was the misfortunate who'd have to break the news to me.

'The manager wasn't impressed.' He said, with great solemnity. 'He wasn't happy, Ned. And I have to say, nor am I.'

I remained silent, trying to process what this all meant and how it had come to this; two grown men standing in a tunnel in Buckinghamshire late at night, having a shitty conversation about something to do with me being racist.

'You'll understand that we'll have to take action. It's not something we can simply let pass.' The press officer was nearly done. 'I'll be in touch.'

A few weeks later, ahead of a Champions League home match we were to broadcast on ITV4, and shortly after we had requested from Chelsea an interview with Mourinho, it was made known to me that I was banned from interviewing the manager. He wouldn't speak to me, either pre- or post-match. As an embarrassing consequence, an extra reporter was called in, simply to talk to Mourinho, and would then withdraw to allow me to conduct the other interviews.

This was, all in all, one of four separate occasions on which I had received bans, either from specific managers or entire clubs, when I worked in football. To Alan Pardew I could now add José Mourinho and latterly Ken Bates (during his time at Leeds), as well as Martin Jol for asking him if he felt under pressure just before he was sacked. Jol's actual sacking came so soon after my ban that it was effectively rendered null and void.

Though in theory ITV had my back, there was a limit to their support. Broadcasters don't tend to strongly contest the position of the clubs. Not often do they actually risk upsetting the clubs further by questioning their right to behave as they do. There is a prevailing and puzzling unwillingness to upset the very institutions to whom they are paying vast sums of money. This deference to football clubs is far from being unique to ITV. All the major broadcasters, in my experience, share the same reluctance to ruffle feathers, lest they somehow lose the right of access. Never mind the hundreds and hundreds of millions of pounds that they shell out; a fact that ordinarily would put them firmly in the driving seat of a non-dysfunctional agreement, but the power dynamics in football are such that you are never quite sure who's working for whom.

Or maybe it was just me; too thin-skinned, too sensitive, too confused by the unwritten rules of the game, the invisible trip wires and apparent breaches of footballing etiquette that could be unilaterally determined on the spot and on a whim. It wasn't that I went out of my way to create trouble or to make a fuss. I just found that it came to me, often when I least expected it.

Even the most thoughtful of football managers has been lulled into a misunderstanding about the role of the football journalist. For some reason few interviews are not proceeded by a list of authorised topics for discussion being agreed with the press officer before the cameras start to roll.

'What do you want to talk about?'

'Oh, the upcoming match and whether or not Player X will be sold.'

'The match, fine. But let's leave the other bit, OK. I'd rather you didn't.'

'Well, I have to ask.'

'In that case, no interview.'

Their gaff, their new rules.

But Chelsea were in some ways the incubating chamber for the way 21st century football changed. They developed a self-contained, ruthless, winning culture which they could not contain. Home and away, match after match, I saw them win. Over and over, we'd wait, along with the nervy Chelsea press officers, for John Terry to come, shirtless, to the interview area. Mostly he obliged, though on one or two occasions he made it known that ITV could 'fuck off', in his words. We never knew why this would happen or when. And certainly not a word of explanation or contrition ever came from the club's officials for the words of their highest-paid employee.

I could see why they played the way they played for Mourinho. It was, of course, the coming of age of Terry and Lampard, with Robben flying down the wing, Makélélé doing everything in centre-midfield and then, in 2005, with Drogba, the ultimate spearhead. Didier Drogba was, in the time I was a regular correspondent at the club, the apotheosis, the ultimate Chelsea player.

His last kick for the club, after seven seasons that had seen him bulldoze and explode his way to goals, was a penalty kick in front of a colossal bank of fanatical Bavarian fans. His perfect penalty beat Bayern *at* Bayern, triggering the single greatest deflation phenomenon I have ever witnessed in a giant stadium like the Allianz Arena. The 2012 Champions League Final brought Abramovich the one last trophy he'd craved and its success was Ur-Drogba; effective almost beyond measure, resilient to the bones and determined in ways that few can understand and still fewer hope to emulate. Drogba and Chelsea were success incarnate. But whether they were likeable or not depended on everyone's individual understanding of the game. They were frighteningly effective to watch, something that had to be applauded, then respected.

That was also Chelsea, back then.

*****

Sometimes, visiting my parents at their home, I'd find myself in conversation with Dad about Chelsea, the modern Chelsea, the way things suddenly were as they bore down on back-to-back league titles for the first time in at least a generation.

Dad, of course, had just turned 14 when Chelsea had last won the title, in 1955. To my mind, I could envisage almost no connection between the two clubs, locked into their respective decades and separated by 49 years of human history, save for the obvious, misleading accident of geography and restrictive town planning that meant that Chelsea still played football at Stamford Bridge. Only this core of fact sliced vertically through the layers of time seemed to connect the two clubs, the two teams, the two achievements.

Yet, there was another connector. Dad. He walked on the same legs, saw with the same eyes and felt for his club across that long, long stretch of time. That much, I had underestimated. I had interpreted, on his behalf, a jadedness with the Chelsea project that he didn't share, in reality. I even went as far as to invent a narrative on his behalf.

'Dad's a Chelsea fan,' I used to tell people. 'He was a season ticket holder back in the day. But, recently… well, he's lost interest really since the Russian took over. Too much money, too much success. Not the Chelsea he knew.' I even imagined a bit of detail in my semi-fictional version of where I thought my father's affections lay. 'The last player he really liked was Gianfranco Zola.' I honestly don't know how this misapprehension that I created came about. But for some reason, in my imagination, this interpretation of his feelings stuck.

I was wrong. It was only relatively recently, as Chelsea were preparing to hand over the managerial reins once again from the underwhelming Maurizio Sarri to a now-retired Frank Lampard, that I asked him about it again, as we watched the telly together; me, non-plussed, he, more attentive.

'Do you even care?' I asked him. 'I mean, deep down. Does it even matter anymore, what Chelsea do?'

He looked honestly surprised by the question, almost affronted. 'What do you mean?'

'If they win the league. Or the cup or whatever. Does it matter?'

'Yes,' he said, defensively. 'Of course.'

'Really? Well, who was the last player you genuinely loved watching then? It was Zola, wasn't it?'

'Nope.'

'Then who?'

He paused for a long time before answering. 'Drogba.'

I was amazed. Dad shook his head briefly in admiration for what he'd remembered. 'He was some player, Drogba.'

'Drogba?' I scoffed at him, incredulously. 'You serious?'

'Yup,' he repeated. 'The Drog.'

And in that moment, I knew there were as many ways of understanding football as there are voices in the stands, fists in the air or fingers on remote controls; that each of us relates to the game in their own way; and that every one of these relationships is born from a personal past, present and future that is as unique as the game itself. One attacking move may look much like another, one quickly taken corner may be well rehearsed. But no two moves can ever be the same. If 40 years of the word 'Chelsea' being in my life had taught me anything at all, it was that no two 'Chelseas' were alike. Dad's and mine were wildly different and his, on balance, was a happier one.

16

The Skipper

LIVERPOOL 3–3 WEST HAM (LIVERPOOL WIN 3–1
ON PENALTIES).
13 May, 2006. Millennium Stadium, Cardiff.

In which the fates conspire.

Back in my formative years on *Soccer Saturday*, the show had an arrangement, brokered largely through the influence of Alex Ferguson at the League Managers' Association (LMA), that we would award a new prize every month. The Young Player of the Month award no longer exists. It should probably never have existed anyway, to be perfectly honest. Consisting of nothing more than a cut crystal bowl of around about the right size to serve a rum punch for the Christmas party of a very small company, this award was underwhelming. It was, however, a very convenient bit of leverage by which we could get hold of interviewees we might have otherwise struggled to persuade.

In short, because Fergie was so involved with the LMA, everyone fell into line. If the award was won by Michael Carrick, Harry Kewell or James Beattie, then Michael Carrick, Harry Kewell or James Beattie duly stepped up to the plate and accepted the award, at the same time (and here was the kickback for our editorial content) providing an interview for *Soccer Saturday*.

All this was a long time ago and the award didn't last for very long. In order to cross-reference certain dates and winners, I have searched for evidence of its existence online, only to find that it has left no discernible digital trace. Even the website of the LMA appears to have discreetly forgotten it ever existed. Under the heading 'Who Won What', it appears that no one ever won the Young Player of the Month award.

Yet I beg to differ. I was a witness.

Having made his debut for the club the previous year, it was in 1999 that Steven Gerrard started to impress and set Merseyside, or at least the red half, talking of the next home-grown Liverpool great. It was some time that autumn, conveniently for us at *Soccer Saturday*, that the LMA chose Gerrard as the recipient of the punch bowl.

So it was that I was duly dispatched, with the glassware boxed and placed in the footwell of the passenger seat of my ridiculous little car to take its chances along with the sweet papers, almost empty coffee cups and oily burger wrappers that proliferated in that ungodly space. I drove to Melwood carrying the precious award.

Once admitted to the training ground, the cameraman and I set about making the glass bowl look suitably important and fit for the winner of such an honour. This involved balancing it precariously on a bar stool we'd somehow located, draped in black cloth, and bathing it in diffused and carefully angled shards of white so that it caught the eye with its beauty. In the final shot, it would appear, dazzlingly out of focus, just over the right shoulder of the award-winning interviewee.

Once the traditional extra three-quarters of an hour had elapsed, Gerrard came into the room in the company of Liverpool's beleaguered press officer, whose naturally pale demeanour would blanch still further as the Houllier era came to a close and the Benitez era began. These were the years that would define the startling career of the young lad in a tracksuit, who sloped in reluctantly to take his place in front of the camera. Steven Gerrard had only just finished that damaging growth spurt that had stretched and distorted him to such an extent that, for such an unequivocally athletic man, he often looked cumbersome and ill-suited to the test. He shot a shy, defensive glance in my direction, extended his hand in slightly awkward greeting, plonked his designer shower bag on the ground at his side and almost, fleetingly, smiled.

Of the interview, I remember nothing. This early example of the Gerrard genre, should it still exist in the vast Sky Sports archives, would reveal the same Lady Diana-like shyness within the lanky kid from the Bluebell Estate, whose sole purpose on the planet was to win games of football against other people who weren't on his team. Even when his long-striding pace started to desert him, the trademark hammer of a right foot softened and that famous dynamo motor would start to silt up, many, many years in the future, the determination in his game never let him go. My suspicion is that, with the imperceptible waning of his powers and Liverpool's succession of near misses in the Premier League, the thing that made him special also became his curse; not winning is kryptonite to people built with Gerrard's singularity of motivation.

The interview came to a close.

'Thanks very much Steven.' I dropped out of 'interview' voice. 'Thanks for your time.'

'No bother,' he muttered, pleasantly enough, but clearly relieved that the ordeal was finished. He retrieved his bag, allowed us to unclip his microphone and stood to go with one final handshake. Then he walked off.

'Steven,' I called him back. He turned, at the door. 'You forgot to take your trophy.'

Gerrard looked genuinely surprised. 'Seriously? Do I get to keep it?'

I wasn't sure if he meant this or was being sarcastic. But he rushed back to the glass trophy and looked at it properly for the first time. 'It's got my name on it!'

'Yes,' I confirmed. 'It's yours.'

He looked, in delight, at the press officer. 'Mum'll be made up with this.' And with that, Steven Gerrard departed, carrying a shower bag *and* a glass bowl.

The following month, wouldn't you know it, Gerrard won the LMA's Young Player of the Month Award again. Armed with another piece of engraved glassware in a navy-blue cardboard presentation box, I set off once more for Melwood in a bewilderingly accurate carbon copy of the precise sequence of events from the previous month. Everything followed the same course, from shower bag to clip mic, save for the very end of the encounter.

Gerrard had gone, before I had noticed that, once again, he had walked away from the interview without his trophy. This time I ran to the door, opened it, and looked down the Gerrard-less corridor that led to the inner sanctum of the training ground. I knew that I could go no further. There was a force field, invisible to the naked eye, that kept reporters at bay.

We packed up, hoping that someone from the club might return to the room and take care of the forgotten trophy for us. But the press officer was already in another meeting and didn't reappear.

So, packing it away again in its blue box, the trophy suffered the indignity of another few hours in my car, before being plonked under my desk at Sky's London offices, where it remained for months. Fed up with mistakenly kicking it, and fearing I might damage it permanently, someone finally arranged for it to be sent up to Liverpool, to chase the young player who had so tellingly left it behind him.

*****

That's the Gerrard I remembered. It didn't take long until he grew into the Liverpool captain who forced the great AC Milan side – Shevchenko, Gattuso, Maldini, Pirlo, Seedorf and all, almost inexplicably, to wilt. There he was again; that brooding, self-confident young man with the thick straw-coloured hair and the low frown, this time shaking the European Cup at a world that extended far beyond his imagination. Flanked by the team that seemed to act as a foil to his presence, it was a rudely brilliant place to stand.

Some time in August 2005, after the glitter had settled and the open top bus had been parked up again in a depot on Merseyside, I was asked to take part in the making of a documentary about Steven Gerrard. The idea had been generated by a producer who was closely in touch with Gerrard and with his representative, Struan Marshall, an intimidatingly well-presented football agent. That summer Gerrard had recommitted to Liverpool, signed a new £100,000 a week long-term contract and put behind him forever the impulse to sign for either Chelsea or Real Madrid. He had muscled, hustled and blasted his way to the very top and now was at the very peak of his powers.

Quite why his management team decided to endorse the making of a long-form fly-on-the-wall documentary I am still not entirely sure. They earned money from it, for sure. But the kinds of sums paled into insignificance when stacked up alongside the other revenues Gerrard was commanding by now from sponsorship and other personal deals, as well as a salary that was paying him millions of pounds every year. Perhaps it was sentiment that prompted them to go along with it; the honest desire to record a special period of one's life for posterity. Perhaps it was vanity. That would have been perfectly understandable.

But one thing became very clear quite quickly; they didn't immediately realise what they had got themselves into. The deal they struck with the production company meant that Gerrard would give access to the cameras on about 25 occasions over the course of the 2005–06 season, ending on his expected departure to the World Cup in Germany. How, where and when these days were allotted would be up to the producers, in close collaboration with Gerrard himself.

Liverpool Football Club had given the project their muted blessing (they didn't really have much of a choice I suspect) and so many of the usual hurdles that bedevil filmed coverage of footballers' lives behind the scenes were removed, courtesy of Gerrard's untouchable status. It was a unique opportunity.

Access, genuine access, was slow in materialising. It took a while for Gerrard to relax into the project. At first, and as if it were some sort of ancillary space pod designed to latch onto the Gerrard mothership, we were granted access to his Range Rover, a stepping stone to entering his house. The mansion which lay behind the huge wooden gates that swung open on silent electric hinges remained as yet hidden and out of bounds. But, appearing through the opening, the silver car with its famous driver stopped on the unmade road and a window rolled down.

'Morning lads,' that familiar voice emerged from those familiar and serious looking features. 'Do youse wanna jump in?'

Gary Caine, a short, plain-speaking, good-natured and brilliant Liverpool supporter whose camerawork had been a staple of the output of almost every football broadcaster for as long as anyone could remember, hoisted his camera kit and leapt into the back of the car. Together, he and I would work on the bulk of the documentary that was just beginning to show signs of life.

Once in the leathery Gerrard car, discretely scented with something that smelt a bit expensive and coconutty, and cruising down the dual carriageway from Formby to Liverpool, the Liverpool captain already seemed to be a more forthcoming character. We passed Sami Hyypiä, listening to music and unaware that we'd reared up alongside him, which was the cue for windows to be opened and mutual abuse, shared at 60 miles per hour.

Whenever and wherever we filmed, we were almost always joined by Gerrard's best mate. Paul McGrattan was a lively lad with slicked back hair and an honest wit. It was his principal job to keep Gerrard company, fetch him sandwiches and be the butt of his endlessly testing jokes. The two men were very easy in each other's company, having met when 'Gratty' ran a sunbed parlour near the training ground that a teenage Gerrard used to frequent. They had a riotous shared history, they had a thrillingly rewarding present and at least one of them had a potentially astonishing future.

Gerrard, it became apparent, the longer the filming went on, had two main ambitions left in his playing career: to win the league with Liverpool and to win the World Cup with England. In the end, neither dream achieved fulfilment. And nor would Gratty's. He would never become the Hollywood 'A-lister' he wanted to be.

Gratty wanted to be an actor – and he was deadly serious. He had no qualification, nor experience of acting, and lived with his mum near Huyton. That's not to say he wasn't any good; he might well have been. It's just that no one knew, because he'd never done any actual acting. That didn't stop him for a second from believing that a major film role was within his grasp and nor did it stop Gerrard from mercilessly exposing the potential flaws in Gratty's celebrity masterplan.

'Would you say you're ready to take a big part in a film, Paul?' Gerrard would ask him with bone dry deadpan.

'Yes, Skipper,' Gratty would answer, aware that he was being teased, but not completely certain of how to play it. 'I do.'

'Do you think your lack of any experience at all might be, like, a problem?'

'Not really. If you've got it, you've got it.'

'So, do you think you've got it?' Gerrard would counter, stony faced.

'I *know* I've got it,' Gratty would say, looking directly at Gerrard. 'What do you know about it, anyway? All youse do is kick a football around all day.'

'That's true, that.' Gerrard would nod, impassively. 'Would you say you're like the typical actor, you know…?' Then he'd search for the correct word. 'Bubbly?'

Gerrard could be relentless and very funny. Many of these exchanges took place in the car, some of them captured on camera. But none of them made the final edit in the film. The rest of the Gerrard operation sought to minimise Gratty's input. I thought he was stellar.

Bit by bit, week on week, Gerrard started to relax into the making of the film and appeared to accept that a certain intrusion behind the scenes was now required. We had done all we could in the car, including a terrifying few hours during which he entrusted his prized Range Rover to me, so that Gary and I could film additional 'B-roll' shots from the car window of the Liverpool skyline, for use at some unspecified point in the emerging film. Gerrard had literally thrown me the car keys at the training ground and I'd driven away, very nervously, through the ever-present gaggle of autograph hunters who peered at me behind the wheel of their hero's car with barely concealed rage that I was in the Liverpool skipper's car.

Now it was time for Gerrard to throw open the gates to his house. I had never been anywhere like it. It smelt, for a start, amazing, like the plushest hotel foyer you've ever been in. The rooms were huge and, despite a large amount of faintly oversized and oddly-shaped furniture, still somehow seemed to contain acres of carpeted, empty space. There was a swimming pool, really quite a big one, into which Gerrard would routinely flop and muck around with his young kids. There were saunas (plural), from which a slightly pinkened Gerrard would emerge from time to time and pad off in his flip flops. There was a huge kitchen that produced, as far as we witnessed, no food save for the occasional cheese, or ham, or cheese and ham sandwich. These appeared periodically, sometimes crafted hurriedly by Gerrard himself in his occasional fits of excessive friendliness, before the emotional shutters would once again come down and everyone felt it was time to go.

Gratty's cheerful presence became, in a surprising manner, fundamental to the success of the film. He was always there, seemingly on the Gerrard payroll simply to be present, like a court jester, in the nicest possible way. Sometimes he was handed a real job to do, like nip down to Formby to get something from the shops. This was a fairly frequent occurrence and was born out of the seclusion in which Gerrard lived his life.

The walls of his house and the training ground were indeed the extent of his everyday life, it seemed. His fame and the veneration of at least half a city held him captive, to the extent that he couldn't really step out in public for fear of being mobbed. Nights out for Gerrard and Alex, his wife, when they happened at all, mostly involved choreographed arrivals at restaurants or clubs, and being whisked away into private dining rooms at the rear. It was a life lived in luxury, but under suffocating pressure and relentless scrutiny. But it was what Gerrard had wanted and, by and large, I think he enjoyed it.

Perhaps because of the walls, both physical and psychological, that he had built around him, it proved stubbornly difficult to break down Gerrard's resistance to speaking candidly when the cameras were on. Until, that is, we decided to interview Gratty. Under a barrage of abuse from the Skipper, Gratty took a seat right in front of the camera, in the middle of the living room. Gerrard, perhaps having forgotten that he was still wearing a radio mic from some previous filming, decided to lounge around on a couch, directly behind Gratty and in full, if out-of-focus, view of the camera.

Perhaps it was this unorthodox arrangement that triggered Gerrard to drop his guard. No longer in the spotlight, he must have subliminally forgotten his caution. He started to speak in a completely different register about his upbringing, his relationship with the city, a disturbing encounter with a fan who'd burnt his shirt on Sky Sports News in protest at the offer Gerrard had received from Chelsea, how very, very close he'd come to leaving simply in order to win trophies and how he'd had a late change of heart when he realised what he'd be leaving behind. 'I could win a load of medals there. But when it was over and I came home, who'd I show them to? Who'd care?'

'Not done too bad for a kid from the Bluebell Estate, have I?'

Gradually, we found ourselves stepping ever further into his world. On the one hand, the longer I spent filming with him, the more ordinary he seemed; a regular young man, the kind we all pass by every day, on the street, at petrol stations, using cashpoints, buying crisps. But on the other hand, that was only half the story.

His was, for example, the only house I have ever been in that boasts an extensive top-floor trophy room. The centrepiece, as Gerrard showed me, contained a life-size replica of the European Cup, flanked by two headless mannequin torsos; one wearing the red Liverpool jersey he'd worn on the pitch in Istanbul, and the other one dressed in white, with the name Shevchenko emblazoned on its back.

'Look at this,' said Gerrard, bending down to press a button discreetly built into the wooden cabinet at knee height. Immediately, the cabinet was flooded with soft yellow light, and the Gerrard torso began to rotate.

'Shevchenko's broken,' he apologised. The decapitated Milan captain was stuck.

Our guided tour of his trophy cabinet continued, meandering slowly back into that portion of his career that already lay in the past, a silver-plated procession of trophies of various descriptions, memorabilia from a range of pre-season tours and a huge collection of champagne bottles with a blue sticker saying 'Barclays' where it should have said 'Laurent Perrier'. These were his many unopened Man of the Match Awards which Geoff Shreeves had been handing him at regular intervals for six years.

We reached the furthest extent of the built-in cabinet, which contained souvenirs from his days at the Liverpool Academy and his breakthrough season in '99. And there, on display, were both the LMA Player Of The Month glass bowls which I had driven up to Melwood and presented to him. We both stopped in front of them.

'Remember them?' Gerrard looked at me. 'You gave me them.'

I had been just one of hundreds of football reporters whose path had crossed with his. But I realised that even such little things can matter and stick in the memory. Reflected in the world around him he saw his own achievements. I was just a part of that mirror. Big players do not live in such a bubble that the outside world does not exist, they simply have to forge a different relationship with it.

Sometimes it felt as if everyone in his house was on a form of unspoken probation, as if privileges could be withdrawn at the drop of a TV remote or the shutting of a distant door in one of the many bedrooms far away at the top of the house, as Gerrard left the scene. He would sometimes very suddenly stop wanting company. You simply knew, somehow, via a complete change in the temperature of the house, that it was time to go.

Once, this happened on a rain-swept wintry day in March. Gary and I had been in the house all day, filming bits and pieces, when it became very clear that the Skipper had had enough. We scampered through the rooms in our socks, hastily gathering up all the bits of clothing and kit we'd left scattered through the various rooms. Though no one was anywhere to be seen downstairs we shouted our thanks and goodbyes to an empty stairwell, before rushing out into the pouring rain. As we crossed the drive the big garden gates opened, on the push of a button operated remotely from inside the property. They closed again behind us, leaving us fumbling for our car keys on the unmade road outside, which was rapidly turning into a quagmire under the downpour.

It was only as I was starting my car and padding my pockets that I realised what I'd left behind. In my mind's eye, I could see my laptop, perched on the drinks cabinet at the far end of the Gerrards' expansive family lounge. I'd taken it out to show him something and in our rush to leave I'd forgotten it.

I looked to the left, out of the window onto which the rain was being thrown by the winter wind, as it grew dark outside. Then I got out and ran back to the gates, knowing that, much like pulling off a plaster, this was simply something I had to get done as quickly and unthinkingly as possible. I pressed the buzzer and waited.

I didn't have to wait for long, but it was enough time for the rain to soak through my collar and start running cold down the back of my neck. Then the gates opened, wordlessly acquiescing to the insistence of my buzzing. As soon as there was a shoulder's-width gap to dive through, I was away and sprinting back across the drive to where the front door already stood partially open to allow me back in.

I stood in the empty hallway. 'Hello?' I called. But there was no answer. 'Steven? Alex?'

'Sorry about this,' I explained to the silence in the house, 'I've just realised I left my laptop in the living room. I'll fetch it and get gone.' Then, just for good measure, 'Sorry!'

I bustled across the hall, and straight into their long, rectangular living room. Then I strode purposefully across their snow-white carpet towards where my laptop lay at the foot of an ornate bouquet in a vase. It was only as I picked it up and turned to walk back that I understood the gravity and error of my action. Across the entire length of the luxuriant, deluxe, white carpet, I had trodden thick, claggy, wet mud prints. They were huge and brown, and there must have been 20 of them.

I stared at the disfigured luxury carpet, immobilised by its incontrovertible reality. Mentally, subconsciously, I was adjusting to the calamity. Very, very slowly, I bent at the waist and, lifting each leg up, one after the other, I took off my shoes. It might have been far too late to make any difference, but it felt like the right thing to do.

Silently I returned to the hallway, not daring to look back, nor making my presence felt any further, and yet, though I dearly wanted to run as fast as I could from the scene of my shame I stood there, stock still, not daring to leave.

'Steven?' I knew I needed to shout a bit louder. 'STEVEN?'

A distant voice replied from upstairs. 'What is it?'

'I'm afraid,' I paused, 'I'm afraidItrodmudalloveryourlivingroom.' I let that sink in.

A distant voice swore from upstairs. 'Fuck's sake.' We both let that sink in.

'I'm really sorry, it was totally my fault. Can I arrange to get a cleaner straight round?'

'No. Just get off to London. We'll sort it.'

'You sure?' Silence. 'OK, then.' More silence. 'Sorry.' I made for the door.

I was just about to pull it closed and walk in my stockinged feet back out into the rain, when I heard Gerrard calling to his wife from a distant room.

'Alex!' he yelled.

I closed the door and left the scene. Many hours later, I got my first and only text message from Steven Gerrard. 'Don't worry about the carpet, mate. Hope you got to London OK. Enjoyed today, Skipper.'

The only England player's mobile number I ever had. And I never once dialled it.

*****

In March 2006, we were asked to meet Gerrard at the special bit of Liverpool Airport where the private planes go from. Gary Caine, Gerrard, Gratty, Rick Parry (Liverpool's chief executive) and I were going to be flying to Paris with the European Cup. Liverpool had already been knocked out of the Champions League and this trip was simply the fulfilment of their obligation to hand the cup over to the host city of the following year's Champions League Final, at a glittering ceremony in the centre of Paris.

There wasn't much room on the private jet, not with Gerrard's long legs and bony knees, and the European Cup wedged between us. I looked around me as the plane soared clear of the Merseyside cloud cover and into the kind of brilliant blue morning that existed through an aeroplane's window.

'I don't want to give this back,' said Gerrard softly, looking at the cup, locked away in its travel box. 'I want to keep it.'

Both Gerrard and Gratty fell fast asleep, in Gratty's case emphatically enough for his snoring to be permanently audible just above the high-pitched whine of the little jet's engines. How the hell had I ended up here? It was beyond odd.

We were met at Le Bourget airport by a special detail of the border police who had driven across the apron to greet us as we got off. After our passports were nodded through by the gendarmes with a smile and quick pose for a photo, we were bundled into a minibus and set off at speed into the heart of Paris, accompanied by a motorcade of at least three police bikes, sirens wailing.

The traffic in the capital was, as ever, stuffed up. Gerrard and Gratty, sitting up front, were like two little kids on a school trip, while Rick Parry made sure the trophy didn't fall over as the minibus tore along, swinging through bends, leaping speed bumps and dashing through implausible gaps. Ahead of us, one of the police bikes misjudged a non-existent space between two cars and took the wing mirror off an oncoming vehicle as it passed, much to the delight of the Liverpool skipper, who shouted, 'Oooh! Clippage! Actual clippage!' He was enjoying himself, like any 25-year-old might, given a breakneck police escort through Paris.

Things got no less surreal when we finally screeched to a halt in that famous courtyard at the back of the Mairie in Paris in which you often see world leaders greeted by presidents of France. This time, there was only Michel Platini, in a dark blue suit and a head that sported something that looked suspiciously like a comb-over. From there, and with the clip and vim of a well-organised speech day at school, our party of visitors was ushered into the main hall where the ceremony would begin immediately upon our arrival.

I watched the show get underway as Gerrard was introduced onto stage. He strode on, holding the European Cup, which, after much speech-making (not on his part, it should be stressed) was handed over to the Mayor of Paris, who thanked him in French and had his thanks translated into English to Gerrard, who thanked him in English.

It was at some point in these proceedings that the host of the television show, a very competent, multilingual woman, asking a question about Liverpool in English to Gerrard, suddenly started to slow her sentence down until every individual word became stretched and slurred. At which point, she fell over and collapsed at his feet.

Steven Gerrard, the Liverpool captain, had never looked so awkward. One hand tentatively stretched out towards her prone body and his back bent somewhat forwards in a vague gesture of sympathy, if not assistance. He looked like he was helping Paul Scholes up off the ground after a crunching challenge. Other people rushed onto the stage from all angles to help. It was only much later, when we'd all established to everyone's relief that the woman had simply fainted in the heat and was fully recovered, that Gerrard could laugh about his own inadequacy in the event.

Piling into a grand fin-de-siècle ballroom, where there was a huge buffet of hors d'oeuvres and champagne flutes, the two old friends came bounding in, roaring with laughter. 'What a man!' shouted Gratty. 'What a fucking hero! The Liverpool skipper has a woman fucking collapse at his feet and just stands there doing fuck all!' Michel Platini, who had half of what looked like a muffin in his hand, the other half in his mouth, started nodding vigorously in agreement and nearly spat out his food as he, too, was overcome with laughter. 'Oh, mate,' continued Gratty. 'It was priceless. Your face!'

And so we left Paris, and Steven Gerrard's grip on those famous handles loosened, in the strangest of circumstances. We all flew home together, cupless, and all laughed out as the skies grew dark over Europe. At some point over the English Channel, I think I fell asleep, too.

*****

Liverpool weren't actually very good that year. They had probably (and improbably) overachieved by winning in Istanbul, and the following campaign was a lot of huff and puff in comparison.

Our sunny documentary about Gerrard's golden year butted up over and over against the hard reality of results, and the ensuing mood that flowed from the biggest defeats. Getting knocked out of the European Cup at an early stage was a big anti-climax.

But losing again to Manchester United in the league was just gloomy and predictable for Liverpool fans.

One Sky Sports *Super Sunday* afternoon, they were soundly beaten at Old Trafford. Gary Caine had been filming pitch-side at the match, getting into an increasing lather of fury about the ineptitude of the performance, particularly with Liverpool's almost-quite-good-but-not-really-trying Djibril Cissé. Gary had always been a Liverpool fan and cared intensely about their fortunes.

When the match was over, he drove to Liverpool and met me at a hotel in the Albert Dock. The following day we were to have an early start, filming behind the scenes with Gerrard as he shot a Carlsberg commercial.

I went early to bed leaving Gary and our old friend, the poet (and fellow Red) Keith Wilson, to enjoy a few 'scoops', as Keith put it. They ended up in a nightclub in the docks, into which, well after midnight, Djibril Cissé walked, no doubt in some expensive and possibly rather elaborate clothing.

Gary, who has on occasion been known to back himself in a car park/nightclub face-off (most notably with a former Nottingham Forest manager outside the City Ground), and despite being about 5ft 7in at most with a very distinctive high-pitched Lincolnshire voice, decided to let Cissé know in some detail where exactly he thought the Frenchman's prodigious shortcomings lay.

'Oy, Cissé! You need to get a grip, pal,' he launched at him. 'What are you doing in here? You had a shocker today!' And then he had to be pulled away. Cissé had apparently looked at this ball of fury flying at him with amused bewilderment. Gary was escorted from the nightclub. He was nearly 50 when this unfortunate incident occurred.

Over breakfast, Gary sheepishly told me about his encounter with the Frenchman. Though I was listening, I was more concerned with getting to the appointed location on time to meet Gerrard, and so I hurried Gary through his fry-up and out onto the film set. We met up with the Liverpool captain, who was in a Winnebago having his make-up applied. He, too, looked ill-slept, though perhaps for a different reason to Gary, and was clearly in a foul mood after losing the previous day to United.

'Do you know how this is going to work today, Steven?' I'd asked him, trying to figure out what we might get out of the day's shoot. 'Who's in this advert? Is it just you?'

'No,' he said, as a make-up artist tousled his hair with some sort of wax and Gary buzzed around him getting some footage. 'There's a few of the lads coming down: Alonso, Jamie, Pepe Reina…' And suddenly both Gary and I knew what was coming next. Out of the corner of my eye, I could see that he had taken the camera off his shoulder and was already backing towards the Winnebago door. Gerrard continued, '…Cissé.'

The door opened and Gary walked out. Gerrard looked round. 'Where did he go?'

We'd film with Gerrard on just a few more occasions. Once in his penthouse at the Grosvenor House Hotel in Park Lane where he was getting changed ahead of the PFA Player of the Year Awards (which he won). And once more, in May, though that shoot very nearly didn't happen. Had Liverpool failed to beat West Ham in the 2006 FA Cup Final at the Millennium Stadium, there wouldn't have been a special party organised at a Liverpool restaurant to which we briefly had access and into which Gerrard, dressed in his grey cup final suit and red tie, strode with the FA Cup in his grasp. He'd won the 2006 final almost single-handedly, with two thunderous long-range strikes, the second of which still astonishes when you watch it.

I'd spent the afternoon listening to the match on the radio, while I made slow progress up the M6 in my car. As the game had ebbed and flowed, I'd repeatedly stood down and then re-booked the cameraman who was waiting in Liverpool. At one point I even pulled over, turned my car around and started heading home. That was when Gerrard did his thing, and I had to leave the southbound carriageway and turn back again towards Merseyside, racing the Liverpool team as they celebrated the cup win and then boarded a private jet from Cardiff. I have a blurred picture of me and Gerrard taken late that night, his red club tie is loosened and we are each holding a handle of the cup. But only one of us had any understanding of what it really meant.

The final day we spent with him was the morning he left for the 2006 World Cup. The FA were sending a car to come and pick him up and drive him to England's training camp in Hertfordshire. Alex, who had been a quiet, cheerful presence throughout the months of filming, was drifting around the house, while her footballer husband faffed about trying to find his toothbrush and remembering his phone and laptop chargers. He'd be going away for at least a month, maybe longer if England progressed through the tournament. But it was his socks that were really bothering him.

All those years of proximity to players, tiny blades of grass plastered to the sweat on their brow and breathing heavily after walking from the scene of victory or defeat, had done little to make me feel that theirs were real lives being lived. Even standing directly in the presence of the best in the land, I still felt that they seemed not quite three dimensional, as if unable to make the leap from the flat screens of their televised life: a fiction. Or were they actually trapped in the lens and neither here nor there, like flies in amber?

My understanding of the game had thickened and changed. Certain impressions had already begun to recede to a faraway place. A nostalgia of stink from grilled Bratwurst and Prince Denmark cigarettes, lit by the unreal colours of the adjacent fairground. Not to forget the Guinness from the darkly cloistered Shamrock pub over the road from Feldstrasse U-Bahn station, which started tapping the pints as the second half kicked off, so that by full time there were a few hundred on the bar. This was how I discovered a love for the game, these the things that had first held me in their thrall.

But now I'd seen football laid semi-bare, I was no longer allowed to view it through the smoky haze of watching from the stands. Sometimes I yearned for that distance again, for the space to imagine what was going on behind the scenes, what it might be like to see the players for who and what they were, rather them how I wished them to be.

Was I getting close? Or not close enough?

'Alex!' He yelled from upstairs. 'How come I can't find any matching socks?' I stood back so that Gary could get a clean shot of the staircase he was about to come loping down.

Eventually, with a bulging hold-all in the hallway, Gerrard said goodbye twice. Once for us to film, a camera-ready demonstration of family unity. And once more, as we left him to it, this time in private and just to his wife and children. Even as he left for what he hoped would be the summer to define his life, he carefully balanced those two identities.

The last words he spoke on camera were something along the lines of wanting to 'go and win the World Cup now. Why not?' And with that, a black limousine with a three lions logo visible on the windscreen pulled away from his home, with the expensive sound of crunching gravel as it went through those gates that opened and then closed on the other-worldly world I'd been briefly invited to see.

17

Fußball Comes Home

ENGLAND 0–0 PORTUGAL (PORTUGAL WIN
3–1 ON PENALTIES).
1 July, 2006. Gelsenkirchen, Germany.

In which old truths are examined.

The *Bundesrepublik Deutschland*, with its slightly insipid domestic
league, organic muesli shops and love for British slapstick was
where Steven Gerrard was heading in his FA limousine. And it was
where I was due to spend six weeks of the summer, too. In 2006, my
haphazard career in football had finally deployed me to a World Cup
and in doing so had unwittingly landed me back in the country that
had first inspired me with a love for the game.

Not many in the production team shared my unbridled sense
of wonder at a prolonged stint of commuting between gloomy-
sounding locations like Bremen and Düsseldorf. Perhaps they felt
that they were condemned to spend their summer in a country stuck
in the 1980s, celebrating a football *Mannschaft* built on nothing more
joyful than winning algorithms. Germany was about as far away as
it was possible to get from the *tiki-taka* of their dreams or the Nike-
parading, ball-juggling carnivalesque of the Brazil team sashaying
their way through an airport. Football was sold to a willing world as
a sparkly Latin thing that rose from the everyday like the encrusted
spire of Gaudi's cathedral. Germany, in comparison, culturally
and footballistically (to coin a Wengerism) was like watching the
freshly painted grey hull of a battleship dry. Where Barcelona had
'philosophy', Bayern simply had 'method'.

Mostly I kept my thoughts to myself, not wanting to raise my own expectations too steeply of what a return to Germany might mean. But in my imagination, being at an actual World Cup would be like encasing oneself in a block of sunlit, suspended time. It would feel like the endless first summer after leaving school when days just loop around instead of loping onwards. I expected to see Ecuadorians mixing with Russians, Belgians with Brazilians, drumming in the streets, and sharing songs and beers on leaf-dappled warm Berlin avenues in hot and joyful union.

As the tournament grew closer, I'd watched with wonder the rash of bewilderingly high-tech new stadiums that sprang from the ground, from Frankfurt to Munich and Hamburg to Gelsenkirchen, unseating Germany's welter of brutalist concrete bowls that had hitherto housed its great clubs. The architecture of the past had been rewritten, in the case of the 1936 Berlin Olympic Stadium, quite literally.

The Germany I had left behind in '95 had been far from perfect: a nation under immense strain, wrestling with the aftermath of reunification and riven by a deep divide where the Iron Curtain had fallen. This wasn't just socio-economically, but politically and philosophically too. This culture war had been a big part of my football baptism at the brown-and-white painted concrete font that was FC St Pauli's Millerntor Stadium; where a vagabond mixture of working-class dockers, artists, piss artists, drag artists and general layabouts loosely self-identified as 'autonomous'.

They stood, inasmuch as they could stand after five litres of Holsten Pils, for everything that challenged the accepted norms of the establishment. Their hatred for the bad guys compelled them to carry with them wherever they went a fistful of 'St Pauli Fans Against Nazis' stickers, featuring an iconic design of a big fist smashing into a swastika. If you look carefully as you walk through the underground networks and bus stations of London, Rome, New York or Cairo, you will see these stickers from time to time. They have spread unevenly across the globe like a haphazard antifa virus.

In the early 1990s that Pauli rabble took to boarding buses early on a Saturday morning and taking interminable beer-sodden journeys into the heart of old East Germany in order to confront the enemy, both on the pitch and off it. Whether it was Dynamo Dresden, VfB Leipzig or Carl Zeiss Jena, it mattered little. Pauli's fans wanted to wave their fists, always clutching a smouldering Rizla, at their new brethren from the East, known dismissively as *Ossis*. Most of these *Wessis* viewed their new compatriots not so much with brotherly or sisterly solidarity, as with outright suspicion. And that suspicion was reciprocated.

I made my one and only away trip with a group of St Pauli supporters to see our team succumb meekly to an entirely predictable two-nil defeat away at Hansa Rostock, newly relegated to the second division. But the trip to and from the bus station to the terrifyingly exposed Ostseestadion, long since demolished, had been a grim and unfriendly trudge to the accompaniment of a phalanx of green-jacketed, brown-trousered officers of the Polizei, with a few snarling Alsatians thrown in for extra dispiriting effect. Nothing bad happened, apart from Pauli's chronically disappointing striker Leonardo Manzi missing an open goal. In fact, it would have been somehow more disappointing if Manzi *hadn't* missed.

While there was so much more to my years in Germany than just bleakness, there was nevertheless a core of disruption, a sense of the close possibility of violence that exposed the political nerves in a country still terrifyingly young and uncertain. I also had a sense of seeing history as a living thing; an organism that evolved with staggering pace. This unsettled and excited me about life there.

All those years later, I was eager to see what had changed. In 2006 my senior ITV colleague Gabriel Clarke was to be stationed with the England team in Baden Baden, nicknamed Pardon Pardon because of the lack of mobile phone signal. Gabriel's onerous task was to elicit something broadcast-worthy out of the England camp every single day and sometimes twice a day. That's an awful lot of sifting through the thoughts of Sven-Göran Eriksson on Wayne Rooney's metatarsal for any man to reasonably bear, even if that man is Gabriel, who can listen to football people talk, without cease, for the rest of his life.

My job that summer was to go where I was told. With John, an extremely hard-working and talented producer from St Helens, and accompanied by a rotation of camera crews, we were cut loose around Germany for the entire duration of the tournament, covering pretty much every team that wasn't England. Every day we'd phone HQ in Munich, where the central broadcast operation was based, to discuss the following day's agenda. Often they'd only confirm late at night which German city we'd be flying or driving to the following morning. At the group phase of the tournament, before team after team started to get knocked out, the choices were almost endless. The best bit of a World Cup, I discovered, is always the beginning.

We made our base in Wiesbaden, a spectacularly well preserved and elegant spa town not far from Frankfurt. It was rumoured that Wiesbaden had been spared the carpet bombing which had almost completely destroyed neighbouring cities like Darmstadt, chosen for an attack because it was believed, rightly, that its preponderance of wooden-built medieval houses would burn so readily as to form an unstoppable conflagration. The story was that King George had taken Arthur 'Bomber' Harris to one side and asked him to keep Wiesbaden from suffering the same fate, since the family rather liked going to the famous *Kurhaus* there to take the waters. Sadly, this turns out to have been complete nonsense. The British did in fact attack it in 1945 with 500 planes and destroyed a fifth of it. It could have been much worse had cloud cover not spoiled their aim. Most German towns and cities have a similar tale to tell. Close to 20,000 tons of bombs were dropped on nearby Frankfurt, killing 5,500 civilians. It was there, outside the *Hauptbahnhof*, that I stood in the crowds before England's opening match against Paraguay and watched visiting fans fill the city centre with their traditional song reminding their hosts of the bombing campaign waged by the Royal Air Force. Frankfurt's passers-by, going about their everyday lives, walked inscrutably past the singers, keeping their feelings hidden.

From our Wiesbaden base we started criss-crossing the country by train, car and plane, and were bowled over by the open, workable, pleasurable, welcoming ease of it all. Things functioned. Ideas came to fruition. People tried to help. When it came to covering the German national team itself, I hit a tiny little jackpot.

The *Deutscher Fußball Bund's* press conferences were huge affairs, broadcast live across several TV stations, with a full studio rig, as if they were the *X Factor*. The first time I attended, I was, to my great surprise, picked out to ask the first question. This is a witheringly small achievement, but in the fragile little world of the football reporter's ego, it matters greatly. It also invited comparison with the many press conferences I had witnessed with England and English teams, in which questions from the foreign media are often an afterthought, greeted by the football clubs and the home press alike with a vague amused dismissiveness or impatience.

In German, Harald Stenger, the head press officer of the DFB, started the press conference and, after introducing Miroslav Klose and Michael Ballack alongside him, signalled towards me.

'I'd like to call upon our international colleagues first, and would ask our friend from the BBC, Mr Bolton, to start the press conference.' Undeterred by hearing my new name and employer, I stood up and live on TV across the German nation asked something a bit daft in German about Klose being a typically German striker. That made Ballack laugh because Klose spoke German with an identifiably Polish accent.

This iteration of the German national team had started to represent for the first time the growing variation of the host country's increasingly multi-ethnic population. Jürgen Klinsmann, the sleeves of his crisp white shirt forever rolled up his handsome forearms, flanked by Joachim Löw, the man who would go on to replace him as well as continue the trend for natty suits, curious hair and huge success, had started to benefit from a new definition of nationality. Players with Ghanaian heritage, such as Gerald Asamoah (ex St Pauli, staggeringly for such a talent) and David Odonkor broke into the German national team, having, in Asamoah's case, assumed German citizenship. In 2001, he had become the first African-born player to represent Germany. In this 21st-century team these two players, and others to follow, took their place alongside the *Deutsch-Polen* Klose and Lukas Podolski.

It wasn't all entirely unproblematic, of course. In fact, the match between Poland and Germany that had ended with an injury-time winner from Oliver Neuville had been one of the few encounters during that World Cup to have attracted isolated outbreaks of trouble on the streets outside the Westfalen Stadium in Dortmund. I'd been travelling in a taxi across Nuremberg as the winner had gone in that night. Our driver, a first-generation Turkish immigrant who I'd spent our ride chatting to, was, rather terrifyingly, watching the match on really quite a big screen strapped to his dashboard as he drove. When Germany scored he screamed in victory and repeatedly punched an invisible opponent about three inches above the steering wheel from which his hands had now been entirely removed. I screamed with him, astonished to be in the company of a Turkish man so completely captivated by the fortunes of a host country that had done precious little to make his community ever feel welcome. I also screamed because I thought he was going to kill us.

Instead of ploughing into an oncoming tram, he dropped us off outside a big, grand hotel near the railway station. England fans had gathered in large numbers in a street at the side of the building. What had drawn them to that spot was the light coming from a room on the second floor. There, standing on the balcony, and just about visible, were three of the England squad who, the next day, were due to face Trinidad and Tobago. I could just about make out Frank Lampard and Wayne Rooney. And then, honing into view, the unmistakable silhouette of Peter Crouch 'doing the robot'. And down below, his sunburnt disciples replied in kind. 'Let's all do the Crouchey! Let's all do the Crouchey!' they sang. 'La-laaa-lala, la-laaa-la-la…' And no one was throwing any glasses or plastic chairs anywhere. Nor were they, at least for one night, singing about WWII.

Something good was happening, or half-decent, at least. Germany was not only delighting its many thousands of visitors from around the globe, as well as the countless millions whose experience of the event was being filtered through television, Germany was also delighting *itself*. From the moment in the opening game that Philipp Lahm ran onto the ball on the left wing, cut inside, dumped a Costa Rican defender on his arse, and then curled a right-footed splendour of a goal one hot, sunny afternoon, Germany decided to throw off half a century of knitted brows, wrung hands and occasional self-loathing. But this uncomplicated celebration of a short, clean-cut full-back's poise, pace and placement had moved a tense nation to express itself with an unfettered joy it hardly recognised in itself. The flags were waving; those three powerful and unlovely colours, the *Schwarz*, *Rot* and *Gold*, suddenly radiant against the white of their flags and shirts. Germany decided, collectively, simply to have fun.

With the tournament in full flow, our trajectory across the country picked up speed. One day we were sitting down in Würzburg with the erudite and talented Stephen Appiah, the Ghanaian talisman, whose metronomic passing game and silver earring had caught the eye. And the next day we'd be off again, this time to Herzogenaurach, to hunt down Diego Maradona, at his record plumpest and hobbling around on those arthritic legs, playing to the cameras as his accompanying circus descended on the training camp he was notionally in charge of.

One sunlit afternoon (and it was a glorious, endless June), we watched Maradona walk the 50 yards across a training pitch to the changing rooms, all the time keeping up a tirade of abuse aimed at persons unknown in the Argentinian press pack, gathered in the stands in his honour and soaking up his disgust with total indifference. It must have taken him 10 minutes to get it all out, by which time most of the attendant media cortège had lost interest and wandered off, except us. We gazed on in fascination.

We travelled down to Nuremberg again, to watch in growing disbelief as Portugal and the Netherlands contrived to earn a collective tally of 16 yellow and four red cards in their group match. I can't even remember the final score and I think I was still laughing as I made my way down to the tunnel area, showing my full panoply of accreditations (and still getting stopped every 10 paces), to interview Cristiano Ronaldo, who'd limped off after half an hour, thus avoiding being sent off later like most of the rest of his team.

Even the USA were great, riotous fun. I found myself, for reasons I cannot remember, being filmed watching one of their games at a USAF base near Frankfurt with Greg Proops, whose improvisational wit I had admired on *Whose Line Is It Anyway?* That programme, when I had been living in Germany, had seemed to my rose-tinted emigrant eyes to define the difference between my host nation and my home, a kind of self-deprecating cultural sophistication that Germany could never match. This assumption, like so many others, was founded on a fundamental misunderstanding of where Germany was heading and what England really was.

England. Stolid, square old England. Despite Ray Winstone's motivational presence as some dubiously titled 'fans' ambassador' in Cologne, they still huffed and puffed. We'd interviewed the arch cockney actor at 9 o'clock on the morning of the game, at his express command, since after that he'd wanted 'to get on it with the lads'. I'd got the impression he meant it. Only once did that team I always willed to excite actually manage to excite. It was against Sweden and, even then, it only flickered for a moment.

I was stressed, that day. My arrival at the stadium had been delayed by the nasty legal aftermath of me shunting our van into a brand new Mercedes on the big approach road to the ground. Being the only German speaker, as well as having been actively and obviously to blame for the crash, I was left behind to talk insurance policies and wait for the police. I got to the ground just in time to see Joe Cole's career hit and simultaneously pass its peak.

It lasted no more than a few seconds, but, like a darts player hitting a perfect 180 down the pub, there was at that precise moment no better footballer on earth than Cole. He volleyed the ball past the keeper and into the Swedish net to ensure that England somehow, painfully, progressed further in the tournament. I felt a strange, deferred pride and a certain inexplicable jealousy towards the mercurial yet straightforward Cole. It was the delusional sense of ownership that sometimes blights the judgment of journalists who think they have something in common with their subject simply because they might have written or spoken about them; a kind of journalistic Stockholm Syndrome or Munchausen by Proxy.

England had reached the round of 16 and then, after dispatching Ecuador 1-0, another quarter-final. On the day of their fateful slog against Portugal, commentator Peter Drury, 'Big' Sam Allardyce (he was only ever referred to as 'Big') and I were driven over to Gelsenkirchen from our hotel in Berlin where, the previous afternoon, we'd watched Germany creep past Argentina with an inspired penalty shoot-out. Allardyce had worked as a pundit on that game with Peter commentating and me reporting. The Bolton manager was travelling with us.

It was a long journey right across Germany's nondescript central belt. We were, however, being driven in one of those posh cars that, a bit like London taxis, have a passenger section in which you sit facing one another. Peter and I had our backs to the direction of travel, leaving the future England manager to luxuriate on his own opposite us, his colossal retired centre-half's legs, in a dark blue suit, splayed out. For over 300 miles we were presented with an unenviable choice about where to place our legs, relative to his, which, angled at 45 degrees to his pelvis, seemed to extend to fill every square inch of the car.

This journey was not the first prolonged spell of close contact I had had with Big Sam over the course of the tournament. Late in the evening, after England's group match against Trinidad and Tobago, we had all dined together in some Nuremberg restaurant. It had been one of those messy corporate evenings out where too many colleagues try to cram around too few spaces at a table, different factions develop uncomfortably in the seating arrangements and ordering takes far too long.

But the one man who'd seemed blithely unfazed by any of these irritants had been Allardyce, whose appetite was matched only by his ability to hold court. Most of the content of his monologue was Sam Allardyce-based. After all, as he impressed on us, lest he left any room for doubt, he was at the height of his tactical powers. 'The Chess Master,' he'd said with sullen certainty and not a flicker of irony, as he moved salt and pepper pots around the table. 'That's what they call me.' Though who exactly 'they' were he'd left slightly less clear.

On the road to Gelsenkirchen, Big Sam was expounding once more on his sporting philosophy. For hour after long hour on the autobahn, Peter and I listened attentively to the Allardyce Vision for Football, like a TED talk of no proscribed duration. In fact, it would have quite fitted the moment if he'd been wearing the trademark headset microphone for which he had become well known. By Hannover, we knew all about his attitude towards referees. By Bielefeld, it had become apparent to us that he wasn't expecting to do much business in the transfer market that summer.

At one point his phone rang and for a while we listened to one half of a pretty sparing exchange.

'Yes... no... yes... not really,' then he hung up. We looked at him with curiosity. 'Benni McCarthy,' he intoned with world-weary gravitas. 'Not for me.'

At one point, on the outskirts of Münster, we stopped at a service station. Allardyce stepped out to stretch those immense legs while our driver filled the car's vast petrol tank. Once Big Sam had closed the door behind him, Peter looked at me and asked, 'Do you think he knows our names?' I howled with laughter. It was true, he'd not even asked.

Our only other stop, and Allardyce's only other pause in his monologue, came as we approached Gelsenkirchen. We pulled up at an Italian restaurant – having ill-advisedly drunk a coffee at the previous stop, we were all three desperate for a toilet break. We minced through the dining area like Olympic speed walkers, after which all three of us entered a cavernous male toilet area at a canter. Peter and I turned at once towards the urinals.

Big Sam turned left.

We heard a cubicle door slam shut, the soft sound of a pair of suit trousers and the metallic clang of a belt hitting the tiled floor, and then what I can only describe as a cry of victory from the Bolton Wanderers' manager. Peter Drury and I dared not look at each other for fear of what might happen. Instead, wordlessly, we finished up and got out of the loo as soon as we could, only subsiding into helpless laughter when we were back in the safety of the car.

Later that sultry afternoon, Ronaldo winked, Rooney sweated and England lost another penalty shoot-out. And that was that.

The following morning I was up early to head off to some other part of the country. Hastily eating breakfast in the hotel, I briefly sat down next to a few colleagues who'd been working at the England match, the latest in the long, unbroken lineage of English quarter-final penalty shoot-out defeats. We were chewing over the whole ghastly inevitability of it all and how England had appeared uninspiring throughout the World Cup.

I stuffed one of those very small, very over-baked and consequently very dry mini-chocolate hotel croissants in my mouth and I washed it down with a bitter swill of coffee. Then, half standing to go for my luggage and waiting taxi, I ventured a not totally controversial opinion.

'Beckham,' I said, and flicked a bit of croissant flake off my bottom lip, 'I hope that's the last we see of him for England.' I turned to leave, but was interrupted.

'Why do you say that?' asked Terry Venables.

Venables had overheard my comment from the table next to me where he sat with Andy Townsend. He'd been part of the studio team of pundits, high up in the stadium the previous night. I hadn't spotted him in the breakfast room at first. But there he was, looking smooth, friendly, a bit like someone you think you know extremely well, but then realise you've never actually met. I fought off the urge to tell him that my dad used to have a dog named Terry Venables.

Brutally exposed, I now only had myself to blame. Ordinarily, and especially in the presence of actual football people, I make a point of never expressing an opinion. It seems unwise, because, frankly, it is unwise.

'Well,' I began, not knowing what I was about to say next. 'When he starts, it looks like the opposition knows exactly how England will play.'

'Which is?' Venables countered, with an unexpected and growing curiosity.

I really wasn't prepared for this level of analysis. 'Quite… slowly?' I suggested.

Venables looked at me for a disconcertingly long time. 'Would you pick him for the next England squad, then?'

This had already gone way deeper than I'd been prepared for. But there was no obvious way of backing out.

'No.'

The twist in this innocent tale was that soon after Venables was announced as part of the new England manager Steve McLaren's coaching staff. On 11 August, 2006, McLaren announced his first England squad and there was no place for David Beckham.

It is simply bizarre to be in close proximity to great football names, something I never got used to. This surrealism was never more apparent than after we'd all worked on a match between Germany and Ghana. Adjacent to Dortmund's Westfalen Stadium, where they'd just played, is an athletics track that encloses a hockey pitch. A game of football had been organised there between the English and German TV companies. It was due to kick off a couple of hours after the final whistle in the actual game. That was the proud day I represented England on the field of play against Germany.

A notable difference in the general approach of the two camps became immediately apparent. The Germans were all wearing football kit. Admittedly, none of it matched. But they had shorts on and running shoes and football jerseys. Our team, a rag-tag assortment of video technicians, directors, producers, camera operators, commentators (Peter Drury was a very voluble presence in goal) and reporters (me) were mostly in the suits they'd been working in all day. But, and this was key to our chances, the England team boasted three loan signings in Andy Townsend, Ally McCoist and Ruud Gullit, who was immaculately turned out in slim-fitting Gucci and some frighteningly precious-looking shoes.

Townsend, as he had done for Ireland and Aston Villa, admirably anchored midfield and shouted a lot. Drury commentated his way through the entire game, a lone, unamplified voice from our backs that sometimes became self-referential ('Drury's off his line... makes himself big... and gets down well'). McCoist played up front and looked for all the world like an estate agent. And Gullit bestrode the entire defensive quadrant, master of all he surveyed, never once breaking into a run, let alone a sweat. Occasionally, languidly, he'd scoop up in his winklepickers a fantastically weighted long pass up the left wing for some idiot like me (me, in fact) to trip over rather than control.

'Fuck's sake, man,' came the understated assessment from the former AC Milan and Holland legend. 'It was to your feet.'

'That was the problem, I think, Ruud.' I flashed him what I thought was a winning smile, but he angrily brushed it away, batting dismissively at thin air.

Germany won by some humblingly comfortable score line and by dint of being younger, better than us and wearing the right shoes.

But all the players from both sides lingered together for a long while, at the end of a day's work, as the hot sun started to dip lower in the sky. Photos were taken, stories exchanged, beer cans were snapped open. Football seemed to me, as I stood there marvelling at two halves of my life colliding, a perfectly uncomplicated pursuit of pleasure. Laughing at our collective incompetence, giving credit where it was due, with a simple clap on the shoulder, all relieved of pressure, the pitch became a secular communal meeting place for strangers to convene and deal with the tricky roll of a ball. A damn sight better than No Man's Land on Christmas Day 1914.

Though England were out, Germany weren't.

Their semi-final against Italy was played at night some weeks later, but at the same cacophonous venue. Borussia Dortmund's iconic football ground is the result of nothing more than ambitious, unembroidered scale. It's massive boxiness is its great virtue, without any of the curvatures, tarpaulin-style roofing or oval bowl-shape of so many of its more aspirational equivalents across the world. It stands as a blockish symbol of the very city that gave rise to its construction in the first place, a place where the people have, for generations, dug for coal to power the factories of Germany's admirably resilient backbone of heavy manufacturing.

There is in that little-understood prefix 'Borussia' (the Latin name for Prussia) a direct call to the industrial revolution that swept across the disparate Hapsburg lands and created the modernising impulse for Germany to be born in the first place, for better and for worse. Unlike their great rivals in Munich, whose Catholic homeland aspires to the Renaissance and drips with Baroque, Dortmund only knows the value of labour and the tangible results it can generate. As much power station as football ground, it was the perfect setting for this young, exciting Germany team to plug into the fervour it had generated.

Arriving a long time before kick-off, I toured the huge area inside the ground, adjacent to the dressing rooms, that had been partitioned off and subdivided to accommodate the demands of the world's TV stations. As the tournament had narrowed to the final four, so the numbers of media outlets attending each match had risen. A World Cup semi-final was the biggest single game I had ever been lucky enough to attend and I gave my shoes an extra polish, Columbo-style, on the back of my calves, as a result.

We found our designated working zone, an area not much bigger than the oche in a darts match, framed by a backdrop emblazoned with all the logos of the global corporations responsible for pumping in the hundreds of millions being generated by FIFA. Buried within this sea of brands sat a single 'ITV Sport', which meant that this was our patch. All along the line, dozens of other camera crews were locating their pens, from Brazil, Russia, Mexico, India, Saudi Arabia.

Long before the end of the game I made my way down to this position, so that I might be ready at the moment the final whistle went to stick a microphone in the face of whichever player I could persuade to talk. In reality though, these interactions are carefully marshalled. FIFA employ an agency to facilitate the media's requests. This, in turn, results in a clutch of suited men and women, who, with an air of perpetual stress and fear, invite requests from each accredited broadcaster. These are then relayed to the relevant press officers.

'ITV. Who do you want?'

I was being barked at by a Spanish man in a suit who I recognised from many a Champions League match and always in a similar situation. He had his long greying hair scraped back behind his ears in a kind of bob and his chin supported the most neurotically manicured goatee I had been lucky enough to be in the presence of. He was poised with a pen above his clipboard. 'Who?'

'Klinsmann.'

'No chance.'

'Ballack.'

'Come on, be serious.' He walked away, waving a dismissive hand at me.

'Lehmann,' I said at his retreating figure. But already he was talking to the reporter next to me.

'Who?'

'Klinsmann.'

Outside, the game was thundering towards its mighty conclusion. Trapped in this tunnel under the main stand, we could feel the steel and concrete in which we were entombed contract under the pressure of the moment. Above us it was tumultuous. We crowded around the one tiny little monitor that a French TV station had had the foresight (and the budget) to rig down in the interview area. Otherwise, we'd have missed the moment that summer ended for Germany. The Italians scored.

A sudden quiet rushed down the tunnel from the pitch. Distant yells of anguish could be heard from a scattering of German TV crews at the other end of the interview zone, and then the noise of running and screaming. The Italian backroom staff, the physios and kitmen, came running in from the side of the pitch, howling with delight in an area that had otherwise gone quiet. From the far side of the ground you could now make out the more muffled noise of the few thousand Italian fans whose team had just broken Germany's happy-go-lucky hearts.

And then suddenly the Spanish media official went into overdrive. Striding with a furious sense of purpose up the line of reporters and cameramen, he ordered us all back into our designated pens.

'You stand where you should be!' he screamed. 'You do not cross this line!'

Pretty soon, Germany's defeated team would have to walk past us to get to their dressing room. He pointed at a length of coloured tape on the ground. 'When the players come off the pitch, you do not talk to them! Cameramen, point all your cameras at the ground! You will not film the players as they come past!' It was a rare mania. I had witnessed fear and loathing at football matches before; the tunnel at Old Trafford could be an intimidating place to work. But this paranoid rage was on another level altogether. I looked around me to see if the other TV crews were doing as they were told. They were.

Then the German players traipsed past, one by one, in forlorn silence, their eyes downcast. Passing close enough to where we stood for us to catch that acrid smell of cold turf and night air, mixed with the faintest overtone of cordite from the Italian flares that had no doubt been lit. I was standing close to their reality, the irrefutable evidence of their crushed aspirations. The privacy of their hurt was already straining to keep at bay the vastness of a nation let down by events in a game of football.

Finally Jens Lehmann, the last to come off the pitch, walked dejectedly by. Under the watchful gaze of our FIFA minders, I was prevented from asking him for an interview of course. Not one player from the Germany camp stopped and spoke to any TV crew, while the Italians were by now lighting up cameras and microphones, and piling in to each other's joyful interviews.

A long time after the end of the match, we still had no interview. The FIFA official strode over to me and, looking more stressed than ever, demanded to know if I'd already managed to speak to Lehmann.

'No.'

'Didn't you ask him?' he almost screamed at me.

'You told us not to talk to them.'

'Don't tell me what I told you.'

'OK.'

I couldn't wait to get out of there. Even without the excitable exchange with our FIFA prison guard, I realised I actually didn't want to be the person to whom these beaten players would have to speak. I felt profoundly uncomfortable being the suited fool asking the bleeding obvious of them. The 'Jens, you-must-be-very-disappointed' kind of non-question, which is pretty much all you can do in the circumstances.

When big games are won and lost like that, it always strikes me that they are charged with a significance they cannot contain; as if the world has been knocked fractionally off its axis; as if it's taken a tiny whack which has altered its direction. As absurd as it sounds, I have often felt like that after England's serial defeats; that each ignominious collapse or valiant near-thing undermines my own journey through the world, my own faith in progress. And this late defeat for the host nation felt to me like a similar blow. The party was dispersing. The spell of summer was broken.

Germany 2006 came to a close for me as I sat high in the stands of the Olympic Stadium in Berlin, marvelling at the lack of atmosphere in the ground, bored by the grind of a World Cup Final. It was a torpid affair, lit up only as Zinedine Zidane made sure that he would be remembered as much for a headbutt on a player who specialised in being headbutted as he would be for all those magic tricks he hardly knew he was doing with the ball. Italy took the prize, a blithely insouciant team. With Marcello Lippi acting like the head teacher of a school whose student body was constituted entirely by school bullies, they were a quietly confident rock of self-assuredness parading a cup to a country that was busy turning the lights out.

The next day, all booked on the same BA flight back to London as the BBC production team, I queued up to check in behind Gary Lineker and Alan Shearer, who were faffing around with golf clubs and excess baggage. Having started the tournament like a fresh sheet of blotting paper, primed to absorb everything that it could throw at me, I left, perhaps through sheer exhaustion, with a hollow sense of bathos. This time it had nothing to do with England's shortcomings, which had, once again, been manifest.

I'd wanted Germany to win and they hadn't. For convoluted reasons I cannot even begin to unpick, that would have felt like some sort of closing of a circle, a form of self-justification about the choices I had made in life. But it can't have been that complicated, surely? After all, it's a simple game.

18

Trans-Europe Express

MANCHESTER UNITED 1–1 CHELSEA
(MANCHESTER UNITED WIN 6–5 ON PENALTIES).
21 May, 2008. Luzhniki Stadium, Moscow.

In which there is no end in sight.

If you're not a player, not actually on the pitch tearing sinews to get to that cursed ball, then football is simply a story that is told. Some stories are better than others.

Over the course of their faltering, skin-of-the-teeth campaign, I had been on hand almost everywhere to see Liverpool lose in Athens to Olympiacos, lose to Monaco and draw at home to Deportivo La Coruña. I had stumbled along with them through the first full season of Champions League football I'd been sent to cover. All the while, we had one thing in common, I suspect, me and the Liverpool FC of 2005. We couldn't quite believe it was happening to us. Not really.

It was interesting how many times, during the early rounds of their extraordinary march towards the Istanbul final, Liverpool were deemed to be uninspiring enough to be bumped off the main channel and onto the lesser digital platform. This meant that I got to cover them, being firmly part of the 'B team'. Rafa Benitez was, after all, still a relatively unknown Spanish technocrat, except to football 'hipsters' – a term that had not yet been invented. And the team he'd inherited was a slightly underwhelming mixture of not-quite-top-level misfits, plus Xavi Alonso and Steven Gerrard. At least that's how it appeared.

But there we were and there they were. We arrived in Turkey a few days before the Istanbul final and sank immediately into the cultural kaleidoscope of Istanbul, with its languid stray dogs and fuzz of charcoal grills hanging in the early summer air above the Bosphorous mixing with the crackle of prayer from minarets. Already the experience felt unreal. Exoticism, for many a Western thinker through many centuries, had started here. English clubs reaching the final of the Champions League was still a rare thing and hadn't happened for six years, not since Manchester United had won in 1999. For that reason it got the full Big Match treatment from ITV. There was an hour-long preview show to make, as well as a long build-up to the match itself for which further content had to be generated. Gabriel Clarke and I, in a one-off collaborative effort, filmed a rough guide to the great city at the junction between the East and West. This involved a contrived piece to camera at the railway station, where Gabriel muttered something extremely clever about the Orient Express in relation to Liverpool's progress through the competition that I didn't fully understand, and a trip to a barber shop, which again, I didn't fully understand the purpose of. But I got a free haircut out of it and it was good fun to film.

Our interactions with a whole host of different shopkeepers, passers-by, taxi drivers and waiters left us both with a good feeling about this most multifaceted and variegated of cities, its astonishing, sprawling size, elaborate skyline and great, important-feeling place in the sweep of human history. And all the while, Istanbul was beginning to fill up with the oversized flags, ambitious short trousers for the time of year, polo shirts, light sunburn and beery breath of the Liverpool supporters. This match was going to matter in a way that others didn't quite manage.

The red army continued to throng the ancient city, closing in on it like so many armies through the centuries, from all different approach routes, buses through Romania, trains to Macedonia, ferries from Greece. For us, working on the match for TV, there was a heightened air to everything we did. On the morning of the game, our boss conducted a motivational team talk in an anonymous meeting room at our bland suburban Istanbul hotel in which he reminded us of our privileged position, and encouraged us to remember that days like this do not come along very often, and that we should enjoy it. Once again, I had to cast my eyes to the floor and examine my shoes with sudden interest to avoid blushing at the silliness of it all – TV's self-important habit of conflating the principal actors involved with those minions charged simply with making the telly, as if the messengers somehow enjoy the same status as the message, or even the people in the message doing the important thing that prompted the message to be sent in the first place. It's nonsense, but it's beguiling nonsense, and plenty of us have fallen into this trap.

Even as we made our way through suffocated traffic to the barren outskirts of the city, where they'd plonked the brand-new Atatürk stadium, and sensed the onrushing masses of Liverpool fans, outnumbering the Milanese comfortably by four to one, our sense of occasion only grew again. As night fell, the evening started to take its shape. The time difference between western Turkey and the all-important ratings heartlands of western Europe dictated that kick-off wasn't until a quarter to eleven at night. By the time they went into that penalty shoot-out, it was past one o'clock in the morning.

The match took the famous, historical course that it took, with the Milan team greedily eyeing up the trophy as they trudged off at half time with a three-goal lead. After that it was all Gerrard swinging his arms and Clive Tyldesley, who I was sitting very close to high in the stands, with his portentous half-question, half-exhortation, 'Hello!?' as the red tide started to turn. I'd heard Clive shout it out loud against the roar from three of the four sides of the ground. I was despatched downstairs to get ready for all eventualities, as the programme schedulers prepared to over-run again.

When Andriy Shevchenko's shot was somehow blocked by Jerzy Dudek and the Liverpool team had indeed won it, I was standing right by the side of the pitch, not far from the Liverpool bench. Everyone associated with the club, all the staff who might otherwise normally have been working behind the scenes, the kitmen, and medics and ancillary workers rose as a single entity. In one surge I was almost swept off my feet by the tide of bodies sprinting, against every possible UEFA regulation, right onto the pitch. Unless for whatever legitimately partisan reasons you couldn't bring yourself to enjoy it, it was a moment of astonishing power. Liverpool had done something huge and everyone knew it, even those who couldn't bring themselves to admit it.

Even when the last interviews had been done and when I had been ambushed by Rafa Benitez outside the Liverpool changing room and bear-hugged to within an inch of my life (I think he must have mistaken me for someone he actually knew), even when I had loosened my tie and made my way to the little minibus which was going to take the production team back to our hotel for a few hours' sleep, I knew already that I'd never see anything quite like it again. Sitting on my own I wiped my hand to clear the steamed-up window and catch a glimpse of Liverpool-supporting inebriates staggering around trying to find an international airport in the dark suburban streets. I sat back and listened to the euphoric chatter from the row behind of Steve McManaman, who'd been part of the ITV studio that night, and the mate who he'd brought along for the ride, Robbie Fowler, as they cracked open another can of beer.

Some of us slept for two or three hours, before reconvening on board a flight back to Heathrow. By breakfast time in the UK the following day we were gazing blearily at the baggage carousel in the airport. As we stood there glumly eyeing up luggage, the head of ITV Sport received a phone call from the controller of ITV informing him that they'd cleared an hour in the schedules for a one-off special studio show to celebrate the astonishing victory. All they needed right now was a name for the programme, so they could let their press department know.

'Can anyone think what to call it?' he asked, as we all stood around, looking wanly at the moving belt dreaming of seeing our luggage. 'Oh, and by the way, Matt, you're presenting it from the studios.' He was talking to my colleague Matt Smith, who, as a Liverpool fan, had been enjoying the flight every bit as much as he'd enjoyed the entire evening before with Robbie Fowler. He swayed his response, rather than speaking, and grinned vacantly at our boss. 'So, get yourself to a hotel, get your head down and get to the studios for seven.'

'*Midnight Express?*' I ventured, thinking of the late hour and the black night sky above the ground, more than any association with the heroin trade.

The boss now turned to me. 'What's that supposed to be?'

'*Midnight Express*,' I repeated. 'The title of the show. How Liverpool got out of jail in Istanbul.'

'No,' he said.

'*The Kop Final*,' said someone else, more suited to the job than me. Clearly, I had just over-reached, *again*.

The show went out that evening, presented by an immaculately groomed and sparklingly sober Matt Smith, and it was called *The Kop Final*. Not *Midnight Express*.

*****

Liverpool's night of high emotion in Istanbul had been my introduction to the unmatchable intensity of the Champions League. No games that followed ever quite came close to its shock and awe.

The victory had ramifications, of course, horribly so for their Merseyside rivals Everton, who now had to pre-qualify for the Champions League, though they'd finished above Liverpool in the league table. They were knocked out in a fury of frustration at the home of one of the most esoteric clubs in Europe, Villareal. Time and time again, over a period of two seasons, we returned to their eccentric home on an unlovely stretch of the Spanish coast.

Villareal was the team that Manuel Pellegrini built, and in which the sultry Juan Román Riquelme lazily starred, the Argentinian misfit with sublime, idle skill. Their slightly ramshackle ground, El Madrigal, sits in the heart of a cobbled-together town in Castillon, an hour's drive north of Valencia. It is far from beautiful, but it is jammed with character in a way that I found completely fascinating.

The first thing you become aware of when you visit this mysterious football institution is that everything is tiled. The strangely undesigned building's walls are tiled both inside and out. The ceiling and roof are tiled. The labyrinthine concourses, tiled. This part of Spain is the centre of the country's substantial porcelain industry and there is little or nothing that is built in Villareal that is not, eventually, tiled. Sometimes, after days of dusty heat, there can be a sudden squally shower along this coast, in whose immediate aftermath no one can possibly stay upright, since the whole of Villareal turns into a freshly polished wetroom. Indeed, the stadium that everyone calls El Madrigal is now both officially and hilariously known at Estadio de la Cerámica.

Villareal hosted, on days preceding matches, chaotic press conferences, which I came to enjoy immensely. Because they were a new club in the family of Champions League regulars and were therefore unfamiliar with the methodologies and regulations of UEFA, who control their crown jewel competition to within an inch of its life, you could feel the fault lines creaking and groaning. UEFA would arrive with its legion of branding officials in the days before the match and would obliterate all visible trace of sponsorship that might conflict with theirs. Therefore, the local Spanish beer company, whose logos appeared in the concourse bars all over the stadium, found itself airbrushed out of existence for the duration of UEFA's tenure at the ground. An army of operatives with blackout boards and rolls of gaffer tape made sure that nothing detracted from Europe's football governing body's main aim of selling a specific beer to the masses.

But although the authorities did their level best to control the environment as they would expect to do at a fully compliant venue like the Emirates or the Allianz Arena, there was something always a bit rogue about covering a match at Villareal. Radio reporters from local stations and newspaper hacks from Spanish dailies, eschewing the need to wear the requisite MD-1 (Match Day Minus One) SADs (Supplementary Accreditation Devices), roamed around the inner corridors of the Madrigal ground as if they belonged there, which is precisely what they normally did.

Such lawlessness drove the UEFA officials to distraction. This pleasing spirit of mild rebellion spread to the ITV staff sent out to cover the visits to Villareal of Everton, Rangers, Inter Milan and Arsenal. Ahead of every single visit we put in a formal request to interview

Diego Forlán, for the simple reason that he spoke immaculate English and was well known to British football fans after his spell at Old Trafford. But, on almost every occasion, we were denied by the club. Undeterred, we simply approached him anyway, as he walked off the pitch from the eve-of-match public training session, usually only open to the press for a quarter of an hour, but, in the case of Villareal, open throughout, because they couldn't find you if you hid well enough.

Poor Diego began to expect it and would anticipate the moment we'd spring from behind a pillar and spirit him away to some broom cupboard where we'd set up. 'Ah, hello, ITV,' and he'd wander off with us to say nice things about British football, while simultaneously scheming to end the European prospects of whichever club had turned up in Villareal.

But of all the visits, it was the Everton play-off match that had the most impact on me. On a warm night, a seething mass of blue-clad Merseysiders, intent on cheering their team home, leapt as one when Duncan Ferguson flew both vertically and horizontally with a geometry-defying angle of attack, and bowed that impressively structured head towards the ball, compelling it by sheer, frightening physics into the back of the Villareal net.

But the joy turned almost immediately to outrage as referee Pierluigi Collina, a man with a fierce reputation, saw a foul that no one else saw and disallowed the goal.

Just before the ref blew for half time, I made my way into the cramped, tiled, tunnel area to observe at close quarters the players making their way into the dressing rooms. This was often extremely revealing, as their pre-match poker-faced guard had by now melted away. The last two protagonists to leave the pitch were Ferguson and then, a little after him, Collina. In fact, Ferguson, instead of heading to the dressing room, waited just inside the tunnel area for the Italian to appear.

'Hey, big man!' he bellowed. 'Big man!'

The world's most famous referee stopped and then slowly approached Ferguson, glaring, but saying nothing. That prompted the

Scot to unleash a full and frank tirade straight into Collina's angular face, until the two of them were virtually nose to nose. Godzilla v King Kong. I found myself transfixed as pure Glaswegian filth filled the hot air inside the tunnel. Then Phil Neville, or someone grown up from the Everton squad, appeared out of the shadows to prise Ferguson away from the brink of a lengthy UEFA ban.

*****

Not often did we get a glimpse of what went on away from the floodlit public spectacle, in the dark corners of these organically ill-designed stadiums. But every now and again, a Champions League door would be left ajar just enough for me to catch a glimpse, as I did of José Mourinho, towards the end of his time as Chelsea manager, leaving the dressing room at his old club, Porto, and indiscreetly confiding to the grizzled ex-army security detail who'd been posted at the door: 'That was the worst half of football they have ever played for me.' The security guy just nodded at him. 'SO bad.'

Mostly, though, such contact as we had with the clubs were restricted to the day before the match and to the immediate post-match mêlée during which we scrambled to get comments from as many of the relevant names as we could.

In 2007, Liverpool made it to the final again and renewed their acquaintance with AC Milan. In the build-up to this re-match, I was asked to write a big booming poem (that tired genre, again!) about courage and revenge which would open the show. I accepted the challenge with enthusiastic pomposity. The resultant short film was then duly narrated by the Hollywood star and Liverpool fan, Clive Owen, who I'd actually never heard of and confused with some bloke from *Dad's Army*. We filmed Owen reciting my words in the velvet seats of an old cinema in Harwich. This gig he did in exchange for free tickets to the match in Athens, though on the night of the final he never bothered checking into the grotesquely expensive hotel suite ITV had booked for him, preferring instead to crash on some mate's yacht in Piraeus.

At the opposite end of the glamour spectrum to Clive Owen was Jamie Carragher. About a week before the 2007 final, we travelled to Melwood training ground to interview him about the game. He was typically Carragher-esque and funny, recounting how his mates from home used to give him stick for owning a wallet when he first started earning a rich-man's wage. 'Nobody from Bootle ever had a wallet. And there was me with a wallet!'

'Do you have one now, Jamie?'

'No, look!' He hauled a gold credit card out of his tracksuit trousers and a dirty tenner.

When that interview finished, I asked Carragher if we could jump in his car and if he wouldn't mind giving us a quick guided tour of the streets he grew up in.

'Sure, no bother lads,' he answered. And yet it wasn't going to be that simple.

'Sorry, hang on.' We looked around. Liverpool's long-serving press officer, who'd been present in the room all the time suddenly intervened. 'When was this agreed?'

I looked at Carragher, who looked back at the press officer.

'Er, just now,' I told him.

'You know the rules, Ned. I can't allow that.'

'Right…' I replied, hastily trying to imagine what rules he meant.

He explained. 'If I let you do this, what will Sky say to me? Geoff Shreeves would never let it go.'

There was an uncomfortable silence in the room. Then Carragher left.

'Sorry, Jamie.' I said to his retreating back.

'No worries,' he said, without looking around. I think it was the last time I spoke to him.

*****

The 2008 final between Manchester United and Chelsea is locked away somewhere deep in my Champions League subconscious.

It was a dark, tortured affair. Even before we got underway there was something naggingly petty about the distant encounter between two English clubs which even the sunny superstar disposition of CR7 struggled to dispel. Back at Manchester United's Carrington training ground four or five days before the match, I'd been granted a one-minute audience with the Portuguese who'd just notched 42 goals for the season and was bound for Real Madrid. He'd nearly swerved it completely, but I'd intercepted him as he tried to scarper.

'Where will you be at the start of next season, Cristiano?' I'd hastily enquired, before my seconds counted me out. He stood by the changing rooms, his boots laced together and slung over his shoulder.

'Only God knows this,' CR7 laughed breezily, in a Ronaldo kind of a way.

'Only God,' I concurred, with an anxious press officer honing into my field of vision. 'And your agent,' I added at speed before he was spirited away.

For some reason, the Manchester United midfielder found that to be enormously funny.

'And my agent!!' he repeated. And then he strolled away from the camera, still shaking his head with mirth. I watched him go and tried vainly to imagine what it must feel like to be Cristiano Ronaldo, aged 23, about to leave for Real Madrid, on a quarter of a million pounds a week and with a decade and more of imperious genius ahead of him.

But before Madrid came Moscow; a fittingly serious backdrop to a game that confirmed the ascendancy of the Premier League to a temporary top spot in the world's pecking order.

I can remember this: once again it was close to two in the morning when the shoot-out began. Gabriel Clarke was detailed with interviewing whichever team ended up winning and I, being the junior reporter, was to be handed the losers. As the fortunes of both teams fluctuated during the shoot-out, Gabriel and I began a laughable choreography, running through the torrential rain to take our place behind whichever bench we thought would be ours, and then criss-crossing backwards as another penalty was saved.

After John Terry's moment of ultimate hubris, slipping on the Russian turf, all I am left with is snapshot memories: Frank Lampard wretchedly departing the scene, the match coming too soon after his mother's death. And the loneliness of Avram Grant, the manager the Chelsea players scarcely acknowledged, without his coat and with frigid Russian rainwater soaking through his grey suit to his skin, looking more like a depressed mortician than ever.

I interviewed him live on the pitch and, as I fully expected, was instructed via my earpiece to ask him if he now thought he would be sacked. This is the football reporter's ground zero question; impossible for the manager in question to respond to, yet, for almost all viewers at home, the only question they want you to ask if they are entirely honest with themselves. So, I had to ask him.

He gazed back at me with great sadness. In fact, there was such a long pause that I could hear the raindrops hammering down onto the foam covering of my microphone. I briefly wondered whether he'd actually understood and was about to ask him the question again, when he muttered something almost inaudible that sounded like, 'It's not my choice,' and then walked away, accompanied by his press officer scowling back at me and shaking his head in quiet fury. I wouldn't see Grant for another two years and never again in the Champions League.

The night ended with a long wait for transport back to our central Moscow hotel outside the Luzhniki Stadium. So long, in fact, that I gave up and started to walk along the Savvinskaya Embankment, only to find that Mark Hughes had decided to follow me and a few of us trudged back together.

As Hughes and I strolled surreally and mostly wordlessly along the dark waters of the Moskva, all I could think about was the guilt I had felt at watching Hughes playing for Manchester United on TV in the European Cup Winners' Cup in 1991, when I should have been revising for my finals. But that ancient memory, and all that it contained, wasn't worth bothering him with. I doubt he'd have cared much.

This was a crazy job I was doing. The Champions League was a crazy place to live.

19

Fick FUFA

SOUTH AFRICA 1-1 MEXICO.
11 June, 2010. Soccer City, Johannesburg.

In which little changes.

A day before the first match of South Africa 2010, I was in a van approaching the centre of Johannesburg.

As the traffic slowed on one of the arterial motorways, I noticed a newspaper headline being held aloft by a street vendor in the middle of the road. It simply read, in bold capital letters that took up the entire front page: 'FICK FUFA!' I laughed out loud, asked the driver to pull over and picked a copy up from the seller.

Even from a long way out, this World Cup had been destined to be different from any that had gone before it. It was a tournament that had the potential to turn the football world, if not the world itself, on its head. Geostationary satellites normally positioned above the population and economic hubs of Europe and North America had to be painstakingly repositioned in the deep, dark night skies above Durban, Cape Town, Pretoria and Johannesburg, that low-rise sprawling city of millions spread wide and flat on the altitudinous plateau at the heart of the country – portentous land, overhung with vast skies.

There was widespread trepidation in the minds of football's European custodians about what the reality of a World Cup in the 'murder capital of the world', as the media often liked to refer to Joburg, might look like. So it was that, weeks before we all departed, many of our colleagues from the BBC were sent off for some form of on-site battle training at a derelict airfield near somewhere like Maidstone. It was the kind of place where ex-soldiers delight in jumping out from behind toilet blocks screaming, 'Get down!', before passive-aggressively pointing out to some traumatised production junior that they'd have been disembowelled by now with a carving knife. We at ITV couldn't afford such an immersive experience, so instead we had a meeting in the canteen. That would have to do, as we prepared for battle.

Our security budget stretched to an ex-army bloke telling us that we were to trust no one. He just stopped short of predicting that only 50 per cent of us could expect to return alive. For the big finale, we were each handed a bright pink baseball cap, which we were to keep with us at all time. If for whatever reason we felt threatened, we should simply, calmly, put the ridiculous hat on and await help. 'We'll have eyes on you at all times and will interpret that signal as an SOS. At that point we will initiate an aggressive exit strategy, eliminate the threat and remove you from harm's way,' I think was the gist of it.

Under the vivid winter skies of South Africa, we set off for what would be our base for the duration of the tournament. Just north of Johannesburg and south of Pretoria lay an isolated hotel complex, owned by some absent landlord and run by a hard-pressed staff who, over many weeks of enforced cohabitation, we got to know. It was dripping with faded colonial grandeur, a collection of more or less run-down rooms set in extensive grounds that smelt of wild garlic, and were populated by peacocks and other slowly patrolling fowl. No respecters of the game, the various birds would defecate all over a hotel golf course which was slowly going to seed.

The mornings were bright and frosty, but by 10 o'clock a fierce sun had lifted the temperature to the low 20s. And every day the weather was the same. As the tournament grew close we started to make a film about how a cross-section of different groups within South Africa's disparate and still deeply uneven population were preparing for the first World Cup on African soil. To do this, we went into Soweto, the historical heart of the ANC and the anti-apartheid movement, and home to over a million mostly extremely football-literate residents; noisy fans of the Orlando Pirates and the Kaizer Chiefs.

We had arranged with a typical 'shebeen' bar in the heart of the township that we would film the reaction of their customers watching South Africa's opening match against Mexico. It was deemed necessary that our security presence was doubled by the addition of a pair of English ex-soldiers. Arriving, as we did, in an excitingly driven but probably unnecessary convoy of two minivans, one of our extra bodyguards decided to open the big sliding door at the side of the vehicle as we swept into the quiet neighbourhood in which the Sowetans were gearing up for their party. He then disembarked the van before it had stopped moving, as if exiting a helicopter, and proceeded to flick his head from left to right to scout out the terrain. Looking out of our windows, we could feel a hundred pairs of eyes watching this elaborate exit manoeuvre with confusion and distaste.

South Africa 2010 got off to a quite wonderful start, though. Sitting among the tightly packed, cheerfully raucous rows of Bafana Bafana fans on benches in the dark back room of the shebeen, we watched the home team grow in confidence, urged on by the drone of vuvuzelas.

Ten minutes into the second half, South Africa broke with the ball, moving at speed over the half-way line before a perfect pass found the feet of the onrushing Siphiwe Tshabalala. And everyone stood up. It went quiet. Now with only the keeper to beat and a continent (it was notable how African nations drew together in solidarity) holding its breath Tshabalala, a 26-year-old from Soweto, took two touches and then thundered his perfect shot past the Mexican keeper.

The net blew out behind him as the ball's trajectory triggered an explosion of noise in our tight little backroom, on the streets around us, across Soweto and beyond. Tshabalala wheeled away in triumph, his arms outstretched, his fingers trawling the hot air and cutting through the sudden noise that engulfed him. Instantly, he became the only story in South Africa. Lawrence Siphiwe Dambuza Tshabalala had gained the status of a national hero in the length of time it took him to lift his left leg and then boot the opening goal of the tournament.

The following morning, we went off in search of Tshabalala's background story. This time, mercifully, we could go about our work without our elaborate security detail and usefully accompanied only by our local security guys, Kevin and John, who were conversant in all of the African languages spoken in Soweto, along with English and Afrikaans. This self-evidently proved itself to be of exceptional value when travelling around the township trying to forge contacts. Before long we found ourselves sitting in the Tshabalala family home in the Sowetan district of Phiri.

It was a brick-built house, which must have been filled to bursting the night before with all sorts of family, friends and general hangers-on. We spoke to Tshabalala's silver-haired, chair-bound grandfather, his mother, his sister, as well as a range of others, all of whom expressed the same intoxicating mixture of unbridled astonishment and touching pride at what their boy had achieved. To be witnessing at first hand the transformational power of a single strike of a football felt like what it was: a rare privilege. The Tshabalala family's collective shock and awe at how their name had been catapulted into such a stellar place banished temporarily the wintry oddness and simmering unfairness of Africa's first World Cup.

For this was an awkward truth. The tournament looked, sounded and felt strangely disconnected. This was not the kind of World Cup that the world was used to. On the evidence of what we had seen in the week leading up to the start, this event was far removed from the summery jamboree of European or Latin American squares, filled with colourful flags, dancers, drummers and the occasional English plastic chair throwers. For a start, the evenings were bitterly cold, which discouraged outdoor partying so that, as the sun dipped down and kick-off times drew closer, the nation hunkered down. South Africa, still haunted in the extreme by racial and socio-economic inequalities, enjoyed little street life at the best of times. Its café and bar culture, certainly in the white community, was very much tucked away. And white folk almost never went into the townships. Add to that the fact that football, as a sport, was alien to the majority of the cricket-loving or Springbok-supporting white population, it became evident that lip service was being paid to football's importance in at least part of the nation's life.

Even in football-besotted Soweto, there was scant evidence of a nation taking a month off to dance in the streets and cheer every goal. In fact, were it not for the standard proliferation of FIFA-sanctioned advertising, as well as the usual football-bombing of every single visible commercial enterprise, you could have been forgiven for not knowing that there was a World Cup in progress at all. This might have had something to do with the necessities of life – holding down a job, looking for a job, getting by, feeding the family and staying well. Such things actually eclipse football.

We had just finished filming the last of the interviews for our mini-film with the ponderous working title, *In Search Of Tshabalala*, and were saying our goodbyes, when one of his uncles collared me.

'Do you think it is possible for Siphiwe to play in England?' he asked, as I loaded up some of the camera equipment into the back of the van. He looked earnestly at me. I'd never been asked anything like that before. Outside his family home, I stopped and thought.

There are plenty of football broadcasters who are on texting terms with multiple football managers, but I wasn't one of them. In fact, I knew none well enough to call up or text, with one exception. Avram Grant, no longer at Chelsea, had just guided Portsmouth FC to an FA Cup Final. I knew him a bit.

A few weeks previously, before the FA Cup Final, and only after careful negotiations, I had flown with a film crew to Israel, where we had spent two surprisingly emotional days with Grant. We'd filmed at his old football club and at the flat he'd grown up in with his holocaust-survivor father, who had only recently passed away. We'd accompanied Grant to various locations and interviewed his famous wife, Tzufit, who was the host of a massively popular late-night TV show in Israel that involved her, for no discernible reason, sitting naked in a bathtub full of beans and drinking her own urine. The visit to Tel Aviv with Grant had been memorable. He'd even bought me a falafel wrap. Now I found myself standing by the side of an unmade road in Soweto sending him a text.

'Hi Avram. Are you interested in signing Siphiwe Tshabalala for Portsmouth?' I found myself writing. 'If so, I can help,' I added, mysteriously. Who did I think I was? Grant was personal friends with the super-agent Pini Zahavi, the man who'd fed the world's super clubs with hyper-inflated players for a decade. I was just a persistently annoying bloke from ITV Sport. I put my phone in my pocket.

I told Tshabalala's relative that I would do my best for Siphiwe, which was all I could do. And as we drove at dusk from Soweto through the endlessly streaming traffic around Johannesburg's darkening centre and back to our hotel, I gradually forgot about the whole charade of trying to broker an international move to the Premier League for a star of the World Cup. It was only when my phone lit up with a message that the altered reality of my situation came back again to surprise me. It was Grant.

'Maybe that's interesting for us.' I gazed at the message, wondering what my next move should be. 'I am in the States on holiday now,' he added. 'I'll contact you. Thank you.' I pictured Grant on a Florida sunbed.

Sadly, this was to be our final communication on the subject. There would have been something perfectly suited to the 21st-century Premier League if Tshabalala had turned up at Fratton Park under the tutelage of Israel's greatest ever manager, but the move never came about.

*****

South Africa spread out before us. With Gabriel Clarke once again on England duty, I was free to chase around the place seeking out all the other stuff that makes World Cups so special.

This TV *libero* role had been created at the England-less Euro 2008. With a less partisan approach to the competition, Gabriel and I had both been free to flit through Switzerland, visit Austrian monasteries, where they'd recorded inspirational football-themed Gregorian chants, spend endless days stalking Guus Hiddink (in charge of Russia at the time), chase Turkey's Kazim-Richards, admire the fabulous haircuts of Spain's golden generation and embark on a month-long and ultimately successful mission to track down and interview Austria's retired all-time greatest-ever-goalscorer-turned-*Austria's-Got-Talent* crooner and designer of truly ghastly leisurewear, Toni Polster.

I'd loved working at Euro 2008 and two years on, in South Africa, I was similarly cut free. Thrillingly, the tournament offered up a chance to renew my acquaintance with the German national team. Shortly before England were due to play them in the last 16, I paid my first visit to their remote training camp in an absurdly well-appointed hotel. We'd turned up at the compound at least two hours too early.

Hotel catering staff had just started to set out coffee cups, though as yet there was no sign of any actual coffee to put in them. Hesitantly addressing one lady as she set out rows of empty saucers, I asked whether there was anywhere I could get a coffee while we waited. She thought about it for a second and then indicated that I should follow her.

She and I left the media waiting room via a fire escape at the back. Following her lead, I walked from annexe to annexe, crossing beautifully manicured courtyards filled by jacaranda and lemon trees, up mysteriously designed sets of staircases, until eventually we reached a landing which was faced at the far end from where we stood by a single, imposing closed wooden door. She indicated with a smile that that was my final destination.

'You can get coffee in there,' she said. I thanked her and opened the door.

My eyes took a second to adjust to the light. Lukas Podolski sat at a computer terminal. Sebastian Schweinsteiger and Philipp Lahm sprawled on expensively upholstered couches, while Joachim Löw was standing up, reading a paper spread out on a table. They all looked up at me and the room fell very silent.

'*Was tun Sie denn hier?*' asked the mop-topped German national head coach, posing the legitimate question as to what I thought I was doing there.

I breezily explained in hastily reactivated German how I ended up there on the premise of getting a coffee. I looked at the coffee machine on the table, a few feet from where Löw was standing, showing increasing signs of anxiety. I contemplated, for a split second, styling it out and brazenly striding towards my goal, as if it were an inalienable right and the most natural thing in the world, before deciding on a more conservative approach. It was the sight of two massively-built security guards starting to move towards me, and the sound of Podolski telling me in a fluent Cologne dialect to piss off, that persuaded me of the best course of action. I took flight the same way I had come in, apologising in a foreign language as I went.

Given the nuisances that we'd severally made of ourselves, I suspect the German football association was hugely relieved when that particular match was over, and England's players went home to pore over Fabio Capello's honest evaluation of them and see what they could learn from the benefit of the £14 million of total Capello wisdom that the FA had invested in their prospects for success. Despite the injustice of Frank Lampard's disallowed goal, England fans knew, deep down, that the golden generation was a bust flush. This had been an England exit that had meant curiously little to me. From the moment the team had underwhelmed against the USA in their opening game, they seemed preordained to disappoint, but this time not even with the usual accompanying contortions of frustration.

For us, in our little broadcast bubble, the big discomfort of that first England match had been ITV's HD service cutting to a commercial break just before Gerrard's goal. It was an error that heaped abuse on our heads from media and supporters alike. ITV had been seen to fail once more and England were a bit rubbish again, which statistically they always were on ITV, as the BBC's Dan Walker delighted in confirming on Twitter. This time we watched England grind to a halt with something like resignation, or even satisfaction. It was arid, tedious. Actually, it was uninteresting.

A few days later, we filmed a piece about FIFA's capricious official Jabulani football, in which Adrian Chiles, Andy Townsend and a few others had all kicked the ball at Peter Drury in a jumpers-for-goalposts goal on a piece of wasteland behind the International Broadcast centre.

After we had completed our pleasantly daft bit of telly, over a coffee I'd talked to Gareth Southgate about this England team. Southgate was a newly signed part of the ITV team in South Africa and a man I'd instantly liked. I remember asking him, the first time we met as colleagues, if he missed being at a football club? 'You have no idea, Ned, how good it is to spend time with people who have other things in their lives. I've been immersed in football since I was a child.' It was an unusual take for an ex-player and I noted it.

Quite what had happened, I asked Southgate in South Africa, to the connection between the country and its football team? I felt it was broken. I remember being surprised, as I moaned on at him, that he didn't seem to feel the same. Though he could understand my ennui, he was genuinely upset by England's exit. I noted that too, I think.

*****

Weeks later, the tournament started to narrow down. By the time the quarter-finals came around, just one African nation was left – Ghana. Solving substantial logistical problems, our camera team flew across the continent to the Ghanaian capital, Accra, to film a background piece on the country's build-up to the big match against Luis Suárez's Uruguay.

Landing in Accra at midnight we were met by a local fixer who breezily collected our passports, none of which contained the correct visas, and reappeared with them a few minutes later, as he ushered us smilingly through no passport checks whatsoever. The following morning we spent all day out and about in the seriously ambitious and busy capital city, pushing through markets and public squares getting misunderstood, welcomed, questioned and, occasionally, lightly threatened. Later in that extraordinary day, filming a sunset on a beach near Accra, a young-ish man appeared from absolutely nowhere and made his way over to our little crew, with a joint smouldering in his right hand, no shoes and hair that was exploding skywards.

'Excuse me,' he'd said, having correctly divined that we were something to do with the World Cup. 'Can you please help me to get a place on one of the football teams in England? I am not perhaps at the level for the Premier League, but certainly for the Championship. I am a very, very good player. I think maybe Ipswich or Blackburn Rovers.'

This was his parting suggestion of how I might help further his career, before giving me his email address then drifting off back to his tent, drawing heavily on his weed, whose sweet smoke enveloped us in unreality.

*****

Back in South Africa, friendships within our little team of sound engineers, satellite truck operators, fixers and in particular security guards deepened as we got to know each other. Kevin and John, our security guards, became good friends, at least for as long as the tournament lasted.

As the weeks rolled on, John told us his story. A short man in his early 40s, with a fairly substantial belly and a cryptic smile, he had been born in Matabeleland in Zimbabwe. He was raised in an Ndebele family, an ethnic group that makes up a fifth of the population and has historically been on the wrong end of aggression from the Shona ruling party ZANU-PF, headed by Robert Mugabe. It is fair to say that John hated Mugabe with homicidal passion.

Day by day, more of his extraordinary story emerged. He had left Zimbabwe as a teenager after his older brother had been lynched and murdered by ZANU-PF thugs. From there he had become a mercenary soldier, teaming up with some of the nastiest operators the apartheid years had ever spawned, in particular Eugene de Kock, the South African Police counter-insurgency commander who went by the nickname, Prime Evil. De Kock was sentenced in 1996 to 212 years in prison for crimes against humanity. On a free day during the week leading up to the final, we all visited Joburg's remarkable Apartheid Museum. In the gift shop I came across John perusing the bookshelves. He was picking titles off the shelf and leafing through the colour plates. To his noisy delight, he found a picture of himself with his old unit standing in front of a chopper, all gathered around de Kock. He came bustling over to show me. 'Look, look,' he pointed. 'It's me!' He seemed weirdly proud. I suggested he put the book back and we leave.

But John had been retired a long time. And in the post-apartheid years, based now in Cape Town, he had started working on a plan to assassinate Mugabe. It had, if he were to be believed, been worked out to a very detailed level, but had never (obviously) reached fulfilment. The tales he told were completely unverifiable, but packed with the kind of astonishing detail that again made this curiously unengaging football tournament seem less and less relevant, and more and more like an expensive distraction, just a plaster to put over the world's deep running sores. He spoke of crossing from Botswana in the dead of night, executing border guards, grooming members of Mugabe's palace staff to collaborate, planned poisonings, smuggled satellite phones into countries and alleged secret meetings in Cape Town with Jack Straw when he was Foreign Secretary. It was extraordinary to listen to. Writing it down now it appears completely bizarre. But it is what he told us, true or false.

As the final drew close, news broke that Mugabe himself was to be among the list of VVIP dignitaries in attendance. Roger, our cameraman, unhesitatingly shared this information with John.

'But I do not have a gun,' was his considered reply. 'I will have to break his neck with a monkey jump.'

None of us knew what a monkey jump was. Roger, who was due to be filming pitch-side from behind one of the goals, asked only that John and he should agree an exact time at which the political assassination would take place. That way he would be the only cameraman in the world who happened to be filming the VIP box at that moment and not Andrés Iniesta.

Disappointingly, perhaps, when the day of the bad-tempered final between the Netherlands and Spain dawned, John had gently dropped his much-vaunted ambition to 'monkey jump' Africa's most notorious dictator.

Roger never got his scoop and Mugabe survived.

*****

I wasn't in the stadium either. I had already said my goodbyes to the remainder of the team. The six weeks I had spent in South Africa had been chastening, enlivening and not always comfortable. And now they were done, I had been released from football duty and was about to board a flight from Joburg to London, then on to France where I would immediately hook up with my colleagues on the Tour de France production to join the race a week late. At the airport awaiting the same flight home as me was ITV's commentator Peter Drury. As we settled into our seats for the long journey home, the captain came over the intercom, welcoming us on board and reassuring us all that he'd be keeping abreast of the developments in the World Cup Final, which was about to kick off.

'I'll let you know over the tannoy as the goals go in.'

Suddenly, from the row in front of me, Peter Drury piped up. Football's irrepressible enthusiast, the son of a vicar and one of the nicest, most positively-inclined colleagues I have ever worked with, shouted, at the top of his goal-celebrating commentator's voice, 'Don't care! Don't care!' Then, for the avoidance of doubt, he added, 'Couldn't care less!'

From my seat behind, I howled with laughter. It seemed absurd, but I knew what he meant. There was the nagging sense that football had overstretched itself, and that the marketing myths of the global game sending a world into simultaneous rapture and smiling delight were exposed for what they were, when they had to live alongside the real injustices of poverty and opportunity that the host country and the host continent has to contend with on a daily, hourly, minute-by-minute basis. No amount of Lionel Messi's mazy head-down, loose-limbed runs were ever going to rewrite the present trauma of poverty, injustice and disease. That task was too great. Even for Messi.

As, eventually, I drifted off to sleep with the news of Iniesta's goal crackling through the intercom, I mulled over Peter's sudden and very funny outburst. It was true. I didn't care either. Maybe it was the drone of vuvuzelas, England's stodginess, the silly dip and swerve of the lightweight Jabulani ball that had beaten so many keepers, the French in mutiny and Luis Suárez cheating Ghana and a whole continent. I could remember almost no games that excited any wonder in me, only frustration. The final fell into line with the generalised torpor.

And yet, when I think back, there'll always be Siphiwe Tshabalala's opening shot. That's the last thing I saw before I fell asleep on the plane. That goal and a brief surge of happiness, like a straw fire on a dark night, before the winter closed in around us.

20

Euro Exit

ITALY 2–0 REPUBLIC OF IRELAND.
18 June, 2012. Municipal Stadium, Poznań.

In which the spark goes out.

Throughout my very English childhood, we had spent a good portion of our summer holidays with my Irish grandmother who, by the 1970s, had retired to a bungalow just south of Dublin. We idled the days away as she chain-smoked John Player Specials and slowly inked in the *Times* crossword while her dachshund howled. I loved these trips and saw Dad again in a different context – his slightly Irish one, and a son, not just a dad. Always Dad changed, according to where he was and who he was with.

Half of my father's family are Irish and, as a result, I was first given an Irish passport at the age of about 12. It was a big one with a harp on the front and the four letters EIRE stamped in gold-embossed characters. I remember being fascinated by the printed Irish-language exhortations to the serried peoples of the world that I might be treated with respect. I was, and still am, at least in the passport-related sense of the word, an Irish citizen, and have never once been the holder of any other nation's identity document, despite actually being as British as a rain-streaked bus station precinct featuring a branch of WH Smith. Not everyone has a football club. Not everyone has a clear-cut national identity.

Mum and Dad had met each other for the first time outside Lansdowne Road stadium after a match, both being students in Dublin at the time. Family legend has it that Dad approached his destiny swinging a bottle of whiskey around, which apparently had made him seem attractive. I'd always had a strong imagination of Dad's time in Dublin as a young man and fed greedily on the scraps of conversational reminiscence he'd toss our way from time to time when he was feeling nostalgic. Most of these centred on sinking pints, entering and occasionally winning meat raffles, and playing carefree darts at a pub called Scruffy Murphy's near the canal in the centre of town, while the swollen corpses of drowned cattle turned over in the river on their gentle seaward trajectory. Sometimes he'd run out of money and be forced to write informal letters to his estranged, famous father, who'd simply reply, 'How much?'

Once, during the Easter holidays when I was a student, on a whim I had hitchhiked all the way to Dublin from a friend's house in Norwich and then called Dad using reverse charges on a payphone from his old pub. 'Guess where I am, Dad?' I'd said, over a crackling line all the way back to the living room in Bedford where I could suddenly picture him frowning. I told him, expecting him to be delighted, 'Scruffy Murphy's.'

'What are you doing there?' was all he had to say. He sounded underwhelmed by my adventure. Perhaps he knew that I'd run out of money a few days later and would phone him again to ask for a sub. But that wasn't the point, isn't the point. The point is this: I don't feel like I belong in Ireland.

One of the very worst things that an English person can do is to exaggerate Irish heritage. Never did I feel more English than sitting in a pub in Bray, listening to my aunt's quite extremely Republican friends talk about the enemy over the water, while the music played. To be a 'plastic paddy' is arguably the most disingenuous identity one can assume as it seeks to retain the inbuilt sense of British self-assuredness while simultaneously benefitting from the rich cultural heritage of the Irish – a deep fake. Yet there was a secret bit of me that I couldn't admit to, which craved association with the land that had accounted for a quarter of my genetic inheritance. An inarticulate little bit of me still wanted to be accepted by the nation of my dad's birth.

*****

Of course, I kept all this nonsense quiet when I was in the company of Roy Keane.

In 2011, the former Ireland captain had suddenly revoked his avowed intention never to sit in a TV studio as a pundit by joining ITV in order to sit in a TV studio as a pundit. I had been warned that Keane could suddenly snap. 'You won't see it coming and you will have no idea why it happened.'

I had that warning very much in mind as I watched him out of the corner of my eye the first time we shared a TV production room, hours before we went on air for the Champions League Final between Barcelona and Manchester United, which was to be Keane's TV debut.

I recalled coming face to face with him many years before that at White Hart Lane. The front row of the press seating used to be right behind the back row of the opposition benches, where Keane was sitting. A very young Cristiano Ronaldo had just flaunted a bewilderingly elaborate display of step-overs (rare and exotic things back then), before falling over, and it had made me laugh involuntarily out loud. Keane had whipped around in his seat to stare at me from a distance of maybe three feet. I hadn't forgotten that look in a hurry.

But, as part of our TV broadcast, a very different character began to emerge. Keane had a dry, laid-back wit and was surprisingly curious about the work we television types did. From time to time, he made us stop in our tracks with an unexpected observation.

On the day of a Champions League match in Milan, I ended up having an early lunch in a trattoria with him. He asked me what I'd been getting up to the previous day, when he'd been twiddling his thumbs, impatiently waiting for kick-off the next day. I told him I'd filmed the press conference, and then I'd been given a short one-to-one interview with the manager and one player.

'Why don't you interview them this morning?' Keane had looked up at me from across his spaghetti carbonara. 'The morning of the game, it'd be better, don't you think?'

'It's match day, Roy.' I was astonished that such a basic rule needed explaining. 'It's not allowed. They won't speak to the media because they're "in the zone" or whatever.'

'Crap. All the players do is hang around getting bored, watching videos.' He loaded a spoonful of pasta into his mouth and took a gulp of sparkling mineral water, then fixed me with that intense look. 'I would have done interviews on the morning of a match. But no one ever asked.'

'Seriously?' I looked at him in puzzlement, fascinated by his claim, and trying to work out if he meant it or not. 'You'd have given us an interview?'

There was a pause while the former United skipper chewed and thought. Another swig of water. 'Nah, I'd have probably told you to fuck off to be fair.'

He was full of tiny surprises and unexpectedly good company when he wanted to be. On a couple of occasions he would treat us to his riveting and very acutely observed account of the explosive moment his Manchester United career came to an end. It involved swearing, shouting, an overhead projector, more swearing, and Ryan Giggs 'ghosting up alongside him' as he jogged around the Carrington training ground on his own to tell him he needed to pack his stuff and leave. Every time he dusted the story off for the telling, he'd have us spellbound. He was still Roy Keane with all the aura you might imagine might attach to that name.

On the eve of the 2012 Champions League Final we had finished dinner in a Munich hotel and were amusing ourselves in the bar by playing a game called 'Where Were You When Southgate Missed?' in the presence of Gareth Southgate, who good-naturedly answered, 'London.' As we all headed for bed, a few of us were making plans to meet early for a run the following morning. Southgate suggested meeting at 7.30 in the hotel lobby.

Keane's ears pricked up. '7.30?' he asked.

'You're not coming are you, Roy?' asked the future England manager, who had once famously been on the receiving end of an on-pitch and fairly violent stamp from the Irishman. Southgate looked concerned. 'You don't run, do you?' Keane often proudly told us that he hadn't run a step since retirement.

'I'll be there,' he warned.

And he was. Even though he was a few minutes late and we were all about to set off without him, there appeared the dread sight of Roy Keane in shorts and running kit, sauntering menacingly down the stairs to the foyer to join us. And so, in cowed silence, and with a watchful eye on the Irishman, we set off.

But, to our collective astonishment and relief, Keane gave up the run after a couple of fairly plodding miles and walked on his own along a river path back to the hotel, muttering something about how boring and pointless it was unless you had a dog or two to exercise.

Later that afternoon, I found myself sitting in a back-room worker's café at the Allianz Arena trying to entertain Keane and Gianfranco Zola. I'd simply suggested we get a coffee as they both looked as bored as I was. It was still hours before kick-off. Unexpectedly, they'd accepted the offer. What made the situation still more surreal was the growing realisation that Keane and Zola had never really met, a fact I found fundamentally absurd. The conversation between two of the greatest players ever to lace up boots for Manchester United and Chelsea respectively was stilted, almost to the point of non-existence.

Keane was evidently still brooding about the morning's run. 'Do you go out running a lot?' he asked me, with that same disarming curiosity I'd come across before.

'Yes,' I told him. 'A fair bit.'

Keane continued to mull it over. It must have been chastening to have been beaten by Gareth Southgate, me, Andy Townsend and Adrian Chiles, in that order. But that was the harsh truth.

'I don't like running out and back, like this morning. It's boring. I prefer going from A to B.' he said. 'I like to have a target to aim at.'

'What,' chipped in Zola, suddenly. 'Like an ankle?'

Keane dropped his teaspoon, went suddenly pale and jabbed a finger at the little Italian who sat smiling opposite him. 'What the fuck does that mean?'

'You liked a tackle, Roy,' said Zola, looking less certain now. 'Just saying.'

'Listen, I could play, a bit, you know?' he glared intently across the table. In an instant the atmosphere had changed. 'Just cos you were like "Mr Fucking Silky Skills". I could play football too, you know,' he concluded, before adding, 'I was a fucking football player.'

The conversation went quiet for some time after that. Then, out of nowhere, the pair somehow started to talk animatedly about London house prices and I could zone out from taking any further part or shouldering any responsibility. It had been one of the strangest half hours of my life.

*****

Later that summer I found out I was to be 'embedded' with the Irish national team for their brief and hapless appearance at Euro 2012, hosted jointly by Poland and Ukraine. I didn't know it at the time, but these were to be my last years working in football and this my final international tournament.

The word 'embedded', of course, is borrowed from the world of news reportage. My filmmaking grandfather, John, had been embedded with the RAF Film Unit during the war, but it's something I more immediately associate with excitable correspondents running around Baghdad in flak jackets generally getting in the way of heavily armed professional soldiers. Perhaps it was no different for my grandfather in 1942, but the notion that these reporters are really in on anything secret or confidential is transparently far-fetched. It just seems like the army give them a packed lunch and tell them where to stand. In this regard, it is not so different with football.

The Republic's team in 2012 was managed, astonishingly, by Giovanni Trapattoni. Under his bizarre leadership Ireland's qualification had been by the skin of their teeth. Hopes of emulating the rollicking greatness of the Jack Charlton years were muted all the more when it was revealed that they'd be in a group with the collective brilliance of Croatia, Spain and Italy.

Once it had been established that I was going to be posted on Ireland duty for the duration of their stay in the tournament, and a week or two before the squad jetted off to their base near Gdańsk on the Baltic coast of Poland, we flew to Dublin to watch their final warm-up game at Lansdowne Road. We also wanted to introduce ourselves to the press department of the FAI with a view to establishing a good working relationship.

On the evening we arrived, we watched the Irish draw stodgily 1–1 against the Czech Republic. The mercurial James McClean made his debut for the national team. But apart from McClean, the team was populated by players I knew precious little about, like West Brom's Simon Cox, who scored the Republic's late equaliser. The lack of stardust and the general apathy in the ground, despite the very watchable histrionics from Trapattoni on the sideline, left an impression that there was something intangible missing from the heart of the affair. A sense of adventure, perhaps.

The following day, after the conclusion of a chaotic and ill-tempered post-match press conference at an airport hotel, in which Trapattoni had been charmingly unintelligible and the Irish press pack had been tetchy, we tried to sit down and talk about the upcoming summer tournament with the smoothly shaved, snappily suited press attaché. He seemed spectacularly unwilling to accommodate us. Wanting simply to introduce ourselves and discuss the summer to come, we were left with the overarching impression that ITV was an encumbrance he could do without.

When, a few weeks later, we all arrived in Sopot, the elegant little spa town where the Irish had their base, the cold shoulder towards British TV really kicked in. We were admitted into the general press conferences, but never allowed any individual access to any of the players or the staff. No amount of soothing talk or appealing to the better natures of the press office seemed to have the slightest effect and our delicate argument that the entire Ireland squad played either in England or Scotland seemed to have a negative effect, if it had any impact at all. Our repeated requests were an expression of British exceptionalism, I suppose, and I understood the resistance towards us from the FAI. But what was I to do? ITV expected more from their embedded reporter than a few distant shots of Robbie Keane in a training bib and a bland quote or two from Shay Given at a press conference.

We followed Ireland limply from defeat to defeat, each one with little sense that they were deserving of any better on the pitch. It was no disgrace, of course, to lose comprehensively to three such accomplished teams, but it wasn't fun. There were no Ray Houghton in New York moments.

During our weeks in Poland, Ireland, the Irish fans and our little team remained on the margins of a tournament that seemed to lack a centre. We were mostly holed up in a brand new hotel right on the Baltic, whose barely salty, hardly tidal waters lapped with a total lack of enthusiasm on the pristine sands of Sopot, where the Irish fans were camping en masse and along which I would run most mornings as I contemplated another day of banging my head against a green corporate wall of non-cooperation.

On one early morning run, after Poland had played the previous night, I was joined by a young Polish man with limited English, no shoes or socks and an astonishingly mismatched array of randomly chosen sportswear. He had also clearly not been to bed.

'Hello!' he'd gasped alcoholically at me after he'd leapt to his feet as I passed. 'Where are you from? Ireland?'

'London,' I said, preferring to think of myself as coming from a city rather than a country.

'London is great.' He panted alongside me, billowing clouds of pre-digested vodka and pickles. 'I am from Poland.'

'Are you?' I smiled across at him, at the exact point he tripped on an empty beer can, and fell instantly and violently face first into the sand.

'I have fallen suddenly!' he shouted by way of explanation as I ran on smiling.

England fell slowly. They bumpily rode their luck under the first of three increasingly hapless summers under Roy Hodgson. It became very clear that no amount of Andy Carroll's hair would be able to turn the tide of a global game that had its gaze fixed firmly on Barcelona and Madrid, and would probably never return. The combination of tiki-taka, high pressing and mesmerising skills were beginning to make the game resemble the rapidly evolving Playstation variants. It was changing faster than the video games themselves could replicate the real thing.

And then there was the branding. Euro 2012 felt saturated once more in a proliferation of licensed products and official endorsements. Wherever we pointed our cameras, there was another global corporation trying to muscle in on the game. Try as we might to present in our little films a cleaner version of the tournament, one that stripped away the contagious need for advertising car tyres, beer and TV sets at every possible encounter with football, we were beginning to find it impossible to frame out the multiplying logos.

We tried, though. We had a little trick. Conducting post-match interviews in our allotted area in the tunnel of a football ground, Roger, the ingenious cameraman, would bring in two cameras – a conventional one with a normal lens for the live TV show, and another one that didn't even look like a camera. It had a cunning lens. We used it to shoot interviews once ITV had gone off the air. This camera had, I was informed in painfully over-simplified layman's terms, a depth of focus that meant we could film a player talking, in sharp focus, but completely blur out the board behind, so that the logos appeared as a mottled mess. The result was an artsy backdrop of the kind used on high-end documentaries, rather than one that amounted to staring at the side of a Formula One car.

It was a small victory against the march of capitalism; piffling, really. But, amid the narrow constraints of UEFA regulations, and leaving the stadium behind us, shedding as we went our multitude of primary and secondary accreditations that enabled us to breathe the same air as Luka Modrić and his mates, we celebrated our small act of rebellion in the same spirit that kept Alec Guinness alive in his *Bridge On The River Kwai* hot box.

We got away with our tiny subversion for a couple of weeks, relaxed in the understanding that those elicit shots were being smuggled into features that were only broadcast back in the UK and were probably not accessible to anyone in Poland or Ukraine who wore a suit. And, besides, surely UEFA didn't care about such a trifle?

We were wrong. Though we continued to smuggle the special kit into matches, we started to become aware that the special camera was drawing increasingly obvious attention, in particular from a Scottish UEFA official who wore the same, frazzled, over-promoted look that was made into an archetype by Matt Hancock during the Covid-19 pandemic. He would walk past our position, very slowly, and eye-catchingly, slightly too often. From time to time he would cast a surreptitious glance at the bewildering array of highly expensive kit that was laid out at Roger's feet. Eventually, and with the pride of a minor postal official in Anschluß Vienna, he spotted the switch and our time was up. We were busted.

'What camera is that?' He pointed at Roger's odd-looking device, lying on the floor like K-9. I could tell that it fleetingly crossed Roger's mind to lie. But instead of telling him it was a toaster, he admitted to it being a filming device, of sorts. 'It's a camera,' he offered as a slightly disingenuous explanation.

'What does it do?'

'It films.' He nodded at the interview position, 'Footballers. Or anything, really.'

'We know what you've been up to, you know.' Suddenly the gloves were off. 'I want that camera out of my tunnel.' The UEFA official seemed extremely agitated. Roger sighed, rather theatrically. Then the man turned his gaze to me.

'Don't think this hasn't been noted. I'll mention it in my match report and I'm sure it will get back to ITV.' Then he nodded curtly and without clicking his heels, even though he might as well have done, he spun on his patent leathers and clip-clopped off down the tunnel to go and harass a Turkish TV crew about something else of terrible triviality. Our two opposing careers, his and mine, suddenly seemed petty beyond salvation.

*****

Meanwhile, the Irish footballing summer continued to be curiously devoid of fight, except for the wonder of their travelling fans bellowing out into the night sky above Gdańsk *The Fields of Athenry*. But by the time the final match in the group came around, and we'd all reassembled in Poznan, the Irish fans were resigned to their fates and the inevitable pointless early exit had already been secured, before they even had to face Italy.

On the morning of their final demise, I sat in the sun and talked at length to a group of Ireland fans from Galway about a famous Irish greasy spoon café in Lewisham. Maggie's dispenses bottomless mugs of tea and, during the Cheltenham Festival, whiskey with its bacon, hash browns, and bubble and squeak. It was what we had in common; not so much a shared Irish heritage, as an intimate working knowledge of a street corner in south-east London, where one could sit behind steamed up windows on cold, wet days and be happy. It was a fine thing to sit in the sunshine and mercantile splendour of Poznan's beautifully restored main square and remember Maggie's extraordinary, idiosyncratic institution, known throughout the London Irish world for watery baked beans and brusque charm. But that wasn't what any of us should have been in town for. The point of the summer was missing.

When kick-off came around, Robbie Keane, Richard Dunne and Damien Duff huffed and puffed and did their best to stem the Italians, who were fighting for their tournament survival. But it was like watching your dad dancing at a wedding, as they flounced with creaking joints through retro moves in half-remembered tunes. The Italians simply strolled. Better though they had been against either Croatia or Spain, Irish hearts were waning. This was not '94, nor was it meant to be. I interviewed Shay Given at the end and didn't know how to talk to a man who had just seen an ending of sorts to all that he'd ever desired. These things creep up on you. Even Balotelli scored. Ireland were out. So was I.

*****

It came to an end. Shortly after we gave up trying to make high art out of a UEFA press conference and accepted that we were exactly where we were and who we were, Ireland limped off home. The travelling army of Ireland fans who'd been such a wonderful presence in the extensive campsites of Sopot pulled out their tent pegs and wound in their guy ropes and, with Roy Keane's scathing words about their general bonhomie still ringing indifferently in their sunburnt ears, returned to normality in Waterford, Limerick, Dublin and Cork. And my tentative foray into another avenue of my family's past petered out. Pretty soon after their dismissal, came ours. Our reporting team was sent for. I didn't realise it at the time, but that defeat by Italy was to be my last day working for ITV at a summer football tournament.

En route to London, we stopped off for a day with our colleagues, who were all based in Warsaw. Demob happy, we swung into the main operations hub where everyone was hard at work preparing for whichever game was going on that afternoon. We generally got in the way, posing for pictures sitting in Adrian Chiles's anchorman chair in ITV's extravagantly baroque studio in the middle of the city. Then we went for a long lunch, staking our places at a modest cafe outdoors in the bright midsummer sun. We ordered big, cold beers and set about reading the menu.

'Ello.' I was suddenly tapped on the shoulder. I looked up at a tall man, whose silhouette I could just make out against the bright sunshine. It was Arsène Wenger.

'Hello, Mr Wenger.' He was one of those managers you would never call by their first name.

'How are you, Ned?' he asked. I was completely startled by his use of my name. The Frenchman had been at the helm of Arsenal by now for 16 years, almost all of which had fallen into the span of my life in football reporting. Interviewing Wenger had become such a familiar process to me, with its own precisions and rhythms. But he'd never once used my name.

Through all the iterations and eras of his remarkable Arsenal reign, and even in the endlessly self-repeating cycle of pretty failure, which increasingly characterised his later years, Wenger had retained a rigid sense of equanimity. He treated everyone alike and never, as far as I could see, used first names with journalists. Unlike a certain type of British manager was wont to do, he did not visibly foster a coterie of chosen ones among the press pack. Nor, like Rafael Benitez would often do, did he stay behind after interviews and brief the interviewer 'off the record' to advance some agenda or other. With us on the outside, he was in command and we knew where we stood.

I found Wenger's mystique fascinating. Once, at the San Siro, when his Fabregas-led team had played AC Milan off the park over the first 45 minutes, I had caught a glimpse of him at half time. The dressing room door was open and he was standing in the middle of the group, shirtsleeves rolled up, tie loosened, and he was imploring them, loudly, swearily, for more. 'You've fucking got this, boys!' I stared at the scene as if I'd caught my parents in bed.

Another time, during a midweek FA Cup replay at Elland Road, I'd been given a pitch-side chair to sit on during the match that was embarrassingly close to the Arsenal dugout. The visiting entourage, complete with Wenger in full zip-up long coat mode, seemed as surprised to see me there as I was. I smiled apologetically at them and, when the match got underway, they forgot about me.

But for the first time I could actually hear the words coming out of Wenger's mouth, as he and Pat Rice shouted at and variously cajoled their players to ever greater heights as they laboured to victory against lower league opposition. Most of the time, the pair were simply bellowing at Nicklas Bendtner.

'Oi, get back, Nick!'

'Man on, Nick!'

'Get on him, Nick!'

'Time, Nick!'

I don't know what I'd been expecting, really. Perhaps something more philosophical. But I liked Wenger all the more for the sheer simplicity of it; just a middle-aged ex-player shouting in frustration into the dark Yorkshire air at a young man who was finding it hard to control a football at his feet.

'Space, Nick!'

Now, here he was again in Warsaw, the same man but different. Wenger chatted away, smiling broadly, wearing a loose-fitting T-shirt and jeans, no suit, no tie, no silly padded coat. He was there to work for French TV and had quite consciously opted to alter his behaviour accordingly. For a short while he talked amiably with me about Warsaw's reconstructed post-war architecture and his affection for Poland. This was a Wenger I had never met before during all those long years of passing acquaintance. Then he shook my hand and asked me if Bradley Wiggins was going to win the Tour de France that year. Now we were talking about cycling!

'He might do, Arsène' I told him, before I'd even noticed that I'd now used *his* first name. Then he walked off, unnoticed by the hundreds of milling tourists. I watched him disappear into the Warsaw backdrop.

I think that must have been the last time I saw Wenger. I didn't know then what that moment meant but I now understand that it was the end of something that I'd shared, in a tiny unreciprocated way, with a man who'd changed the game for good and was unable to change it again. I'd begun in football around the time he'd arrived. Our two stays had overlapped. Something was coming to an end.

As for me, I was invisibly being de-commissioned, or rather I was willingly de-commissioning myself. It was the TV equivalent of presenting myself with a white feather. I drank my beer, ate my lunch, laughed about our month's adventure, kept my thoughts to myself and then left. Like it was for the Irish football team, so it was for me. An exit.

21

Abpfiff

ENGLAND LEGENDS 2–7 GERMANY LEGENDS.
2 May, 2016. Upton Park, London.

In which it ends.

Towards the end of my time spent patrolling the touchlines and the tunnels of Britain's football grounds, I found that I went to work reluctantly and with a heavy heart. Increasingly frequently, it felt like the joy of it all had been knocked out of me. I used to go and clock on for work on live TV simply in the hope that I would not screw it up, get humiliated by a football manager, or produce a slip of the tongue that would make me into an overnight headline buried somewhere in the acres of sports pages. Reporting from a match had become an exercise in damage limitation, before it even got started. And, rather than figuring out what I could do to make it better, I resigned myself merely to hoping it wouldn't get worse.

I'd had inklings of this malaise before, on isolated occasions, over many years. It would manifest itself in a blunt, unspoken desire to see the match abandoned. Heavy rain could sometimes threaten to get the job done, but never quite did. Gazing up at leaden skies with my windscreen wipers going into overdrive en route to Stoke, I'd try to convince myself that the match would be called off. But matches seldom were. Somehow the players negotiated the puddles near the corner flags when placing the ball. And the super slo-mo cameras liked nothing better than to capture the flying fin of rainwater sent up by the sliding buttocks of some hard-tackling midfielder after a mistimed lunge had left him surfing the centre-circle.

A better hope was that the match might be frozen off, and that I could swing the car around in the forecourt of the BP station at Norton Canes and surprise my young family at home by turning up in time for dinner instead of shivering with nerves at Goodison Park, anticipating another stare-off with David Moyes. A frost-hardened pitch seemed like a convenient way out. But global warming, in tandem with sub-soil heating, had made that salvation an increasingly remote prospect.

There was always fog – a rare, but glorious cause of matches being called off. It nearly happened at Southend. Roots Hall was anticipating the arrival of Luiz Felipe Scolari's (yes, I'd forgotten, too) Chelsea for a third-round FA Cup replay.

With three or four hours to go, the old ground was shrouded in a freezing January fog, so thick that the corner flags could not be seen from the centre circle. Ray Wilkins, in a blue tracksuit that seemed several sizes too big for him, had arrived ahead of the team bus that was bringing the marquee Brazilian manager and the Chelsea 'B team'. Every few minutes he poked his nose out of the away dressing room into the players' tunnel, down which the fog was swooping from the turf to fill the empty space. 'Not cleared, yet?' he'd enquire from either me or Peter Drury.

'Not yet, Ray.'

'Oh, dear,' said the former Chelsea captain. 'Oh dear,' he fretted, like some character from a gentle 1980s sitcom. And then disappeared back inside to rearrange the warm-up bibs.

The match's viability was in the balance right up to the moment when the visiting team's luxury coach appeared like the Death Star in a supermarket car park and drew to an undertaker's halt right outside the main entrance to the ground. Out stepped a funereal Scolari, to be greeted by Wilkins. Peter and I followed the duo as they took the requisite 15 steps through to the tunnel, then a further six or seven to the side of the pitch, to discover that the evening was crystal clear, the floodlights were shining brightly over a pitch powdered with their tiny sparkle in each droplet of dew. It was a perfect night for football.

'You should have seen it half an hour ago, Felipe,' explained Wilkins, wide-eyed, and speaking both loudly and slowly so that he might be understood by the moustachioed Brazilian. 'You could not see anything. Nothing. The fog.' Scolari looked impassively around the vacant little ground with its wooden stands and classic post-war proportions. Wilkins made a final sweep with his arm, encompassing the scene. 'It was a pea-souper, Felipe.'

I think that this might have been the only time that Luiz Felipe Scolari and I have been on the same page. I think we'd both rather have been somewhere else.

It was wrong of me. I was in a place of bad faith. One should never want the games to stop.

I 'dropped down a division', as the Champions League rights leeched away from ITV towards a variety of other platforms. For two or three more years I worked Thursday nights on the Europa League. This meant watching Spurs play against a variety of central European curiosities, mainly. I witnessed Gareth Bale at first hand in that glorious, darkest blue box of a ground that has now been bulldozed, as he blasted his way out of White Hart Lane towards Madrid. I saw Andros Townsend briefly suggest he could fill the gap and then Harry Kane, in his very different way, do amazing things. I remember watching the teenage England star-in-the-making going through his paces during open training and, turning to a colleague, saying: 'Don't know what all the fuss is about Kane.' With hindsight, this might have been the moment to go.

The signs were there. Arriving for a production meeting before one of Chelsea's early season games in 2012, I was asked if I knew anything about César Azpilicueta's fitness. I didn't, I said. What I failed to mention was that I'd never heard of César Azpilicueta. My quarter-century habit of osmosing football news, ingesting it as a matter of reflex, like a whale might inhale plankton, had unwittingly silted up.

Or, sitting in a press conference ahead of yet another of Spurs' endless string of increasingly pointless Europa League games, I found myself calling Jan Vertonghen 'Sam'. Not once, but on about three occasions, and to his face. Afterwards their press officer asked me why I'd done it. I hadn't even noticed that I'd been using the wrong name.

So, the weight of evidence was pointing towards the exit. In 2014, I waited until I wasn't asked to go to the World Cup in Brazil. And the following winter my contract with ITV ran out entirely. In fact, I was sent an email which landed just before Christmas Day, telling me that I had an appointment to see the Head of Sport at ITV as soon as the office opened for the New Year. When January arrived and I trudged in to meet with my fate, it wasn't a long meeting. The gist of it was that, with all the football rights that ITV had been forced to cede, there really wasn't any work left for me to do. And so, after just under 20 years of working in the game, football, and my little part in it, suddenly stopped.

The last game of football I covered was for Channel Five. It was a charity England v Germany 'Legends' game at the old Upton Park, shortly before it, too, was flattened. The England team featured Jack Whitehall, Angus Deayton and Ben Cohen. Michael Ballack was the captain of a Germany team that hadn't got the memo about it being 'a bit of fun'. Once they'd stuck away seven goals, they finally got the message. After 90 minutes and a little bit more, Dermot Gallagher blew the whistle for the end of the match. *Abfiff*, as they say in German.

My last ever football interview was with Gallagher, some minutes later. Not quite entering into the spirit of Channel Five light entertainment, he refused to discuss any decisions he'd made on the pitch.

'But it was just a charity game Dermot, a bit of fun.'

'Did you not understand what I said?' he replied, tersely. 'I will not answer any of those questions.'

Minutes later, I was taking off my tie, and leaving the ground and the game behind me for good.

*****

It's November 2020. For the first time, the weather has switched. A wind blows in from the North Sea, down the Thames estuary, whipping the soft, yellowing leaves from trees. The London skies above our house grow quiet. Planes on the approach to Heathrow, reduced in number still by the pandemic, plough in from the west. Their noses are angled into the onrushing cold air that passes over the great city and on towards the broad sweep of England.

It's got to be four years, I reckon, since I have visited a football ground.

I listen to the radio as I peel potatoes for a late Saturday lunch. Reporters are calling in their news from all across the country, entering its second lockdown in 2020. The fake crowd noise fed into the radio feed has become the accepted price we pay for football continuing; our own tacit agreement that reality needs to be kept at bay.

Because for a long time the football had actually stopped rolling. And without it, all we were left with was reality. League tables ossified. They fell into the shadows where they kept their stories in frozen animation. People were lit up instead by the white-blue light of their screens, scrolling through graphs and bar charts, the unfolding trigonometry of a pandemic. One by one, all the building blocks of our assumptions were removed. Cities fell quiet.

One of the few stories my dad ever told me about the films made by his Chelsea-supporting father and uncle concerned a little-known piece called *Seven Days to Noon*. It was a taut, tense thriller, made in 1950 and starring a spectral Barry Jones as Professor Willingdon, a nuclear scientist who holds London to ransom by threatening to detonate an atomic bomb unless the government declares that it will stop building nuclear weapons. The city is evacuated. In the film, there is a haunting sequence of shots of empty London landmarks and streets at dawn. Dad had always been impressed by this film.

When lockdown eased, I used to go for long walks alongside the railway lines that run beside the Den, Millwall's graceless home, flanked by an incinerator and a refuse dump. Through the gaps I could see the pitch, vivid green and triangulated by the dark shadow of the roofs. Untrodden now by a booted foot for six weeks, it looked unnaturally well. It must have been kept perfect by a groundsman or two, coming into work on their own to mow and fork a pitch without portfolio.

A pigeon launched a swooping dive from the top of the west stand and dropped into the middle of the empty space, picking up height again through the imagined line above the centre circle, where the noise of matchday would have risen to meet the sky above the ground. Yet the bird flew through solid, three-dimensional silence, hanging loosely in the chill air.

And all around the ground, in the breakers' yards and timber forecourts, and in the MOT garages and small units tucked into the railway arches under Victorian lines that snake and weave through Surrey Quays and Bermondsey, every approach to the Den was quiet. The same roads that would, on matchdays, fill with blue and white in the summer, or black jackets zipped up to the chin and topped off with a beanie hat in the long and dark London winter, were all de-purposed. An indefinite suspension hung over the scene.

The football is back, but the crowds are not. I can imagine the deserted, cold corner where they sell the soup at Kidderminster Harriers, where I'd once stood in a queue with some Premier League caretaker manager whose name I've now forgotten. I can see London Road, where Barry Fry would bustle to and fro, dispensing foul vocabulary and smiling like a music hall act from the war. I have an image of Ibrox, its vast brick edifice black against a clear Glasgow sky.

The radio announcer goes up a notch. 'Goal at the Etihad and finally Manchester City have broken the deadlock!'

Manchester City, whose rise to the top and high-handedness I had tracked through years of reporting on the reigns of Mark Hughes, Roberto Mancini and Manuel Pellegrini. That the venerable club has gone the way it has seems to epitomise the soulless hollow eating away the core of the game. Another of football's great tribe of underdogs has had to adapt to a world into which they have suddenly been propelled, like lottery winners posing with an oversized cardboard cheque and a magnum of champagne, before being resented by family and friends who might once have held them in esteem.

I can still picture Maine Road, where the big supermarket now stands. I think back to a morning I spent in 1998 accompanying a group of three Manchester City-supporting refuse collectors on their bin rounds. The resultant little film, shown to the amused delight of Rodney Marsh and George Best in the *Soccer Saturday* studios, was intended as a homage to the Granada TV comedy series from 1969 called *The Dustbinmen*. This forgotten gem of a sitcom was set in a Manchester landscape that made the city still look post-war. The series followed the fortunes of a group of bin men whose gently haphazard lives revolved around swinging bins into the back of dustcarts, sipping warm-looking pints of ale and making very mildly reprehensible comments about ladies in frilly nylon dressing gowns in doorways of terraced houses in Moss Side. And when they weren't doing that, they were fretting about the fortunes of Mike Summerbee, Franny Lee and Stan Bowles with exaggerated passion.

My little recreation, some 30 years on, in which the roles of the bin men were played by an amateur cast of enthusiastic real-life dustbin men, sought to pair the class of '69, at least in terms of passion, with the team of '98. They sang of their love for, and frustration with, the great Jamie Pollock, Shaun Goater and Paul Dickov. That year, City slumped to relegation to the third tier in English football for the first time in their history.

Two decades later, that lineage of support seems fractured at best. As with Chelsea's old fanbase, my dad included, I wonder how many Manchester City fans, thinking about those times, wouldn't be tempted to return to Pollock's barrel-chested, almost-out-of-breath presence in a midfield that might at any given moment fall apart, or the Goater-Dickov axis of power, the very archetype of an age that still set much store by the enduring native myth of 'The Big Man, Little Man'? As City's supporters subscribe to a burgeoning number of platforms in order to watch the millionaire heirs apparent to the Joe Mercer generation, what do they feel? Watching a squad that is marshalled and acquired by the ultimate symbol of urbane football modernity, Pep Guardiola, seeing his players jiggle up and down, arms around each other's shoulders amid the confetti on a branded cardboard stage in the middle of the new Wembley to celebrate the acquisition of yet another League Cup, what do those supporters feel?

Was old Wembley, with its shallow-raked seating, its whiff of burger onion and urine, its hint of violence, better in the collective unconscious of the football fan? Does it sit deep in the *animus* of City's identity?

Because it was there, in 1999, just a week after Manchester United's Miracle of Barcelona, that Dickov scored twice within three minutes of injury time to send City into a penalty shoot-out against Gillingham, which they won. I was there. I was in the thick of their celebrations in the Wembley dressing room, with a camera, conducting live interview after live interview for Sky Sports, not knowing how I got there or what was happening to me. It was an experience that left me shaking. I had been party to the hidden world of a celebrating dressing room, deep within Wembley's West Stand; the very same one that Kevin Keegan would flounce from a couple of years later when it hosted its last-ever game, in the pouring rain, when England lost once again to Germany.

Those four hidden walls, with all their stories absorbed into the flaking paintwork and plaster have since been bulldozed and built over.

*****

Often in those early years of reporting for ITV and Sky, flying away from, or into, London down the spine of the country, I'd gaze down on clear days to try and identify the towns and cities we were passing over. I'd pick out railway lines, sometimes a river, acting as a signifier. But just as commonly I'd hunt for the football ground to be sure of where I was. If there were no signs of a town-centre ground, surrounded by rows of terraced housing, then my eye would trace dual carriageways heading out of town. Eventually one of them would lead to the retail park with its sequence of rectangular roofs, ample parking and adjacent stadium.

These places: the unlovely 21st-century sites of pilgrimage for families disgorging from Nissan Qashqais. A pair of 12-year-old friends leading the way with a little dash for the turnstiles to avoid a sudden salvo of wintry rain, the noise from the tannoy mixing now with the growing swell of the first song of the day, as the crowd inside grows focussed, hands rubbing together in anticipation, the scoreline still replete with potential, the defended goal unbreached, the imagined runs down the wing or the raking passes floating across the midfield like unseen spores of possibility spreading across the perfect carpet of watered turf.

And I would know something of each and every place. Swindon, Northampton, Lincoln, Carlisle, Middlesbrough, Walsall, Gillingham: all of them packed with meaning and bearing a badge of identity, set into the map like a jewel. These places were inseparable from my understanding of the country I called home. They'd lodged within me, too. I still remembered a setting sun over Oakwell, still knew where to stop off near Elland Road or Selhurst Park to grab a bag of chips or stand at the pump amid the stink of petrol, bound for Norwich, Cardiff and Sheffield.

Still, from time to time, the old feelings surfaced.

Like they had in 2018 when England, under the stewardship of Gareth Southgate, were about to surprise themselves, us and the world by reaching a World Cup semi-final in Russia. I had started to pay more attention again, had tried to pick up on the backgrounds of so many players I no longer felt connected to. And briefly, I succeeded. Southgate's team seemed different, more human. I had been impressed with the way his young players felt empowered to speak about media harassment, racial abuse and a whole host of issues their predecessors routinely fought shy of.

As England's opening match drew near, and once again the crosses of St George started to appear sticking up from the windows of cars and from the balconies of flats across the land (though in slightly less proliferation than 20 years before), I dug out an old email address I had from the days when the England manager was just Gareth and I worked with him. No beard, back then, nor waistcoat.

I had had no contact with him since towards the end of his time at ITV when I put it to him over a drink that he'd probably be the England manager before too long. That was shortly before he left to take up his first job with the FA.

Now, I found myself writing him an email, not expecting a reply.

Dear Gareth,

I may have drifted away from football and I never had a club side to support, really. So the seasons run away from me a bit.

But I am still enormously, irrationally drawn to the fortunes of the England team every four years. World Cups matter, particularly now in our troubled land. In fact, I'd say they matter almost as much as the Tour de France! I have bought a little England flag for my bike.

I just wanted you to know that the brief years we shared occasional walks and pints and tea and runs on the road with the ITV crew are among my fondest memories of my time in the game 'on the other side' from the one you currently occupy. Knowing how you think and work, I see your approach all across the public face of this happy band you have assembled. It does you huge credit. The fact that you are now the England manager fills me with stupid reflected pride.

You are the best thing that's happened to our game in recent years and I wish you all the best. I hope you can find it possible to enjoy the unimaginable rollercoaster you are now going to experience. May it be full of highs.

All the very best,
Ned

To my amazement, within a day, he had replied.

Ned,

I can't thank you enough for taking the time to write and for your kind words. The recollections of happy days brought a big smile. We will be judged in the end on results, but for me this challenge is about a lot more than that.

I'm enjoying the challenge and hope we can allow you to fly your flag with pride.

Take care,
Gareth

Later that summer, in the middle of my work at the Tour de France, on a scorching evening in Brittany, I sat in a deserted bar in a tiny village to watch his team fall at the semi-final hurdle. Outside, France could not have cared less. They were already qualified for the World Cup Final and en route to another victory within 20 years of the first, a timespan that overlapped for the most part with my stay in the world of football. With indifference all around me, I was left alone with my thoughts as the national anthems played and the camera panned along a line of faces, many of which I struggled to put a name to. Two years had passed since I'd watched any kind of match on TV and, without a club to support, the pace of change in the game left me struggling to identify Jesse Lingard.

The TV pictures cut to Southgate at the side, frowning. Was he really the Alf Ramsey of the age? Was this image of him one that would burn into the collective unconscious of our peculiar, insecure, raucous, passionate island?

Kieran Trippier scored. I didn't really know who Kieran Trippier was. It didn't matter.

But he scored, and though I could not jump up and shout and hug any strangers, my heart started to race as I crammed peanuts into my mouth. Was I watching something I'd never dreamed I would witness in my lifetime; something dredged from my own pre-history? I had to remind myself that I was alone and not by the side of the pitch, as I had been at so many big matches for so long. I had a bag of peanuts, a small French lager and a fairly sullen landlady for company. And it was only a semi-final.

And it was only England after all. First the equaliser, deserved, but gut-wrenching. Then the second half clogging up with all the insecurities that have always characterised an England team on the brink of something historic. All my life, I knew the outcome before the winner had gone in. As I downed the rest of my beer and left the scene of routine defeat for the umpteenth time in my life, it felt fleetingly as if nothing had changed. Football had entranced and disappointed me once again in quick succession. That's what it does.

I stepped out into the indifferent Breton night. A warm summer sky had only just darkened to black and I could hear the village quietly putting itself to rights before calling an end to a day in which the distant drama of 22 men in Russia, in whom they had no stake, had played no part at all. And the distance consumed me, too. I strolled back to the hotel, allowing with each step the weight of disappointment to lift, which, amazingly, it did.

I knew there was a history there. I could not wholly un-write the written narrative or completely un-remember things. I couldn't entirely un-play the game. But all of those years of immersion in football had led me after all to this withered point where I was no longer rooted in its detail and had let its texture recede over the horizon of my life; a line of cliffs disappearing as a ship sets off into open waters.

*****

The windy afternoon outside is softening and darkening, as the kitchen fills with roasting smells. The goals are coming thick and fast now, as they often do towards the 80th minute.

The game has grown too far and too fast for me to want to keep up. I have not been equal to its speed of regeneration. Like the coronavirus, it evolves through generations at a speed which seems unnatural and even to attempt to keep pace would reveal merely that I can't. I'm a marathon runner who cannot hold their place in the pack of leaders, and so I drop away, step by step.

And on it goes without me, filling pitches, radio stations, forums, social media feeds and hours, weeks and years of people's lives. And still the players will emerge, wildly exciting, wildly excited. And still the devotees will suffer with each hammer blow to their hopes for a happier world. It's football, after all: it still matters/doesn't matter.

I open the oven to turn the spuds over in their oil. As the cloud of steam the door releases makes me flinch, I realise with a slight shudder that 20 years have passed since I stood with a shaking microphone in a dressing room that has long since been turned to rubble.

'Goal at Stamford Bridge! But which way has it gone?'

I bet Dad's listening. Some things never change.

EPILOGUE – 2021

I went to Wembley to see the national team beat the Czech Republic on route to the final of the Euros. It was the first time I had been to a football match for five years, and the first time I'd ever attended an international as a supporter and not in a suit. I had no duties to discharge except to support, with exasperation and delight.

20,000 people had been allowed to attend, so the place was a quarter full, at best. But it was noisy nonetheless. From my seat (which I never once sat on) at the opposite side of the ground from where I had always been during my working life, I was afforded a perfect view of Raheem Sterling's first-half goal. In the second half, as England shut up shop and the Czechs sought a goal, we all wandered across to behind the goal Jordan Pickford was defending. It was as if we were at a non-league match and could go wherever we wished. So we did, and we stood there and we cheered.

Turns out I still cared. I howled, in fact. I think at some point I clutched my UMBRO England badge on the T-shirt I'd bought at Tesco for £12. When I finished howling, I squinted across the vast bowl of Wembley to see if I could spot Gareth Southgate. He was standing dead still, with his arms folded. England were through to the knockout phase without conceding a goal.

It was a highly unusual summer in the national life, which would pit centre-halves against home secretaries, which would posit footballers in the middle of a struggle for ownership of the national game. And all this while we had to present evidence of our viral load, or lack of it, on the way to watch a game of football.

Covid had meant that in 2021, and for the second time in successive years, ITV's Tour de France team were broadcasting remotely, from Maidstone Studios in Kent. We shared studio facilities with the ITV Football team who were at the same facility covering the delayed Euros; my former colleagues, similarly held at arm's length from the action by the pandemic.

I renewed my fragile acquaintance with Roy Keane, who, over a breakfast in the Marriott Hotel disclosed his long-standing admiration for cycling (by now my full-time obsession). Lee Dixon dropped by on our production from time to time to question us about the latest events in the three-week battle for the yellow jersey. I resisted the urge to contact Gareth Southgate again, figuring he had enough on his hands, as he navigated a political path never before ventured by any England football manager. So instead I chatted with any number of former friends and colleagues from the ITV Football team about their work, doing the job I used to do. I marvelled at their ability to still care so passionately about the game, as I once had done.

The evening of the final, 11 July, coincided with my birthday. We watched the game in my tiny room in the hotel, a bunch of us overexcited and enclosed in too small a space. I can recall most of it with intense detail before the evening ended with a rancorous and completely futile argument about whether or not Italians were more racist than English.

Before the inevitable-seeming low it had been the same old well-worn trajectory in a way; the same but different. It was a final, after all, so that was at least novel. Yet it *was* agonisingly familiar because wild hope gradually gave way to a stark realism. The difference lay solely in that nagging sense that I was no longer sure how much it mattered.

In the moment, it still mattered, of course. The penalty shoot-out had me hurtling from my chair to bang my fists on the door with every passing and competing fluctuation in England's tortured fortune. And I was left with that same ensuing deep, deep emptiness when it was apparent that, at the age of 52, I had *still* not seen this lovely, unlovely team win anything.

But it was different, too. Because in the midst of all the resultant slew of recrimination, all the unedifying back-tracking culture

246

warriors in government, all the compelling testimony from those at the game and those simply caught up in its bilious aftertaste, that there were good reasons once again for the rest of the world to despise England.

In the midst of all this: Luke Shaw kicked a ball as hard and straight as a brilliant message. It briefly exploded. It was heavy with meaning and, in my addled imagination, it rippled around the world like a shockwave, emanating from Wembley. No other game can do this.

But, then again, it didn't *actually* do any of the above. It was just a fleeting mirage, an incidental delusion that things might permanently change for the better. It was just a game, after all: one that England lost.

So, I find myself back at square one.

ACKNOWLEDGEMENTS

So many people have played a part in the writing of this story, that it's almost impossible to know where to start. From Hamburg-based actor Georg Münzel's innocent surrendering of that fatal matchday ticket for St Pauli which really ignited my interest in football, through to the younger of my two children (they're grown up now), who only last night suggested we go and watch a match at Dulwich Hamlets; so many people have accompanied me on my journey through the biggest game in the world.

There are people whose cajoling support has been formative in my career in TV however, which led me to write this book at all. At Sky (having been introduced by my sister – thank you, Emily), my faltering start in the industry was nurtured by supportive producers such as Nick Moody, Andrew Hornett and Ian Condron, as well as wonderful colleagues like Greg Whelan, Dickie Davies and many, many others. Nick Atkins rescued me from Sky and brought me over to ITV, albeit via the ill-fated Sport Channel. And at ITV, I have worked under three Heads of Sport, all of whom were very good to me, in their different ways: Brian Barwick, Mark Sharman and Niall Sloane.

Over a ten-year period with ITV, I worked with so many genuinely outstanding producers, that to list some would be to omit others and cause offence. Suffice then to say that, for a long period of time, ITV's production team and roster of commentators and presenters was among the very best there's been in televised sport; and their expertise was sought worldwide. Many of them have gone on to bigger and better things since. If they're reading this, I hope at least that they know who they are. I learned so much from each and every one.

Then there are the players of the game. I thank all those who put up with my questioning in the tunnels and training grounds of this football-mad country; even the managers whose ill-temper threatened to break through at any moment! I am grateful that, by and large, they were decent people doing a hard job in an unstable environment.

This book was conceived in part after discussions with Mark Stanton, who set me off on this 'literary' course in the first place, a decade ago. And it has been realised with the support and expertise of everyone at Bloomsbury, but most notable Charlotte Croft and Sarah Skipper. Thank you.

Finally, I'd like to thank Dad. He has listened with patience to my telling of his story; sometimes in alarm, and other times in fits of laughter. I'm sorry I could never follow your love of Chelsea, Dad. But I did after all get football, on my own terms. I think that's what we all do in the end.